Air & Light & Time & Space

HOW SUCCESSFUL ACADEMICS WRITE

Helen Sword

Harvard University Press

Cambridge, Massachusetts | London, England

2017

First printing

Book epigraph: Lu Chi, *Wen Chu: The Art of Writing*, trans. Sam Hamill
(Minneapolis, MN: Milkweed, 2000), 13.

Library of Congress Cataloging-in-Publication Data
Names: Sword, Helen, author.
Title: Air & light & time & space : how successful academics write/
    Helen Sword.
Other titles: Air and light and time and space : how successful
    academics write
Description: Cambridge, Massachusetts : Harvard University Press,
2017. | Includes bibliographical references and index.
Identifiers: LCCN 2016041937 | ISBN 9780674737709 (alk. paper)
Subjects: LCSH: Academic writing. | College teachers as authors.
Classification: LCC P301.5.A27 S94 2017 | DDC 808.042—dc23
LC record available at https://lccn.loc.gov/2016041937

The pleasure a writer knows
    is the pleasure of sages.

Out of non-being, being is born;
    out of silence,
      a writer produces a song.

In one yard of silk, there is infinite space;
    language is a deluge
      from one small corner of the heart.

—Lu Chi, *Wen Chu: The Art of Writing*, third century AD

Contents

The House of Writing

In a poem titled "Air and Light and Time and Space," poet Charles Bukowski addresses writers and artists who fantasize about moving into a studio where they will finally have "a place and a time to/*create*": a large, beautiful room flooded with light. "No baby," Bukowski tells them, "if you're going to create/you're going to create," even if you work sixteen hours per day in a coal mine, even with "a cat crawling up your/back," even while the city around you "trembles in earthquake, bombardment,/flood and fire":

> baby, air and light and time and space
> have nothing to do with it
> and don't create anything
> except maybe a longer life to find
> new excuses
> for.[1]

Bukowski's portrait of the suffering-yet-productive artist hits home for many academics. The circumstances that sap our strength and hobble our writing—heavy teaching loads, tedious administrative duties, judgmental reviewers, looming deadlines—are admittedly less arduous than mining for coal and less devastating than flood or fire. But even if we don't literally have to write with a cat crawling up our back, we often feel as though we do. We long for "air and light and time and space," an architecture of possibilities and pleasure; instead, we find ourselves crushed under the weight of expectations and the rubble of our fractured workdays. And as the walls close in around us, we hear the voices of our department chairs, supervisors, and that annoyingly hyperproductive colleague down the hall: stop whining; just get on with it; if you wait for the perfect conditions to write, you'll never publish a single word.

Are academic writers doomed to a life of misery, slaving away by day in the educational equivalent of a coal mine and tapping out our manuscripts by night in the dim glow of a computer screen? What if we were to bring air and light and time and space back into the picture, reimagining ourselves not as suffering artists but as artisans of language: skilled craftspeople who trade in the written word and draw delight and satisfaction from our craft? Like the nation of Bhutan, which measures not only the gross domestic product of its citizens but also their "gross national happiness," perhaps we can learn to recognize productivity and pleasure as commodities that supplement and enhance each other's value—or, to return to Bukowski's architectural metaphor, as complementary features of the same building.

This book offers no ready-made blueprint for academic success, no skeleton key to a House of Writing where productive writing habits are quick to achieve and easy to maintain. Instead, you will find here a flexible, customizable building plan intended to help you design your own writing practice from the ground up, with words like *productivity* and *success* capaciously defined to include not just publication rates and professional kudos but other, less measurable, academic accomplishments such as craftsmanship, collegiality, pride, and even joy. Just as a house may be entered by different doors, the four sections of the book may be read in any order. I do recommend, however, that you orient yourself first by reading the Introduction and undertaking the diagnostic exercise on pages 8 and 9.

Whatever your route and your pace, I invite you to wander through this book in a spirit of optimism and curiosity, embracing the premise that creativity and craft thrive best in places where the windows are large, the ceilings are high, the outlook is bright, and oxygen and ideas flow freely. For writers in search of that sweet spot where productivity and pleasure meet, air and light and time and space have *everything* to do with it.

Air & Light & Time & Space

Introduction

Building the BASE

When I first set out to write a book about the writing habits of successful academics, I had no real idea what I would find—or even what I was trying to find out. I had already published two books on academic writing: one outlining the key principles of "fit and trim" prose (*The Writer's Diet*), the other asserting that "stylish academic writing" is not an oxymoron but an achievable ideal (*Stylish Academic Writing*).[1] But whenever I was invited to talk about these books with faculty and graduate students, I noticed how quickly our conversations about sentence structure and style strayed to other writing-related issues: for example, work-life balance ("How am I supposed to find time to write stylishly when I've got a heavy teaching load and a new baby?") or power dynamics ("I'd like to write in a more personal voice, but my PhD supervisor won't let me") or emotion ("I love to write poetry and stories, but I find academic writing to be unpleasant and stressful"). Gradually, my scholarly gaze began to lift from the words on the page to the people who put them there, and I realized that my next book would have to focus not on writing but on writers.

Over the next four years, I conducted in-depth, on-the-record interviews with one hundred exemplary academic writers and editors from across the disciplines and around the world—with "exemplary" writ large to encompass a wide range of criteria beyond conventional markers of academic success. Alongside scholarly superstars with distinguished career tracks and prolific publication rates, I sought out other kinds of exemplars: for example, lesser-known academics from underrepresented cultural, ethnic, and gender minorities who have survived and even thrived in academe; scholars who have followed nontraditional paths into and through their disciplines; successful international researchers for whom English is not their first language; pathbreaking thinkers whose writing has taken the scholarship of their field in new directions; academic risk takers who have subverted or challenged disciplinary conventions; effective communicators who have engaged with audiences beyond academe; inspiring teachers and generous mentors who have devoted time and energy to helping their colleagues and students become better writers; and early- to midcareer faculty who contentedly balance their work and family commitments, without the agony, angst, and uncertainty that characterize the writing lives of so many of their peers. (If that's not academic success, what is?) Along the way, I also collected anonymous questionnaire data from 1,223 faculty members, PhD students, postdoctoral researchers, and independent scholars who attended my writing workshops at more than fifty universities and scholarly conferences in fifteen countries. Although they are not the main players in the book, their voices provide the chorus.

At first, I expected that the interviews and questionnaires would provide me with robust comparative data about two clearly demarcated sets of informants: "successful writers" (the handpicked interview subjects) and "struggling writers" (the faculty and graduate students who signed up for my workshops on how to become a more productive writer). Before long, however, I came to recognize the folly of my assumption. Not only did the two cohorts overlap significantly, but pitting successful writers against struggling writers turned out to be a false opposition. Many of the academics I interviewed, including tenured faculty members who had been recommended to me by their own discipline-based peers, responded to my initial approach by protesting, "I don't know why you would want to talk to me; I'm not a particularly prolific writer" or "I'm not a very stylish writer, if that's what you're looking for" or "To be honest, I really struggle with my writing." Conversely, just about every person who attended one of my writing workshops and filled out my data questionnaire could be labeled "exemplary" according to at least one of my interview criteria. Indeed, I hope that all readers of this book will recognize themselves somewhere in my commodious definitions of *exemplary*, *successful*, and *productive*.

If I initially imagined that my research would allow me to make authoritative claims about the characteristic writing habits of specific demographic groups—North Americans versus Europeans, or women versus men, or art historians versus biologists—that fantasy, too, soon faded. I collected a good deal of fascinating qualitative and quantitative data about the backgrounds, habits, and emotions of the academic writers I surveyed, and insights drawn from that data have in turn informed the structure and content of this book. However, within the first dozen or so interviews, I realized that I would never be able to make confident pronouncements of the "scientists are from Jupiter, humanists are from Saturn" variety. Instead, the more I looked for consistent behavioral patterns among the writers I spoke to, the more I was struck by the richness of their difference.

The futility of such scholarly typecasting struck me with particular force on the day I interviewed two colleagues who work in the same discipline and had recently been awarded the same prestigious research prize by the professional society to which they both belonged. Demographically—with regard to their age, gender, native language, educational background, academic rank, scholarly field, and institutional affiliation—they matched each other as closely as any other two academics in my interview cohort. Yet their personal affects and attitudes toward writing could hardly have been more different. One was self-confident, the other self-effacing; one was earnest, the other ironic; one clearly loved to write but spoke mostly about the agonies of writing, while the other clearly struggled to write but spoke mostly about its pleasures. Interviewed back-to-back, these two unique individuals reminded me that, in any enterprise as nuanced, varied, and deeply human as the writing process, personality trumps demography. (For a full account of my research methodology, including selection criteria, interview and questionnaire prompts, and demographic profiles of both survey groups, see the Appendix).

Many books, websites, and blogs on academic productivity convey the impression that there is only one way to be productive—the author's way. Their tone ranges from cheerfully bossy to hectoring, and their dominant verb tense is the imperative: write every day; write in the same place every day; write before you're ready to write; shut up and write. While the methods they promote may prove highly beneficial to some writers, their one-size-fits-all prescriptiveness can also lead to feelings of inadequacy and guilt, especially for aspiring authors who, for whatever reason, fail to thrive under the designated regime. At the heart of much of the self-help literature lurks a puritanical belief that productivity is a mark of personal virtue, while failure to publish denotes a deep-seated character flaw.

This book takes a more holistic and inclusive view. Its key principles reflect the experiences and advice of successful academics from across a wide range of circumstances, and its ethos is one of experimentation, empowerment, and choice. The writers I interviewed share a flexible array of attitudes and attributes that I call their "BASE habits":

Behavioral habits. Successful writers carve out time and space for their writing in a striking variety of ways, but they all do it somehow. (Key habits of mind: persistence, determination, passion, pragmatism, "grit.")

Artisanal habits. Successful writers recognize writing as an artisanal activity that requires ongoing learning, development, and skill. (Key habits of mind: creativity, craft, artistry, patience, practice, perfectionism [but not too much!], a passion for lifelong learning.)

Social habits. Successful writers seldom work entirely in isolation; even in traditionally "sole author" disciplines, they typically rely on other people—colleagues, friends, family, editors, reviewers, audiences, students—to provide them with support and feedback. (Key habits of mind: collegiality, collaboration, generosity, openness to both criticism and praise.)

Emotional habits. Successful writers cultivate modes of thinking that emphasize pleasure, challenge, and growth. (Key habits of mind: positivity, enjoyment, satisfaction, risk taking, resilience, luck.)

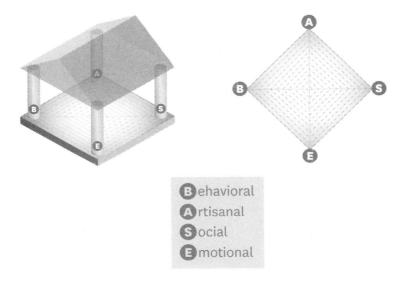

Behavioral
Artisanal
Social
Emotional

Figure 1. "House of writing" with its four BASE cornerstones (behavioral, artisanal, social, emotional).

All successful writers anchor their writing practice on these same four BASE cornerstones. However, just as there is no one-size-fits-all blueprint for creating a comfortable home, no two writers will start from exactly the same foundation or construct their house of writing in exactly the same way. (See Figure 1.)

The BASE model offers a flexible heuristic for visualizing the complexities of the writing process and developing strategies for lasting change. The diagnostic exercise on pages 8 and 9 will help you sketch the footprint of your own current writing practice—keeping in mind that your BASE may change its dimensions from day to day, from project to project, and even from one type of writing to another. (See Figure 2.) As a general rule, the broader and more symmetrical your BASE is, the more stable and spacious your House of Writing will be. Crucially, however, the BASE model does not restrict you to a zero-sum quantity of square footage. Indeed, one of the most effective strategies for broadening your BASE is to expand in several directions at once by leveraging

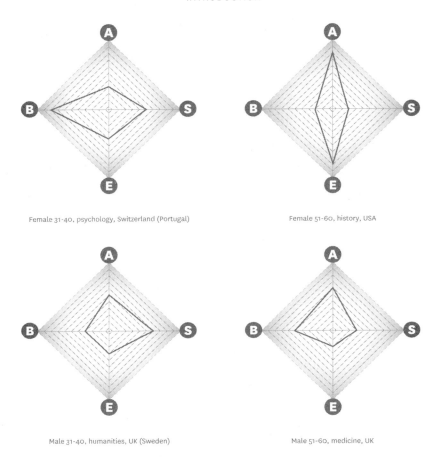

Female 31-40, psychology, Switzerland (Portugal)

Female 51-60, history, USA

Male 31-40, humanities, UK (Sweden)

Male 51-60, medicine, UK

Figure 2. Examples of BASE diagrams completed by academics with a variety of demographic profiles (country of origin indicated in parentheses if different from country of residence).

your existing strengths. For example, if you are the kind of person who thrives on networking and interpersonal relationships (*social habits*), you could organize a writing group that focuses on improving work-life balance (*behavioral habits*) or team up with a colleague to offer constructive feedback on each other's writing (*artisanal habits*) or ask friends and family to support your career by helping you shore up your professional resilience (*emotional habits*).

The BASE habits of the one hundred academics I interviewed are proffered here in all their messiness, contradiction, and variety. I have not filtered out the voices of those whose practices fly in the face of the productivity literature; nor have I excluded those whose energy and outputs arguably impose unrealistic expectations on the rest of us, such as the eminent historian whose legendary penchant for generating 3,500 words every morning has spawned an Internet buzz phrase denoting any aspirational quantity of writing (the "Grafton Line").[2] Several early readers of my draft manuscript urged me to purge such paragons of productivity from the book: "If you profile their writing habits, people will think that you're holding them up as examples of how all academics are supposed to write." Really? I believe that my readers can be trusted to make their own judgments as to the kinds of writers they can reasonably aspire to become. (I, too, would love to leap out of bed refreshed after five hours of sleep and pump out 3,500 words of brilliant new prose before lunchtime; however, long years of experience have taught me that it's never going to happen. Nor will I ever become an Olympic athlete or win the Nobel Prize.)

Interwoven with the stories of the inspiring academic writers I interviewed are my own: the experiences of yet another struggling-yet-successful, successful-yet-struggling author whose BASE habits support a dwelling that is constantly in need of home improvement. More than twenty years after publishing my first scholarly book, I still find academic writing to be a frustrating, exhilarating, endlessly challenging process that never seems to get any easier—but that I wouldn't give up for the world.

DIAGNOSTIC EXERCISE: MAPPING THE BASE

This exercise is intended to be diagnostic rather than prescriptive, subjective rather than judgmental; the contours of your BASE may shift from one day to the next or from one writing project to another. For a digital version of the tool and a range of exercises on which to build, visit the Writer's BASE website at www.writersdiet.com/base.

Instructions:

For each of the BASE habits described below (behavioral, artisanal, social, emotional), assign yourself a ranking from 1 (low) to 10 (high).

B _____

Behavioral habits. My everyday academic writing habits are

9–10	excellent; I am a highly productive writer.
6–8	good but uneven.
3–5	unsatisfactory.
1–2	terrible; I feel unproductive most of the time.

A _____

Artisanal habits. My skills as an academic writer are

9–10	highly developed; I am confident in my ability to write clearly and well.
6–8	moderate.
3–5	underdeveloped.
1–2	very weak; other people seem to be much more competent writers than I am.

S _____

Social habits. I engage in productive conversations with other people about my writing and work-in-progress

9–10	frequently.
6–8	occasionally.
3–5	rarely.
1–2	almost never; I am a "lone wolf" scholar who shows other people my writing only when I feel it is ready to publish.

E _____

Emotional habits. When I think about my academic writing, the emotions I feel are

9–10   highly positive.
6–8   more positive than negative.
3–5   more negative than positive.
1–2   strongly negative; I hate to write.

On each of the four BASE axes in Figure 3 (numbered 0–10), place a dot corresponding to the number you chose for that category. Next, connect the dots. The resulting trapezoid represents the foundation on which your current writing practice rests.

Study your BASE carefully. Is it broad and well proportioned? Diamond shaped? Nearly triangular? How can you expand and strengthen the BASE? Where will you start?

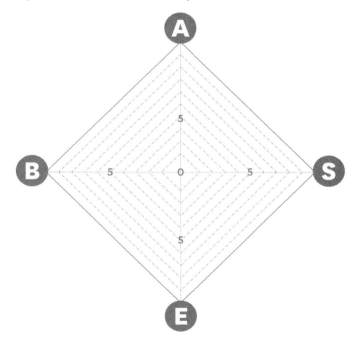

Figure 3. Enter your BASE scores on the diagram and connect the dots.

PART ONE

BEHAVIORAL HABITS

I like work: it fascinates me. I can sit and look at it
for hours.

—JEROME K. JEROME, *Three Men in a Boat*

Ten years ago, I read a book that changed the way I write. In *Professors as Writers: A Self-Help Guide to Productive Writing*, behavioral psychologist Robert Boice describes an intervention study in which he worked closely with three groups of struggling academic writers.[1] Participants in the first group behaved as they always had, "saving up" their research writing for large blocks of uninterrupted time that seldom actually materialized; those in the second group agreed to write in brief daily sessions of around thirty minutes each and to keep a log of their writing time; and those in the third group did the same, with the variation that Boice checked up on them twice weekly at unannounced intervals. The results of the study were astounding: by the end of the year, the participants in the third group had produced, on average, more than twice as many pages of publishable writing as those in the second group and more than nine times as many as those in the control group.

Impressed by Boice's findings, I immediately resolved to develop a regimen similar to that of the most productive academics in his study: I would write every day, log my writing time, and share my time logs in weekly meetings with a colleague. The first part of my experiment was a resounding success. I had already recently taken up the "morning pages" routine prescribed by Julia Cameron in her book *The Artist's Way*:

> Every morning, set your clock one-half hour early; get up and write three pages of longhand, stream-of-consciousness morning writing. Do not reread these pages or allow anyone else to read them. Ideally, stick these pages in a large manila envelope, or hide them somewhere.[2]

It was a relatively easy transition for me to switch from daily personal writing to daily scholarly writing and to extend my scheduled time from thirty to sixty minutes. That early-morning hour quickly became—and remains a decade later—a precious and productive time for me. Typically I roll out of bed around six a.m., plant myself in front of my computer with a cup of tea, and plunge straight into my writing wherever I left off the day before: no prereading, no obsessive editing of the previous day's work, no email check (well, maybe just a brief glance at my inbox . . .). Working at a slow but steady pace, editing and polishing individual sentences as I go but leaving major structural changes for later, I can often lay down a new paragraph before breakfast. Even during periods when teaching and administrative duties devour nearly all my time, those early-morning paragraphs build up one by one, gradually accruing into draft chapters and articles. What's more, my research remains always present in my mind, a faithful companion throughout my working week.

The second part of my experiment—logging my daily research time—also proved worthwhile. After several months, I was able to calculate how many publishable pages I had drafted and edited during my early-morning writing hours; from there, I extrapolated a rough word count. At first, I was appalled to discover that my published research output averaged out to only about one hundred words per hour. One hundred words! That's less than half the length of this paragraph. However, I soon came to realize that my new self-knowledge, albeit dispiriting, was also empowering. Now, if a colleague asks me to contribute an eight-hundred-word blog post or newsletter column ("You're a good writer, I'm sure you can bash something out quickly"), I know that it will probably take me at least eight hours to produce and polish. Armed with this knowledge, I have become much more realistic about planning my workload, more disciplined about carving out dedicated writing and editing time, and more confident about achieving my goals. Ten hours per week of writing can add up to an eighty-thousand-word book manuscript in less than two years.

The third part of my Boicean experiment, unfortunately, did not pan out so well. In an effort to re-create the sense of accountability imposed by Boice on the participants in his most successful group, I recruited a colleague to meet with me once a week to exchange time logs and discuss our respective goals and progress. However, my "writing buddy" stuck to his daily writing routine only for a short time; after that, our weekly meetings disintegrated into a morass of apologies and excuses, until we gave them up altogether. Over the next few years, I tried several times to resurrect the arrangement with other writing partners, but with no luck. Boice insists that keeping a daily writing log is critical to mastering a productive writing routine: "Sometimes the chart alone, especially the guilt of posting up a wasted day, is stimulus enough to get people writing."[3] But that guilt wasn't stimulus enough for my colleagues, apparently. One after another agreed to a weekly exchange of writing logs and supportive conversation; but one after another, despite my enthusiasm and encouragement, they soon fell by the wayside. Remorse and self-flagellation invariably followed: "I know I'm supposed to schedule daily writing time like you do, but I just don't seem to be able to keep it up. You're much more disciplined than I am. I'm sorry I've let you down."

In retrospect, I should have taken my colleagues' resistance as a warning signal. Instead, relying on my own positive experience rather than their negative ones, I became an eager evangelist for the Boicean cause. With a convert's zeal, I began offering productivity workshops at which I tirelessly preached the "Write every day!" mantra. To colleagues who resisted changing their ways—"I can only write when I feel like writing" or "I can't write in the early mornings because I'm too busy looking after my small children" or "I don't like the idea of scheduling every moment of my waking life"—I recommended Paul Silvia's book *How to Write a Lot*, a succinct, witty guide to academic productivity in the Boicean mode. Silvia insists that productivity has nothing to do with pleasure:

> Some kinds of writing are so unpleasant that no normal person will ever feel like doing them. . . . Struggling writers who "wait for inspiration" should get off their high horse and join the unwashed masses of real academic writers.

"I'm too busy" is just a "specious excuse" for avoiding daily writing:

> Like most false beliefs, this barrier persists because it's comforting. It's reassuring to believe that circumstances are against you and that you would write a lot if only your schedule had a few more big chunks of time to devote to writing.

So is an aversion to scheduling:

> Binge writers spend more time feeling guilty and anxious about not writing than schedule followers spend writing. . . . When confronted with their fruitless ways, binge writers often proffer a self-defeating dispositional attribution: "I'm just not the kind of person who's good at making a schedule and sticking to it." People like dispositional explanations when they don't want to change.[4]

Silvia's no-nonsense, pull-your-socks-up advice clearly resonated with many of my colleagues; they headed back to their offices with eyes bright and shoulders squared, determined to give daily writing a try. But how many of those enthusiastic disciples, I wonder now, were still writing every day a year, a month, or even a week later? And how many others slunk away from my workshops in brow-beaten silence, feeling even more "guilty and anxious" than before?

When I first started researching this book, I assumed that my findings about academics' writing habits would affirm the advice of Boice, Silvia, and the authors of other best-selling productivity guides, which aligned with my own experience as a devoted dailyist. The successful academics I interviewed would tell me, mostly, that they write every day; the colleagues who enrolled in my workshops in search of effective writing strategies would tell me, mostly, that they do not; and I would be able to publish persuasive empirical evidence that daily scheduled writing is indeed the magic bullet that Boice claims it to be, the secret elixir that ensures academic success. As the interview transcripts and data questionnaires began to pile up, however, they yielded some unexpected results. Only a small percentage of respondents in both groups—13 percent of the handpicked interview subjects and 12 percent of the self-selected workshop participants—reported that they systematically schedule daily writing time throughout the academic year. Put another way, roughly seven out of eight academics surveyed admitted that they do *not* write every day. Daily writing, it turns out, is neither a reliable marker nor a clear predictor of productivity.

Boice's highly prescriptive formula works well for some writers, particularly those hobbled by self-doubt and plagued by procrastination. But the Boicean way is not the only way, and academics who resist the evangelistic fervor of Boice's "missionary work" are by no means doomed to fallowness and failure.[5] Productivity, I discovered, is a broad church that tolerates many creeds. Some successful academics write daily, others sporadically; some at home, others at work; some on trains or airplanes or during children's sports practice, others in distraction-free environments; some on a word processor, others in longhand or using voice-recognition software; some whenever they have a few minutes free, others only when they have cleared hours or days of uninterrupted time. Some map out a detailed topic outline before they start writing; others write to discover what they have to say.

The three chapters that follow lay out a sheaf of renovation ideas rather than a single behavioral blueprint. Time regulates the first chapter; space structures the second; and rhythms and rituals animate the third. Every one of the strategies described in these chapters has worked for some writer somewhere; at least some of them are bound to work for you. Keep in mind, however, that behavioral habits of daily diligence are likely to crumble over time unless they are shored up by the other three foundation stones of your BASE: *artisanal habits* of craftsmanship and care, *social habits* of collegiality and collaboration, and *emotional habits* of confidence and pleasure.

1

FINDING TIME TO WRITE

You can't lose time behind the back of a sofa or discover a forgotten stash tucked away in a kitchen drawer. You can't mint it like coins or spend it like cash. Nevertheless, academics talk constantly about *making* time, *finding* time, *carving out* time to write. We fantasize about having more of it, and we bemoan our chronic lack of it. But from what—or whom—can we slice it away without doing damage to something or someone?

Proponents of daily writing offer a simple solution to this dilemma: by scheduling as little as half an hour of research writing into your calendar every day, you will ensure that your writing time never needs to be "found," because it's already there waiting for you. Email doesn't generally count as research writing (unless you are, say, communicating with a coauthor or journal editor); nor do administrative or teaching-related documents such as course syllabi, annual reports, or student references. Beyond that, however, the jury is out as to what kinds of activities qualify as "writing every day." For Robert Boice, "writing" is the composition of new sentences on a page, whether or not those words are intended for publication. For Paul Silvia, on the other hand, scheduled writing time may also include reading, note taking, editing, and data analysis—any research-related activity that moves the writing project forward. For Patricia Goodson and Joan Bolker, "every day" actually means five or six days a week, with occasional days of respite allowed. And for the novelist Stephen King, every day really means every day. King confesses that when he is working on a new novel, he writes for four or five hours each morning, no matter what: "That includes Christmas, the Fourth [of July], and my birthday."[1]

There are many compelling reasons why you might consider adopting a daily writing routine:

- *Daily writing prevents procrastination and blocking.* Instead of complaining about how hard it is to write, you simply sit down at the appointed time every day and do it; no more putting off starting until you have read just one more article or sharpened a few more pencils.

- *Daily writing demystifies the writing process.* Academics who write every day—even if only to sum up an hour's worth of reading or to record some preliminary thoughts about their data—have no fear of the blank page.

- *Daily writing keeps your research always at the top of your mind.* However cluttered your schedule may become with meetings, teaching, administrative tasks, and other obligations, a daily writing jag guarantees that you have spent at least some part of every workday thinking deeply about your research.

- *Daily writing generates new ideas.* As scientist Linus Pauling famously remarked, "If you want to have good ideas, you must have many ideas."[2] Writing prompts new modes of thought, activating parts of the brain that might otherwise lie dormant.

- *Daily writing adds up incrementally.* If you write just three hundred words per day five days per week, by the end of the month you will have a six-thousand-word article or chapter that might otherwise have remained just a gleam in your eye.

- *Daily writing helps you figure out what you want to say.* In the words of playwright Henry Miller, "Writing, like life itself, is a voyage of discovery."[3] Sometimes we have no idea which way we are headed until the sails have been hoisted and the wind kicks in.

For most people, however, daily scheduled writing is neither an intuitive habit to adopt nor an easy one to sustain. As any drill sergeant or Mother Superior can attest, few humans possess the intrinsic self-discipline required to adhere to a strictly regimented routine day after day and week after week, no matter how beneficial its effects. The vocabulary of academic development—"writing coaching," "writing cloisters," "dissertation boot camps"—hints at this all-too-common human failing. Even Boice, who devoted his scholarly career to enticing skeptical colleagues into "the congregation of satisfied and productive" daily writers, acknowledged the danger of "backsliding," a term he associated with straying from the strict rules of religion.[4] Little wonder, then, that academe is filled with lapsed dailyists who wear hair shirts of scholarly guilt as a result of their apostasy. The logic goes something like this: "I have been told that productive academics write every day. I tried for a while but failed to keep up the routine. It is therefore my own fault that I am not as productive as I would like to be. I am a bad person."

In fact, only a few of the writers in my interview sample told me that they adhere to the kind of strict, unbending, same-time-every-day schedule recommended by the most prescriptive "write every day" proponents. Even self-declared dailyists, I found, tend to take a more individualistic approach to their writing routine. For example, they may aspire to lay down a specific number of new words each day:

> I'm a morning person so I try to do my writing then, and I try to have a daily amount. (*Matthew Clarke, Education, University of New South Wales*)

Or they may aim for a certain page count:

> I try to write a page every day. I tell my students to think of inspiration as something inside your computer—so you have to turn it on and let it out. (*Lena Roos, Religious Studies, Uppsala University*)

Or they may declare themselves satisfied with just a small amount of forward progress:

> Even when I find it hard to write, I still try to get at least something down every day. It could be a paragraph. It could be two sentences, but it's just the feeling that you're actually moving ahead. (*Stefan Svallfors, Sociology, Umeå University*)

"The trajectories your ideas could take"

KALERVO GULSON

School of Education, University of New South Wales (Australia)

When sociologist of education Kal Gulson became a father, he was forced to rethink his writing habits:

> Previously, I would write in bursts. If I had a paper, I would just write that, and I would put off everything until I was finished. Having children made me realize I had to work in different ways—in shorter periods of time, with more planning.

Inspired by Paul Silvia's book *How to Write a Lot*, Gulson began blocking out daily writing time in his calendar, just as he blocks out meeting time and teaching time:

> I don't schedule any meetings before 10:30 a.m. If people ask, I say I'm writing. I try to talk about writing as an important part of building a research culture, a reinforcement of what you do. There is nothing wrong with making writing and research a core part of your work, as important as anything else that requires the same level of effort and protection.

Gulson still "writes to think" without necessarily knowing where his ideas will lead him, but now he tries to do so within a more structured framework:

> What I hadn't thought through was that in my reluctance to plan, I wasn't writing as efficiently as I could be. I think the act of planning particularly helps you see the trajectories your ideas could take. Ideas still come out of serendipitous moments, but the planning exercise can tie them together a little more quickly.

Paradoxically, he uses administrative systems to help reduce the burden of administration:

> Now I'm doing things that I never thought I'd do, like using an online management system that sets milestones and records day-by-day tasks and all those sorts of things. Because I hate administration, my aim is to do it as efficiently as possible in order to free up more time for writing. So I've actually moved admin into my writing; I now manage my writing in the same way I manage the rest of my life and work.

Nor did I observe much consistency in preferred writing times. Some writers follow a strict "write first" approach:

> I wake up in the morning, and I start working right away. I sit with my computer on my lap, and I drink my coffee, and I write. That's when I'm at my smartest. I think it's the coffee. (*Margery Fee, English, University of British Columbia*)

However, rising with the larks is not—to mix morning-based metaphors—everyone's cup of tea. For every productive academic who claimed to write best before breakfast, I spoke to others who favor later times of day. Some prefer afternoons:

> I'm not very good first thing in the morning, so I like to do not-so-challenging things then. But between three and seven p.m., between afternoon tea and dinner, that's when the best writing comes. (*Alison Gopnik, Psychology, University of California Berkeley*)

Some prefer evenings after dinner:

> I write in the evenings, and it keeps my sanity. After these days of meetings and dealings with budgets and this boring stuff, there is a total switching of gears. Some other people may play the violin instead. People escape in different ways. (*Sun Kwok, Physics, University of Hong Kong*)

Some prefer the middle of the night:

> I got used to writing late at night when my son was small. He would go to bed around ten, and then I got into the habit of staying up until two or three and writing at night. As he grew up, in fact, he would sometimes wake up like at one in the morning and say, "Mommy, are you writing?" "Yes." It was very comforting to him to know that I was still awake. (*Ruth Behar, Anthropology, University of Michigan*)

Before retirement, literary scholar Susan Gubar drew her dividing line not at a.m./p.m. but at "before teaching/after teaching":

> Because teaching requires an enormous amount of concentration and adrenalin, I can't write before I teach. But if I was done teaching at two or three, there would be an hour or two where I would really want to be at the computer. This was not any kind

of puritanism or discipline; this was looking for pleasure and delight. (*Susan Gubar, English, Indiana University*)

A few of the academics I interviewed—very few—possess the seemingly superhuman ability to write at any time of the day or night, with little need for rest or sustenance:

> The book I've just finished was primarily written from about eight thirty at night till about twelve thirty, and then I got up again at around five o'clock in the morning for a couple of hours and then on the weekends. It's the way I've always worked. I got ruined when I was doing my PhD, because I had little kids, and it took me seven years. And the only time I could find was after hours. I never really learned to sleep again. (*Shelda Debowski, academic leadership consultant, Australia*)

For most of us mortals, however, sacrificing sleep for the sake of scholarship is not to be recommended. Māori studies scholar Ewan Pohe recalls what happened when he started getting up to write at what poet Sylvia Plath called the "blue hour," that spookily silent predawn period "before cock crow, before the baby's cry, before the glassy music of the milkman, settling his bottles":[5]

> Three o'clock in the morning—that didn't really work. It's dead quiet; you can get a lot of focused thought done once you get used to it, but it gets you completely out of sync with your family, because you have to go to bed by seven o'clock in the evening. (*Ewan Pohe, Māori Studies, Victoria University of Wellington*)

Pohe's story highlights a theme that surfaced again and again in my conversations with successful academics: the intimate entanglement of their writing lives with their family lives. Some admitted that their preoccupation with writing may cause challenges for their loved ones:

> When I get really deep in a project, I can't do anything else. Stopping and washing dishes is really painful, and that can last for a long time—months. That's when it's really hard to find balance, and most of the time I wander around in a craze and complain to my family about how hard my life is. So they get really annoyed with me. Not only am I ignoring them and not available; I'm

"Simultaneously with both hands"

KURT ALBERTINE
Department of Pediatrics, University of Utah (USA)

Anatomist and physiologist Kurt Albertine started teaching in an era when there was no such thing as PowerPoint. Instead, lecturers learned to "draw beautifully, simultaneously with both hands" to illustrate the details of human anatomy:

> For example, if a cross-section of the spinal cord was to be drawn, you took a piece of chalk in each hand, bellied up to the chalkboard, placed the two pieces of chalk side by side as high as your reach allowed, and pulled the chalk pieces along arcs from above your head and outward and then inward to meet at your navel. The result, with some practice, was a perfect outline of a cross-section of the cervical spinal cord.

These days, when marking up papers on airplanes, Albertine chooses his writing hand based on which side of the aisle he is seated on: "This is a flexible solution to avoid crashing my elbow into the person sitting beside me."

Albertine's ambidextrousness reflects his two-handed approach to academic life. His workday begins at five a.m., when he rises to phone his lab and check on the preterm lambs. Next, he exercises for an hour and a half before heading to the office to squeeze in an hour of writing before anyone else arrives. The rest of the day, he confesses, "is a disaster, like everybody's day." But in the evening, after dinner at home with his wife, he gets a second wind. Around ten p.m., he allows himself to nod off for twenty minutes or so: "Catnaps refresh me, and physiological data suggest that they improve alertness." Then he sits down and writes like a "holy terror" until well past midnight:

> I am bright eyed and bushy tailed, completely awake. I write from eleven until one every night. These are my two hours of focused, uninterrupted writing. I typically do the writing with closed eyes. I visualize what I compose. Of course, typos are rampant. But I find that if I get the story line recorded the first time, tidying up is easy.

In the morning, he is up again at five to check on the preterm lambs, and the cycle begins anew.

complaining all the time and wanting them to be nice to me and nurture me. (*Mindy Fullilove, Clinical Psychiatry, Columbia University*)

Just as frequently, however, I heard stories of family lives enriched and enabled by academics' writing lives, often in unexpected ways. Educator and poet Carl Leggo described an idyllic sabbatical leave structured around the daily needs of his intergenerational family:

> I drove my son to work every morning. He's thirty, but he didn't have a car at the time. So he and I would have that time together, driving some distance—almost a half hour—to get him there and talking most of the way. Then I would pick up my granddaughters at about three thirty in the afternoon. In between, I would write and again in the evenings. The rhythm of that was perfect. (*Carl Leggo, Education, University of British Columbia*)

Rather than forcing his family to march to the drumbeat of his writing schedule, Leggo allowed the lilts and cadences of his household to set the pace for his writing.

The unbroken rhythms of a research leave can, to be sure, be challenging to sustain during a busy teaching term. Some writers create weekly minisabbaticals by working on the Sabbath:

> I tend to write book reviews on weekends. I try to just sit down with the late morning or early afternoon ahead of me, and dinnertime is the time by which I have to have the draft. (*Anthony Grafton, History, Princeton University*)

Others mark out a weekly writing day and guard it with sacred devotion:

> I try to be very religious about keeping Monday completely free for research. It would have to be a summons from the vice-chancellor or something like that to draw me out. It would have to be the place burning down, or something of great seriousness. (*Michael Reilly, Māori, Pacific, and Indigenous Studies, University of Otago*)

> I have been absolutely religious about having at least one day a week at home specifically for my research. I am just not available for meetings on Fridays, full stop, and people work around

that. (*Sarah Maddison, Social and Political Sciences, University of Melbourne*)

Many of my interview subjects cited the long summer break as the most fertile period of their academic year, a time when articles get written, book manuscripts get completed, and the well of scholarship gets refilled:

> My main strategy has been when there's a break—whether it's a week or a couple of weeks in the winter or the longer break in the summer—to absolutely clear the decks before I get there, to take care of any teaching or administrative responsibilities and to have as little grading as possible going into them, so that I can have concentrated writing time. (*Lesley Wheeler, English, Washington and Lee University*)

But not everyone wants to spend the summer hunkered down over a keyboard. Irish-born literary scholar Enda Duffy, whose family summers in Italy, recalls the grilling he received from his department chair upon returning to campus one autumn:

> He said, "What did you do in summer?" He wanted me to give a full report on the three articles I had written plus the research I had done for my next important volume. But I said, "I sat on the terrace reading the *Herald Tribune*." (*Enda Duffy, English, University of California at Santa Barbara*)

Experimental psychologist Cecilia Heyes learned the hard way about the importance of taking a break:

> When I was a graduate student, finishing up my PhD, I had been working seven days a week for months and months; then I went home to see my mother, and I actually fainted for the first and only time in my life. At that point I realized okay, this seven-days-a-week thing doesn't really work for me. Since then I have always made a point of taking at least one full day a week off from work, often two. (*Cecilia Heyes, Psychology, University of Oxford*)

As journalist Ferris Jabr reminds us, time out from writing can also be time well spent: "Downtime replenishes the brain's stores of attention and motivation, encourages productivity and creativity, and is essential to both achieve our highest levels of performance and simply form stable memories in everyday life."[6]

For the vast majority of successful academics, writing is neither a daily routine nor a rare occurrence, neither an immovable constant nor a random event. Writing is the work that gets done in the interstices between teaching, office hours, faculty meetings, administration, email, family events, and all the other messy, sprawling demands of academic life. Economist Janet Currie described a fantasy harbored by many of the colleagues I spoke to:

> If I had a whole week where I didn't have to do anything else, I could sit down and write a whole article from beginning to end, and that would be very beautiful. But I hardly ever get to do that, so the best I can do is to find a day here and there. I just have to take whatever time I have and be very disciplined. (*Janet Currie, Economics and Public Affairs, Princeton University*)

Note how the language of self-regulation ("I have to be very disciplined") mingles here with the language of desire ("that would be very beautiful"). Words like *pleasure* and *challenge* cropped up frequently in my interviews, suggesting that successful writers do not rely on externally mandated discipline alone:

> I associate writing with pleasure in ideas, in communicating with people. I think writing is the ultimate challenge, and that's why I like it, because I can't resist a challenge. (*Ludmilla Jordanova, History, Durham University*)

Perhaps what we need is a radical reconceptualization of time: not as an adversary to be vanquished (*a race against time*) or a criminal to be tracked down (*fugitive time*) or an employee to be disciplined (*time management*) or a commodity to be squandered (*wasted time*) but as an expansive, fluid entity that will always resist our efforts to contain it. Time can enrich our lives (*quality time*), transport us to new places and paces (*island time*), and help us out in moments of need:

> If I can't find the time, the time finds me. (*Margaret Breen, English, University of Connecticut*)

"Squishing everything in"

JANELLE JENSTAD

Department of English, University of Victoria (Canada)

Janelle Jenstad likes to do "a little bit of teaching, a little bit of research, and a little bit of service every day," writing whenever and wherever she can: "on the train, on the plane, in airports, in coffee shops." She sometimes goes to bed at the same time as her young children—"like eight thirty, nine"—and gets up at four a.m. to write: "It's sacred time. The house is quiet. Everybody is asleep." Her current research files are kept pinned to her Microsoft Word menu so that they are always ready to open: "I'll write at the kitchen table if the kids are busy playing with Lego. I'll pop open that file and add a few more words."

A "terrible perfectionist" by nature, Jenstad has learned to write "drafty drafts" full of holes: "I give myself permission to write, 'I don't know what I'm doing here. Come back later!'" Borrowing vocabulary and metaphors from her husband, a building tradesman, she distinguishes during the editing process between the "roughing cut" and the "finishing cut":

> If you're cutting a piece of metal to make a shape, the very first thing you do is give it a roughing cut, where you just get rid of most of the excess metal. Once you've done that, then you do your finishing cut. I've used the concept a lot in my writing and with my students when they come in for editing sessions with me. We'll start to wrestle with some little detail, and then I'll say, "Hang on, we're not finished with our roughing cut yet. We don't know what the shape of this project is yet, so let's not niggle over the details. We'll save that for a finishing cut at the end."

Despite the challenges of juggling many different personal and professional roles—scholar, teacher, mother, wife, writer, blogger, academic colleague, and more—Jenstad contends that she is not particularly interested in maintaining "work-life balance":

> Every aspect of my life is invested in reading and writing and words and texts. When my kids are older, we'll probably be going to the theater together, and I'll probably be writing about that experience of introducing children to Shakespeare. It's not about balance. It's about squishing everything in.

Whenever and however often you write—whether you find the time or the time finds you—there is no "right" time for writing. The best time to write is any time you do.

THINGS TO TRY

Routinize

Many books and articles on productive writing recommend that you establish a daily or weekly writing routine, particularly if you are prone to procrastination or suffer from writer's block. The basic principle is simple: decide how many hours per week you will devote to research writing (however you may choose to define "research" and "writing"); schedule those hours into your calendar; and keep your appointments with yourself just as faithfully as you would keep an appointment to teach a class or visit the dentist. Later chapters of this book will help you develop the artisanal skills, social networks, and emotional confidence to stay on track with your new routine—or, if daily scheduled writing doesn't suit your style, to ditch the rulebook and try a different approach altogether.

Remix

Experiment with writing at different times of the day: mornings before breakfast, evenings after dinner, afternoons at the hour when you normally start craving a postprandial nap. ("It's a time when one's body . . . is quiescent, somnolent," notes novelist Anthony Burgess, "but the brain can be quite sharp.")[7] Make a brief note about how you felt and what you wrote each time. Do you find that different types of writing-related tasks—brainstorming, data analysis, drafting, revising—work better at different times of day? If yes, can you leverage that knowledge into a productive writing routine?

Write at a time that feels "wrong"

For example, you could close your office door for an hour or two on a busy teaching day or slip away with a notebook during a family holiday. Pay attention to how that "transgressive writing" session goes. Did you find it more productive than "routine writing"? If so, how might you harness that subversive energy in your everyday writing life?

Read a book

If you like the idea of establishing a regular writing routine, there are numerous books, blogs, and other resources available to help you plan your productive new life. For a punchy kick-start, try Robert Boice's evangelical *Professors as Writers*, Tara Gray's energetic *Publish and Flourish*, Paul Silvia's slothdom-busting *How to Write a Lot*, or Eviatar Zerubavel's sensible *The Clockwork Muse*. There are also writing guides tailored especially for doctoral students (such as Joan Bolker's *Writing Your Dissertation in 15 Minutes a Day*) or focusing on specific academic genres (such as Rowena Murray's *Writing for Academic Journals*) or promising a particular publishing outcome within a set amount of time (such as Wendy Belcher's *Write Your Article in 12 Weeks*). Studies of writer's block (such as Keith Hjortshoj's *Understanding Writing Blocks*) can provide insight into the complex psychology of time management. And finally, books with inviting titles such as *Thinking, Fast and Slow* (Daniel Kahneman), *Slow Professor: Challenging the Culture of Speed in the Academy* (Maggie Berg and Barbara Seeber), and *The Art of Procrastination: A Guide to Effective Dawdling, Lollygagging and Postponing* (John Perry) remind us of the value of slowing down.[8]

2

THE POWER OF PLACE

In our daily lives as teachers, researchers, administrators, and students, we are constantly shunted from one prescribed venue to another: lecture theaters, meeting rooms, offices, laboratories, classrooms. But writing is a movable feast, an activity that academics can carry with them wherever they go—and they do. The colleagues I interviewed write at work:

> I've always done my writing in my academic office. I felt that once I started working at home, I'd never stop working. (*Stephen Rowland, Higher Education, University College London*)

And anywhere but work:

> I've hardly ever written anything good here in my office. It always happens in the middle of the night or in the morning in a summer cottage or at strange places like the train. So I tell my students, "You should go to the forest or down to the beach to write." (*Thomas Aastrup Rømer, Education, Aarhus University*)

And at home:

> I have a lovely office on campus, but I basically can't work there because it's too distracting. (*Kwame Anthony Appiah, Philosophy, Princeton University*)

And anywhere but home:

> I don't and can't write at home. It's just impossible. My family would just never let it happen. My son will say things to me like,

"I hate your computer," which is devastating coming from a two-year-old. (*Stephen Ross, English, University of Victoria*)

And on the road:

A large part of all my books have been written on airplanes and then airports and hotels, when the rest of Japan is asleep, that sort of thing. (*Keith Devlin, Human Sciences and Technologies, Stanford University*)

And in the bedroom:

My computer is not far from my bed—it's a laptop—so if I have a brain overdrive in the middle of the night, I'm up at two o'clock. Usually an hour of typing will put me back to sleep. (*Poia Rewi, Māori, Pacific, and Indigenous Studies, University of Otago*)

And in beautiful, faraway places:

The year I was translating *Eugene Onegin*, I traveled a lot. For instance, I did some stanzas up in the Sierras in California while hiking. One in a meadow. I was sitting in a tree, on a low branch in the tree, by a lake with wildflowers. I did a bunch in Paris. I also did a bunch in Italy—Florence, Siena, Trento, and other magnificent spots. (*Douglas Hofstadter, Cognitive Science, Indiana University*)

And in venues close to home that remind them of beautiful, faraway places:

We can't go to Paris every time we want to write productively (Paris being the site of our most productive writing/thinking sessions), but we've been trying to re-create what works for us on those trips: combining short, collaborative writing bursts with reading/brainstorming sessions and physically moving to different writing locations rather than our offices: Special Collections at the library, the Bibliocafé, other cafés. (*Lisa Surridge and Mary Elizabeth Leighton, English, University of Victoria*)

And whenever or wherever they can:

I'll write on the couch. I'll write while the TV is on. I'll write while I'm at the table. I actually get itchy if I can't write. (*Inger Mewburn, Director of Research Training, Australian National University*)

"Go a little wider"

STAFFAN ANDERSSON

Department of Physics and Astronomy, Uppsala University (Sweden)

Staffan Andersson's daily writing habits have been shaped by his family life. Even before he had children, he found it difficult to work in his university office:

> If you sit in your office and write, you have to have a big, red light, kill your phone, rip out the computer cord, and shut down the wireless. You have to be unreachable, because if you don't do that, you can't write. You can start writing, but then after a maximum of forty-five minutes, someone turns up with a question about this or that.

Now, on a typical weekday, Andersson leaves his office around three p.m., looks after his children for a few hours before dinner, and helps prepare the evening meal with his wife, who also works full-time. Later, from seven thirty onward, he writes for an hour or two in a small outbuilding away from the household fray. Andersson and his wife have published a book together, an educational volume written in their native Swedish and aimed mainly at students:

> Some people said, when we had our third kid at the same time as finishing our book, "How can you do it?" But having the kids actually helps you prioritize how you do things—a lot better time management. We've been juggling two careers for fifteen years, so to actually do the juggling together was nice.

Andersson brings a "copy-adapt" philosophy to his academic writing: "I learn the rules, and then I ask, can I transform it in some way? 'Go a little wider,' as we say in Swedish?" Upon completing his PhD in molecular physics, he decided to make a "mad leap" and publish a reader-friendly version of his thesis:

> I wrote a popular scientific summary, with a nice layout, some pictures, mainly for my aunts and parents, and printed one hundred copies. That actually that went out quicker than the thesis did, because people just grabbed it. You didn't do that sort of thing back then—but I did.

Having initially trained as a journalist, Andersson understands the core principles of effective communication—"Begin with your audience, always"—and dislikes scientific conventions that demand the quenching of individual expression. He now publishes mainly in physics education, a field in which "you're allowed to have a voice": "It's more narrative. It's a lot more personal. I enjoy that writing a lot more."

In her 1929 book *A Room of One's Own*, novelist Virginia Woolf described the female imagination as a richly diverse collection of architectural spaces:

> The rooms differ so completely; they are calm or thunderous; open on to the sea, or, on the contrary, give on to a prison yard; are hung with washing; or alive with opals and silks; are hard as horsehair or soft as feathers.[1]

Likewise, the physical and metaphorical spaces of academic writing vary as much as the backgrounds, habits, and emotions of those who inhabit them. Paul Silvia scoffs at unproductive colleagues who bemoan the lack of "their own space" for writing:

> I'm not sympathetic to this creaky excuse. I've never had my own room as a home office or private writing space. In a string of small apartments and houses, I wrote on a small table in the living room, in my bedroom, in the guest bedroom, in the master bedroom, and even (briefly) in a bathroom.[2]

Yet the annals of creativity are filled with stories of writers who have insisted on working in solitude. Ian Fleming produced his James Bond novels during the two months he spent every winter at his cliff-top estate in Jamaica; Maya Angelou famously drove every morning to a rented motel room that she kept as bare and ascetic as a monk's cell; Gustav Mahler, William Butler Yeats, Rainer Maria Rilke, and Carl Jung all produced some of their best work in stone cottages or towers, cloistered within elemental walls.[3] "You can read anywhere, almost," muses novelist Stephen King, "but when it comes to writing . . . most of us do our best in a place of our own."[4]

Some writers say that they can write practically anywhere if they have to:

> I remember once being in a motel in California somewhere. It was a very cheap motel—that was all I could afford then. I had to rearrange the furniture in order to get a space to work, but once I'd done that, I was away writing. (*Brian Boyd, English, University of Auckland*)

Others insist on the importance of establishing "the right place to write":

I was on study leave and tried to write in Melbourne. I couldn't write a thing. It was at a modern black-and-white hotel. All the furniture was black leather settees and white lampshades and white Formica desks. It was just the wrong space. I need an attic and a leather chair and an old-fashioned writing desk. (*Tony Harland, Higher Education, University of Otago*)

Cognitive psychologist Ronald T. Kellogg explains that spatialized rituals can amplify performance by inducing "intense concentration or a favorable motivational or emotional state," triggering "retrieval of ideas, facts, plans, and other relevant knowledge associated with the place, time, or frame of mind selected by the writer for work."[5] When psychologist Mihaly Csikszentmihalyi and his colleagues polled individuals from diverse populations around the world to learn the conditions associated with "flow"— states of high concentration and creativity—they discovered that, for 40 percent of respondents, "the performance of the activity was enough to trigger the experience."[6] For example, if you take your laptop to the university library every morning and write for an hour while sitting at a desk with a view of a courtyard garden, you are likely to get "into the flow" more quickly each time you go to that same spot to write. After a while, you may even find that sitting at *any* desk in *any* library or looking through *any* window to *any* garden or even just opening your laptop in *any* public place can trigger a similar response.

For many of the academics I interviewed, music has a similarly evocative function:

There was a particular piece of classical music—I can't remember what song it was—that was about eight minutes long, and in the last throes of my PhD, when it was going really well, I would just play this while I was writing. It would be at a particular time of day or a couple of times a day, because it made me feel a particular kind of way and it gave me a high. (*Kalervo Gulson, Education, University of New South Wales*)

According to Don Campbell in his book *The Mozart Effect*, Baroque music with a pulse of around sixty beats per minute— Mozart, Bach, Handel, Vivaldi, Corelli—can "raise performance levels and productivity by reducing stress and tension, masking

"Hunger for the time"

REBECCA PIEKKARI

School of Economics, Aalto University (Finland)

Picture the following scenario. Your family owns a summer cottage on a remote northern lake, a place where your writing flows freely. Your parents, who happen to own the cottage next door, have offered to look after your children in the mornings while you work. Your afternoons are spent berry picking with the kids, swimming in the lake, or relaxing in the sauna; at night, you share leisurely dinners with family and friends under the twilight glow of the midnight sun. Does that sound like a life of blurred boundaries and endless work stress—or does it sound like paradise?

For Rebecca Piekkari, summer holidays at the family cottage in Finland offer the best of both worlds: an opportunity for relaxation that is also a time for focused writing. Working in an academic field dominated by quantitative researchers, she brings qualitative methodologies and an experimental ethos—"innovation, creativity, pluralism"—to her writing:

> For example, while teaching a research methods course to graduate students, I noticed that the discovery process is at odds with the format of a standard research paper; so I started to experiment with unconventional forms of research writing. I'm currently working with a student to write a theatrical play. And although I usually publish in English, I recently wrote a piece in Finnish for businessmen; that gave me a chance to let loose with a more playful writing style, to feel the wind beneath my wings.

In an article with the delightful title "Herding Cats from Uppsala to Sigtuna," Piekkari worked with coauthors from seven countries to produce a collaborative research paper about the pleasures and challenges of writing a collaborative research paper with coauthors from seven countries.

Piekkari's summer writing sessions are made possible by a supportive family economy even while they contribute to that economy. If she were to emerge at lunchtime each day in a terrible mood, her husband and children would almost certainly rebel and order her to take a break. But for Piekkari, writing *is* a break from her hectic routine as a teacher, supervisor, mentor, colleague, and (at the time of our interview) vice dean for research and international affairs at Aalto University. Sitting in her Helsinki office during a busy workweek, she spoke longingly of her "hunger for the time" to write—an appetite assuaged every summer at that cottage by the lake.

irritating sounds and contributing to a sense of privacy."[7] But rap, reggae, or rock can have much the same effect:

> I listen to music, often with headphones, and I turn off email and everything. I try to put myself in a cocoon. There are only five bands that I'll listen to when I'm writing. If I'm listening to something I know really well, it drowns out all the other sound and allows me to focus and concentrate. (*Eric Hayot, Comparative Literature, Pennsylvania State University*)

Stillness, too, can be a kind of music:

> I can't write when my kids are playing the piano in the background or yelling at me or when students are knocking on my door. I know other people can write and have music on, but I can't. I have to sit in total silence. (*Deborah Kaple, Sociology, Princeton University*)

For writers who dislike ambient noise, Mozart on the stereo may create as much of a distraction as a boisterous child or a demanding student.

The trope of the unplanned visitor appeared often in my interviews with successful academics:

> When my kids were small, I often stayed home with them if they were sick. I realized that their naptime was a good time for writing, because I could use those free hours to produce as much as I would have if I had been here in the office and disturbed by people knocking on the door. (*Christer Nilsson, Ecology, Umeå University*)

I'm reminded of the proverbial "person on business from Porlock" who interrupted Samuel Taylor Coleridge just as he was writing down his visionary poem "Kubla Khan":

> On his return to his room, [the poet] found, to his no small surprise and mortification, that though he still retained some vague and dim recollection of the general purport of the vision, yet, with the exception of some eight or ten scattered lines and images, all the rest had passed away like the images on the surface of a stream into which a stone has been cast, but, alas! without the after restoration of the latter![8]

Coleridge's unwelcome visitor has come to symbolize any un-wanted disruption of creative inspiration: the student, colleague, or family member who demands our attention just as we were about to write something brilliant. (Or were we secretly hoping for a scapegoat on whom to blame our lack of productivity?) In the age of the Internet, of course, the new person from Porlock is email, which sneaks into our studies without even knocking:

> I think email has been a disaster for all of us. The idea of letting the inbox determine your order of priority is utterly ridiculous, but it's very, very hard to resist. (*Michèle Lamont, Sociology, Harvard University*)

Email tempts us with instant gratification:

> We're all waiting on those little bits of external validation that usually come in via our inbox—an invitation to something, a review, something nice. (*Sarah Maddison, Social and Political Sciences, University of Melbourne*)

And it ambushes us wherever we go:

> I try to stay off the Internet when I'm writing. But then there'll be the thing I have to check in an email message, and I'll open it up—and, of course, all the other email messages will pop up. (*David Pace, History, Indiana University*)

Literary scholar Leah Price recalls how, during a research leave in California, she woke up every morning to find her inbox already full of messages from East Coast colleagues:

> But then when I went on research leave to France a few years later, there was no new email in the mornings, so my time there was much more productive. (*Leah Price, English, Harvard University*)

That was when she learned the importance of "unplugging" to write.

Some academics find that the best cure for Porlock syndrome is to go "on retreat," preferably to a place without Wi-Fi: a cabin in the woods, a campground caravan, a beach house, a motel room. A solo writing retreat lacks the collegial ethos of a group retreat (see Chapter 9, "Writing among Others") but can provide many of the same benefits: protected writing time, a sense of freedom,

"Here at this very desk"

ROBERT POULIN

Department of Zoology, University of Otago (New Zealand)

Growing up in French-speaking Canada, Robert Poulin started reading English novels as a teenager, "because they were half the price of French books." An influential high school teacher taught him how to structure a persuasive essay:

> He would draw an upside-down triangle—that was the introduction—then there was a rectangle for the main body of the work and another triangle for the conclusion, which should end at about the same level of generality as the introduction. This is still how I structure my own scientific papers, and it's how I teach my postgraduates to do it. No one has ever criticized the structure of my writing.

Later Poulin attended McGill University, where he made "all sorts of English-speaking friends—from the States, from the rest of Canada." Now, he says, "I write much, much better in English than in French." Poulin enjoys scientific writing and especially relishes the challenge of crafting a persuasive grant proposal:

> I actually find it fun and exciting to sell your ideas and make sure the explanation is crystal clear. In one page, you have to convince people who are not expert in your area that, yes, they should give you a million dollars.

However, leading a research group of fourteen people leaves him little time for his own writing:

> If I get an hour of free time to write, that's a good day—that's a good week, even. So what I try to do is find blocks of time, small blocks of maybe two or three hours. Ideally, I find several of those in a period of a week or two weeks, and that would be what I use to write. It's all done here at this very desk. I don't write at home. All my writing has been done sitting here at this computer during my normal work hours.

Although he often closes his office door when he is writing, Poulin does not turn off email:

> I just let the emails come in, and I'm curious—I look at them every time I hear the little ring. It's an addiction, but it doesn't seem to interrupt my thoughts. I can just stop for five minutes, reply to an email, and get back to the writing. A brief interruption will not make me forget what I've been thinking about for days.

a change of scene. Even when family responsibilities, teaching schedules, or budgetary constraints make leaving town impossible, overworked academics can rig up smaller-scale, close-to-home versions of what Bruce Rogers calls the "writing cloister": a place where, monk-like, "you do nothing but write" for hours or days at a time.[9] For example, if you once spent a productive sabbatical on an island (real or metaphorical) far away from the hurly-burly of your usual workplace, you may discover that you can achieve a similar sense of productive solitude by taking your laptop to an art gallery on a Friday afternoon or by renting a motel room for an intensive weekend of writing, sleeping, and take-out meals.

Just as our bodies all differ in their responses to physical stimuli, so too do the places where we prefer to station them. Voltaire wrote mostly in bed; Wallace Stevens composed some of his most innovative and influential poetry while walking to work; Ingmar Bergman retreated to a remote Swedish island to write his film scripts; Jane Austen surreptitiously penned her novels in between neighbors' visits to her drawing room.[10] Whether you work in an airy studio, a stone tower, a bathroom, or even a bed, there is no "right" place for writing. The best place to write is anywhere you do.

THINGS TO TRY

Escape

The idea of retreating to an island every summer is all very well; but how can we dodge interruptions and distractions the rest of the time, in our everyday working lives? One strategy is to identify your personal Porlocks and allow them no opportunity to knock on your door. At home, turning off Wi-Fi for a few hours may do the trick. In a public venue or open-plan office, you could try facing a wall or window and donning a pair of headphones; not only will you be shielding yourself from visual and aural distractions, but you will also be signaling to other people that you do not want to be disturbed. Even in an academic department with an open-door culture, there is nothing wrong with closing your office door for an hour or two and posting a laminated sign proclaiming "Writer at work, please return at ___ o'clock." Alternatively, try swapping offices with a colleague for the afternoon; your door will remain collegially ajar, but when people pop their heads in and see that you're not there, chances are they will go away and come back later.

Beautify

Does clutter drive you crazy? Do certain colors nourish your senses? Do you write best in a room with a view? Forget all those people who tell you that "real writers" don't care about the scenery. Indulge your aesthetic sensibilities by clearing your desk, decorating your study, or taking your laptop to a place where you can spend an hour or two in beautiful surroundings. If you work in a windowless cubicle, you can tack up some colorful postcards or display scenic photos on your computer desktop to encourage and inspire you while you work.

Take it outside

William Wordsworth composed much of his best poetry during long walks through the Lake District of northern England—and there are sound scientific reasons why. As Richard Louv notes in *The Nature Principle*, the benefits of physical exercise (which stimulates the senses and promotes blood flow to the brain) are multiplied out in nature: when we crunch over autumn leaves or face the sea breeze, we breathe in particulates that literally make us feel good.[11] If long walks in the wilderness are not a viable part of your daily routine, are there places closer to home—parks, urban walkways, pleasant neighborhoods—where you can re-create that same winning combination of fresh air, exercise, and physical regeneration on an everyday scale?

Read a book

The physical world shapes our memories and stirs our senses—and so can books about writing and the physical world, from Anne Morrow Lindbergh's evocative *Gift from the Sea* to William Zinsser's charming *Writing Places*. Before you start reading about space and place, however, consider the places and spaces where you read. A colleague of mine keeps a comfortable "reading chair" in her office—a daily reminder to sit down, take a deep breath, and let her mind shift into reading mode. My own reading habits, by contrast, have become increasingly itinerant in recent years; much though I love the seductive physicality of printed books, I now carry a whole library of e-books on my computer and keep a few audiobooks queued up on my smartphone. Recently, while traveling by ferry to spend a few days in my writing studio on New Zealand's Waiheke Island, I pulled up William Butler Yeats's "Lake Isle of Innisfree" on my laptop screen:

> I will arise and go now, and go to Innisfree,
> And a small cabin build there, of clay and wattles made:
> Nine bean-rows will I have there, a hive for the honey-bee,
> And live alone in the bee-loud glade.

Later, walking on the beach, I listened to the opening passage of Henry David Thoreau's *Walden*:

> When I wrote the following pages, or rather the bulk of them, I lived alone, in the woods, a mile from any neighbor, in a house which I had built myself, on the shore of Walden Pond, in Concord, Massachusetts, and earned my living by the labor of my hands only.

The landscapes so evocatively described by Yeats and Thoreau have now become inextricably linked in my mind with the seascapes of another hemisphere: the ferry pulling into Matiatia Bay, the waves breaking on Onetangi Beach.[12]

3

RHYTHMS AND RITUALS

Time and place will remain empty containers for failed ambitions unless you fill them with your writing. But even once you have established *when* and *where* to write, so many other questions remain. How often should I write, and for how long? Should I shape my sentences as I go, or should I write first and revise later? Should I draw up a detailed outline, or should I plunge straight in and "write to think"? Should I separate research tasks from writing tasks, or should I write surrounded by my books and notes, looking up references along the way? Should I brew myself a cup of tea or go for a run before I get started, or should I resist procrastination and "just write"?

This chapter does away with *should* and focuses instead on *may*, a lovely old-fashioned auxiliary verb that connotes possibility and permission. *May* I discover my own writing rhythms and develop my own writing rituals? Yes, you may. *May* I be released from the guilt of feeling "less disciplined" than my colleague in the office next door, who writes to a daily schedule and posts a weekly word log proclaiming his progress? Yes, you may. *May* I ignore the advice of all those productivity-pumping books, articles, and websites that tell me I should write in a certain way, at certain intervals, for a certain length of time? Yes, you may. Alternatively, you may choose a prescriptive formula and follow it to the letter, if doing so works best for you.

The chapter is sequenced as a series of oppositional metaphors (some of which will return in different guises in Chapter 12, "Metaphors to Write By"). As you read, you may want to question and collapse these oppositions, probing the nuances and shadings in between. Day or night—how about twilight? Black or white— what's wrong with shades of gray? Sink or swim—why not float instead?

Blast or sculpt?

"Write first, revise later" is a strategy frequently recommended by writing experts as a cure for the twin evils of procrastination and perfectionism. The idea is that you should turn off your critical internal editor, get some words onto the page, and leave the revising and shaping for another day—a process optimistically labeled "spontaneous writing" by Robert Boice, "generative writing" by Rowena Murray, "effortless writing" by Dorothea Brande, and "freewriting" by Peter Elbow.[1] The academics I interviewed preferred explosive words such as "blast" and "breakthrough":

> I'm a fast writer. I like to blast something out and then go back and really work on it. (*Andrea Lunsford, English, Stanford University*)

> Often there's a breakthrough time where you write and write and write and write, and it's very bad and there are lots of pages— fifteen pages or more. (*James Garraway, Higher Education, Cape Peninsula University of Technology*)

Or they imposed directional metaphors such as "flow" and "in the groove":

> I have ideas, I start writing, and the more I write, the more I get into the ideas. And it sort of keeps flowing. So once I get into a groove, it keeps moving in that groove. (*Marysol Asencio, Sociology, University of Connecticut*)

Or, less poetically, they called it "blatting" or "blgggh writing":

> I tend to sit with a blank Word document and try and blat some ideas out; then I leave it for a day or two and think about it at night, on the bike, walking around. Eventually a structure emerges, so that it all hangs together and has a bit of grace and style to it. (*Sam Elworthy, Director, Auckland University Press*)

> I'm a "blgggh" writer, as opposed to a "fiddly writer." A fiddly writer is someone who writes a sentence and goes back and

checks the sentence is exactly as they want it before they go to the next one. Whereas I just write frantically and then go back afterwards and revise and edit and chop and change. (*Bill Barton, Mathematics Education, University of Auckland*)

Charles Darwin had an even less elegant description: "I scribble in a vile hand whole pages as quickly as I possibly can."[2]

Many writing guides insist that you *should* (there's that word again!) blast first and edit later, never fiddle-as-you-go:

> Your first drafts should sound like they were hastily translated from Icelandic by a nonnative speaker. Writing is part creation and part criticism, part id and part superego: Let the id unleash a discursive screed, and then let the superego evaluate it for correctness and appropriateness.[3]

> You should not, and cannot afford to, worry about concision when you are just starting to write. . . . If you cut and prune too early, you'll slow yourself down.[4]

However, craft-focused writers—let's call them "sculptors" rather than "fiddlers"—may prefer to revise and edit recursively from the moment they start writing:

> I'm one of those people for whom words just don't flow out in a whole sequence end to end. I spend a lot of time writing and re-writing as I go. (*Michael Reilly, Māori, Pacific, and Indigenous Studies, University of Otago*)

And of course there are those who alternately blast and sculpt, and there are those who blast slowly or sculpt quickly, and there are those who neither blast nor sculpt but craft their prose according to a different set of metaphors altogether.

Bungee or map?

For many of the academics I interviewed—particularly those at the humanities end of the scholarly spectrum—writing is an essential part of the research process, a generative task, a form of thinking:

> In literary studies, you cannot really separate out a phase where you do all the research and then you just put it down on paper. It doesn't work like that—at least not for me. The writing *is* the re-

"They have a map"

KEVIN KENNY

Department of History, Boston College (USA)

Historian Kevin Kenny typically spends several years gathering, sifting through, and organizing his research data before he finally sits down to write a book. By that time, he has processed stacks of primary and secondary material into thematically organized files that represent future chapters or sections. He distills these files into a detailed, top-down outline that contains two columns, labeled "Content" and "Evidence":

> I lay out the book as a whole in considerable detail before I write any of it. The analytical building blocks of the book emerge organically through that process.

Determined to make his work accessible to a wide range of readers, Kenny also deploys some "old-fashioned literary techniques" that he learned years ago in a fiction writing course. His most recent book, for example, contains two tightly interwoven plots:

> It has action that rises to a plot point and then falls away and moves to a second and culminating plot point. It has a subplot that is introduced early without the reader knowing why. The subplot recurs on occasion and draws closer and closer to the main plot until it converges.

With a fifty-page outline to guide him, Kenny once drafted an entire book manuscript over a single summer, writing in the mornings, editing after lunch, and joining his kids at the lake by midafternoon every day. So successful is his "outline first, write last" method that Kenny has trained his PhD students to work the same way. While their friends are sweating over draft chapters, Kenny's students are still reading, taking notes, and outlining. But when they do finally start writing, they can be assured that they will finish:

> The beauty of the method is that it demystifies the writing process. There would be nothing more terrifying to them than to sit down in front of a blank screen or blank page and go, "What do I do? Where do I start? This seems impossibly vast." My students will write the dissertation in whatever order they wish, whatever order suits their mood and their emotional framework and their work habits. The one thing they know when they start this process is that they will have a manuscript at the end. They have a blueprint. They have a map.

search. (*Claudia Bernardi, Languages and Cultures, Victoria University of Wellington*)

Studies by cognitive scientists have shown that the physical act of writing, whether in longhand or on a keyboard, forces the integration of neural, kinesthetic, and manipulative processes into new forms of thought:[5]

> Almost all of my writing is trying to understand something in the first place just for myself—just trying to figure it out. So if I wasn't writing, I wouldn't be discovering anything. (*Kwame Anthony Appiah, Philosophy, Princeton University*)

Yet plenty of successful researchers adhere to the oft-maligned strategy of "writing it up" instead:

> I wouldn't say I write quickly or easily. But I basically plan it all out in my head, and sometimes I jot that down as an outline. Then I just sit down and write it, and I don't let myself leave my desk until a certain amount is done. (*Russell Gray, Director, Max Planck Institute for the Science of Human History*)

This "plan first, write later" approach is common not only in the sciences but also in "book disciplines" such as history:

> Before writing something, I need to bathe in the notes. There's the deep-thinking moment where I may reorganize them; I consolidate, I separate. Then I use paper to outline something and pull out what I call "notes on notes." (*Ann Blair, History, Harvard University*)

Here, the activity of "writing to think" has largely been displaced from the drafting process to the note-taking and outlining stages.

Cecile Badenhorst distinguishes between "mapmakers" who plan their route before they begin writing and "bungy jumpers" who dive straight into a project without really knowing where they are going, supported by a blind faith that they'll eventually rise to the surface again:[6] processes sometimes referred to as "plotting" versus "pantsing" (writing by the seat of one's pants). Blogger Inger Mewburn notes the benefits of combining the two modes:

> I've always taken great pride in being a pantser; I think I read Peter Elbow too early: "Plotting stifles the writing process" and

all that. But now I've come to realize that if I ever want to write a book, I will need to plot it first, to figure out the interweaving threads. Then I can plunge in and write each chunk the way I write a blog post: bang, bang, bang, bang, bang. (*Inger Mewburn, Director of Research Training, Australian National University*)

Lines or boxes? Roots or rhizomes?

Compositional strategies such as plotting versus pantsing may or may not map neatly onto structural strategies such as linearity versus modularity (do you write straight through a piece from start to finish, or do you tackle the various components of a project nonsequentially?) and hierarchy versus chaos (do your thoughts branch off from each other in a logical manner, like the root structure of a tree, or do they spread and propagate haphazardly, like a rhizome?)[7]

> I try to create a structure for the whole text, like little boxes you can throw things into: this is a box, and this is a box, and this is a box. After that, I can basically start writing anywhere in the text. (*Stefan Svallfors, Sociology, Umeå University*)

> I don't start writing until I know exactly what I want to say. But it's recursive; I always go through several iterations. Quite often when I'm writing up the statistical analysis, I have a new idea that forces me to redo the whole thing. (*Fabrizio Gilardi, Political Science, University of Zurich*)

Eviatar Zerubavel, author of *The Clockwork Muse*, recommends distinguishing between "A-Time" writing, when new words are produced, and "B-Time" writing, when you undertake tasks that are directly related to your writing project but require less focused concentration, such as reading, note taking, or editing.[8] Depending on your way of working, A-Time and B-Time sessions could be either planned ("I write in the mornings and edit in the afternoons") or spontaneous ("I don't feel like writing the discussion section right now, so I'll work on the graphs.")

Snack or binge?

"Snack writing" is the practice of writing for short, unscheduled periods of time between other tasks—for example, while you're

"A threshold to step over"

MAJA ELMGREN and ANN-SOFIE HENRIKSSON

Division for Development of Teaching and Learning, Uppsala University (Sweden)

Trained in physical chemistry and law, respectively, Maja Elmgren and Ann-Sofie Henriksson work with faculty from across their university on a range of teaching-related initiatives. When a publisher invited them to coauthor a textbook on educational development—the first of its kind in Sweden—they seized the opportunity, even though Henriksson's teaching contract included no provision for research time: "I officially couldn't write it." Their solution? Snack writing. Most of the book was produced, Henriksson explains, "in odd bits of time left over between meetings or something":

> When I had half an hour, I wrote. I took every half an hour and quarter of an hour or whatever I could get, and wrote on the book, and got as far as I got. That's different from what I used to do earlier, because earlier I was under the illusion that there's no point even starting if I don't have at least a week or more.

Elmgren adds that they were both "thinking about the book all the time," cross-fertilizing ideas even when they were not actually writing:

> We got feedback from each other all the time in many different ways. We learned from each other's way of thinking. It has really been good to come from two such different subject domains.

Despite their mutual support, both authors encountered frequent moments of hesitancy and doubt; for example, starting a new chapter or section could feel "like a wall to climb over" (Elmgren), "a threshold to step over each time" (Henriksson). But when one author got stuck, the other took over, with Henriksson's "inspiration to write a lot" complemented by Elmgren's careful "weighing of words."

Elmgren and Henriksson both worked on every page of the book, gathering feedback along the way from colleagues whom they invited to take part in seminars focusing on the structure and content of each chapter. "We've worked with teachers from all over the university," notes Elmgren, "so we knew our audience well. But we really wanted to make sure we included all their voices. That was a challenge."

waiting for your children to emerge from their piano lesson or during a twenty-minute gap between meetings:

> I can start writing at any old time. I really don't believe in that "clearing a whole day to write" thing, because I've wasted many a whole day on writing when I could have got more done in ten minutes. (*Julie Stout, Psychology, Monash University*)

Experienced snackers say they suffer no major transition issues when they dip in and out of their writing, because they never really leave their research behind. However, many of the colleagues I interviewed insisted that snacking, pecking, and sound bites could not possibly work for them:

> I need to write in chunks at a time, and I need a chunk of time to get into it and do it—and that doesn't just mean days. (*Gillie Bolton, freelance writer in literature and medicine, United Kingdom*)

Instead, they prefer to dive deep and stay underwater for a while:

> I find it almost impossible to peck at my writing. I need a week off or a month off to do it and do nothing else. (*Alison Jones, Education, University of Auckland*)

Proponents of daily writing label this underwater approach "binge writing" and warn in dire tones against its evils:

> Avoid writing in binges. Abandon the notion that writing is best done in large, undisrupted blocks of time.[9]

> Many scholars still hold stock in BIG BLOCKS OF TIME, INC. To write daily, you must sell your stock.[10]

Yet academe, I discovered, is full of successful binge writers:

> When I'm seriously writing—a grant proposal for example—I will sit for twelve hours without moving. (*Patricia Culligan, Engineering, Columbia University*)

> The pieces I've been most happy about writing were always written when I was in a tunnel—when I was so excited by an idea that I got deeper and deeper into it. (*Martin Fellenz, Business, Trinity College Dublin.*)

I like writing intensively. I pick a day to start a project and then do nothing else until I finish (except exercise), working day and night, seven days a week until it's done. (*Steven Pinker, Psychology, Harvard University.*)

Rowena Murray notes that combining these methods—writing in occasional concentrated bursts but also chipping away daily—can be "an effective strategy for making time for writing in academic or professional schedules, and still having a life."[11] However, the very vocabulary of "snacking" and "bingeing" (or even the less pejorative "feasting") suggests erratic patterns of behavior rather than a healthy relationship with writing. Perhaps a different set of metaphors is needed?

Sprints or marathons?

Recast as a sporting metaphor, "snacking versus bingeing" becomes "sprints versus marathons" or "speed versus staying power" or perhaps "Hare versus Tortoise." Which mode should you favor in your writing practice? Any athlete could tell you the answer: both. Fitness in any sport requires cross-training, whereby you undertake a variety of workouts in order to build up your strength, endurance, agility, and mental focus. Studies by Hartley and Branthwaite (1989) and Kellogg (1994) suggest that the most productive writers typically write several times a week for one to three hours per session:[12]

> One of the things I've learned about myself as a writer is that even if I have twelve hours for writing, I can't write productively for twelve hours. I can write productively for three or four hours. (*Victoria Rosner, English, Columbia University*)

But you may be in better shape to make the most of those "Goldilocks" sessions—neither too short nor too long but just right—if you have also practiced working in other modes and at other paces.

Carrots or sticks?

Do you respond more readily to threats or to rewards? To punishment or to praise? To pressure or to freedom? Many of

"There is always a fixed cost"
WIM VANDERBAUWHEDE
School of Computing Science, University of Glasgow (Scotland)

Computer scientist Wim Vanderbauwhede believes that writing for short periods every day is inefficient, because shifting gears requires too much "context switching":

> It's a term from operating systems. If you have to do several things, in little bits, and each of these things has a lot of context—things you need to think about to do them—then you have to always change your mindset to do the next task and reacquire the full context of that task mentally. That takes a lot of time to do; there is always a fixed cost.

He prefers to concentrate on a single task for several hours at a time, preferably away from the office:

> I like a change of environment, so I will go to a coffee shop or something and work there. There's no email to respond to or calls and so on, so I will be able to focus quite well. I've never really believed in doing lots of overtime, but I try to be very focused when I'm working.

A native Flemish speaker who developed his English-language skills by reading English novels (in particular, J. R. R. Tolkien's *Lord of the Rings* trilogy), Vanderbauwhede structures each paper in advance and works out what his "story" is:

> When I start writing, I mark each section with square brackets, and I write whatever I think about. Otherwise, I will sit there and try to formulate each sentence exactly in my mind, and that doesn't work so well. If I get the ideas down in bullet points—this is what this sentence should contain, and in the next paragraph, this is the key idea—then it's easier for me to write the full sentences later.

He believes that academics who spend long hours working are not necessarily any more productive than those who do not:

> I do a lot of thinking outside work hours. When I walk home, I'll be thinking about my work, or when I'm just doing the washing up or whatever. So the mind is kind of defocused, and then some thinking goes on at a different level. I feel most of the connections I make are when I'm not actively trying to crack a problem but when I'm relaxed from it.

the academics I interviewed noted the motivational force of deadlines:

> My main pieces have mostly been finished at the last minute. I get a lot done when I'm on a deadline. (*Johanna Moisander, Business Communication, Aalto University*)

Robert Boice once persuaded a group of unproductive colleagues to write out personal checks to a hated political organization under the threat that the checks would be mailed out if they failed to meet their weekly writing goals.[13] Writers who respond to this kind of motivation-through-punishment might benefit from visiting Write or Die (www.writeordie.com), a website that "puts the prod in productivity" by offering a sliding scale of admonishments ranging from polite pop-up reminders soon after you stop typing ("Gentle Mode") to an unpleasant sound that shuts off only when you start writing again ("Normal Mode") to a particularly punitive feature that erases everything you have written ("Kamikaze Mode: Keep Writing or Your Work Will Unwrite Itself").

Writers who prefer carrots, on the other hand—or, better yet, small, fluffy animals—might try Written? Kitten! (writtenkitten .net), a website that rewards you with a picture of a kitten every time you type a predetermined number of words into a text box. ("We like positive reinforcement," explain the site's originators, "so we decided to make something a bit like writeordie but cuter and fuzzier.") Alternatively, for a more sophisticated range of feedback options, you can subscribe to 750 Words (www.750words .com/faq) and earn animal badges:

> If you write [750 words daily] for five days in a row, you get a penguin badge. . . . There are birds associated with long streaks of writing. For writing quickly, or without distraction, many days in a row, you might get a hamster or a cheetah.

Comedian Jerry Seinfeld is said to practice a low-tech version of this technique, sans penguins or hamsters. He advises budding comedians to go out and buy a large wall calendar, make a big *X* with a red marker every day they get some writing done, and take pleasure in watching that chain of *X*s grow: "Your only job is to not break the chain."[14]

March or dance?

Some academics, especially those who struggle to make time for writing, perform best under the rigors of a daily *routine*: a measured march to the drumbeat of a ticking clock. Others prefer the ceremony of a *ritual* for getting started:

> My ritual is to get up early in the morning, put my computer on a huge table, make a cup of coffee, and start writing. Midmorning I have another coffee, and I always have toast with the coffee or, if I'm lucky, a croissant, if there's a croissant in the house. (*Tony Harland, Higher Education, Otago University*)

Rituals offer comfort and ballast in a chaotic world, investing routines with symbolic meaning: "Without them," muses novelist Anne Lamott, "I would be a balloon with a slow leak."[15] They can be used not only for getting started but also for winding up a writing session, a technique sometimes referred to as "parking on the downhill slope":[16]

> Every day when I finish writing, I write myself a note. I write it in third person. I say, "Eric, here's what you're thinking. This is where you are. These are the problems you're leaving yourself with. This is what you think might come next." (*Eric Hayot, Comparative Literature, Pennsylvania State University*)

Like marching and dancing, routines and rituals share some common features. Both are intentional activities rather than passive states; both can be either communal or solitary; both involve not just repetition but change. (Marching takes you to new places; dancing transforms the places where you are.) The point of this chapter is not that "anything goes" but that, within the spacious parameters of a successful writing practice, nearly anything is possible: marching, dancing, swaying, skipping, or even standing still to feel the wind blow past. Whether you prefer polar oppositions or sliding scales, rules or ambiguity, *both/and* and/or *either/or*, there is no "right" way of writing. The best way to write is any way that works for you.

THINGS TO TRY

Refine your rituals

Chronicle your writing rhythms and rituals over several days or weeks, paying particular attention to unconscious or habitual behaviors. Do you quickly check your email every time you sit down to write, even though you have vowed not to let email intrude on your sacred writing hour? Do you get up and go in search of food every time you hit a conceptual block, even when you're not hungry? In *The Power of Habit*, Charles Duhigg shows how undesirable habits can be broken down to their constituent parts and rerouted in more positive directions. For example, instead of heading straight to the fridge whenever you hit an impasse, you could develop a ritual of first recording your thoughts on a sticky note and placing it on your computer screen to await your (refreshed) return.[17]

Interrogate your needs

Academics often describe their writing routines in terms of predestination rather than preference, compulsion rather than choice: "I *need* to carve out big blocks of time"; "I *need* to be surrounded by my books and notes while I'm writing." What happens when you recast your narrative of need as a tale of possibilities instead? For example, "I *prefer* to carve out big blocks of time for writing, but when the semester gets too crazy, I *can* push my writing forward by dipping in and out for half an hour at a time"; or "I *usually* work at my computer with my books and notes close to hand, crafting each sentence as I go, but *occasionally* I sit down in a café with a notebook and pen and 'write to think' instead."

Find your own metaphors

Concoct some new metaphorical pairings to describe your work patterns, for example:

- *Stew or marinate?* Do you tend to work on a project obsessively every day until it's finished, or do you sometimes park it in the back of your mind and leave its flavors to develop? (Other metaphors of gradual transformation: composting, percolating, fermenting, alchemy.)

- *Juggle or bowl?* Do you juggle multiple writing projects at once, or do you prefer to knock down all the pins in the bowling lane before you pick up the next ball? (Other metaphors of workload management: bringing in the big jets first, rocks in a jar.)[18]

- *Track or float?* Do you plot your writing sessions and track your progress, or do you write whenever you feel like it and keep no record of time spent and words produced? (Other metaphors of invigilation versus freedom: boot camp, coaching, improvisational theater, play.)

- *Cloisters or commons?* Do you like to sequester yourself in a private place, or do you prefer to write in the company of others? (Other metaphors of social isolation versus interaction: cocoon, web, burrow, hive.)[19]

Read a book

The writing processes of successful authors can make for fascinating reading, particularly for aspiring writers who are still trying to figure out their own best ways of working. Memoirs such as Anne Lamott's *Bird by Bird*, Annie Dillard's *The Writing Life*, Stephen King's *On Writing*, Dani Shapiro's *Still Writing*, and bell hooks's *Remembered Rapture* offer a compelling mix of autobiography and authorial advice. Alternatively, you might prefer dipping into anthologies of authorial interviews and anecdotes: for example, Robert S. Boynton's *The New New Journalism: Conversations with America's Best Nonfiction Writers on Their Craft*; Gary Olson and Lynn Worsham's *Critical Intellectuals on Writing*; Mason Currey's *Daily Rituals: How Artists Work*; the *New York Times' Writers on Writing* series; or Hilton Obenzinger's *How We Write: The Varieties of Writing Experience*. Books by or about full-time professional authors do not necessarily reflect the daily realities of academic writers, who must often balance demanding teaching, supervision, and administrative loads with the publish-or-perish imperatives of scholarly research. However, reading about the rhythms and routines of other writers may inspire you to attend more closely to your own.[20]

PART TWO

ARTISANAL HABITS

A line will take us hours maybe;
Yet if it does not seem a moment's thought
Our stitching and unstitching has been nought.

—WILLIAM BUTLER YEATS, "Adam's Curse"

False start #1

I learned to write in much the same way that I learned to make jewelry or mosaics, two of my favorite hobbies: by instinct and imitation, by trial and error, with occasional recourse to workshops, books, and expert teachers.

[I could go on here to discuss the intensely tactile and inexact experience of taking things apart and putting them together again: moving beads around, smashing up ceramic tiles, arranging and rearranging and reshaping the fragments until I can no longer find a better way. But are these examples too gendered? Too specific to my own experience? Maybe I should write about Yeats's "stitching and unstitching" metaphor instead?]

False start #2

Academic writers are makers and shapers of language, in much the same way that weavers are makers and shapers of textiles. The very word *text* comes from the Latin word *textus*, meaning something woven, tactile. So it makes sense to think of words as we might think of threads on a loom or beads on a necklace or glass tesserae in an intricate mosaic: infinitely varied forms that can be woven or strung or pieced together in a dazzling array of patterns.

[Unfocused, fragmentary. Needs to be punchier, more consistent. Find a story or anecdote to open with?]

False start #3

Many years after the death of poet Sylvia Plath, her former husband, Ted Hughes, published a vivid [find a better adjective?] account of his wife's creative process: "Her attitude to her verse was artisan-like; if she couldn't get a table out of the material, she was quite happy to get a chair, or even a toy."[1]

[I love the fact that Hughes uses the word "artisan-like" to describe Plath's way of working, and the carpentry image fits nicely with my "house of writing" metaphor. But Plath was a poet, not a professional scholar, so this example may not particularly resonate with academics—and in fact confuses the artist / artisan distinction that I'm trying to make. Also, I'd quite like to save this quote for the "Metaphors to Write By" chapter, where I could contrast the writer-as-artisan metaphor with more violent and destructive descriptions of the writing process: smashing down bearing walls, murdering your darlings.]

False start #4

artist, *n.* A person skilled in one of the creative or fine arts.

artisan, *n.* A worker in a skilled trade, a craftsperson; *esp.* one utilizing traditional or non-mechanized methods. (*Oxford English Dictionary*)

If poets and novelists are *artists* in the medium of language, then academic writers are *artisans*: skilled craftspeople who work in a nonmechanized trade in which quality matters more than quantity [OR: skilled craftspeople who fashion high-quality, distinctive products by hand, usually after years of apprenticeship and training]. In contrast to the suffering genius celebrated in the Charles Bukowski poem with which I opened this book— the inspired artist who continues to create even when "blind /

crippled/demented"—academics must sell their wares in a competitive marketplace and respond to mercantile demands. But unlike skilled artisans in most other trades (carpenters, weavers, jewelry makers, mosaicists), few academics have ever been formally trained in their craft.

[Good to get these definitions out on the table straight away and to make a distinction between creative writers as artists and academic writers as artisans. However, this opening paragraph still feels a bit bland and abstract, even though I've already spent at least an hour shaping and honing it. Also, given that I'm planning to start each of the other three BASE sections with a personal anecdote, shouldn't I do the same here?]

False start #5

I chose the word *artisanal* [pronounced *ar-TIS-an-al*] for the title of this chapter not just because I needed a vowel for my BASE [too glib?] but because several of the people I interviewed [well, only two actually] used the word *artisanal* to describe their own writing process.

[Boring!!]

False start #6

Whether you're a "blgggh writer" or someone who lays down only exquisitely jeweled sentences that you have already sweated over while producing them, chances are you really care about the craft of writing.

[No no no, this isn't working at all. "Lays down," "exquisitely jeweled," "sweated over"—mixed metaphors jumbled into a single baggy sentence. And what happened to my resolve to start with a personal anecdote?]

Start #7 (the "real" one)

The sequence of false starts with which this section begins may appear unordered and chaotic, but in fact these opening pages have been just as carefully crafted as any other chunk of this book (and took me at least as long to write). I started out curious to see what would happen if I pounded out one potential opening sentence after another without worrying too much about coherence or sequencing or argument. However, I found that I could seldom even get to the end of a sentence without retracing my steps to make some small change along the way—in this one, for example, I've just gone back to replace "*before* retracing my steps" with "*without* retracing my steps"; and after that I went back to replace "this *sentence*" with "this *one*"; and then I replaced "and *then*" with "*after that*"—and now I'm reluctant to come to the end of (no, better to say, "I'm reluctant to *place the final period at* the end of") this sentence because I promised myself that I wouldn't tinker with it any more after—oh no, now I've just realized that "*the final period*" would work better as the final thump, so I'd better try again: and now I'm reluctant to come to the end of this sentence because I promised myself that I wouldn't tinker with it any more after placing the final period.[2]

But I probably will anyway. Despite every attempt I have ever made to become a faster and less finicky writer—to forge relentlessly forward, laying down a thousand new words per hour as Rowena Murray suggests that any writer can learn to do—I seem to be constitutionally incapable of drafting even a single sentence without doubling back on it at least a few times to adjust various details.[3] Then, over the next few days or weeks or months, I will return again and again to polish and tweak some more: shifting things around, adding, revising, recasting, deleting. Many of my favorite sentences and paragraphs eventually get binned because I can't find a way to fit them in. For every chapter or article I write, I have a file labeled "junk" crammed with all the rejected bits and pieces—multiple versions, deleted phrasing, unused examples—that will never get made, à la Sylvia Plath, into tables or chairs or even toys.

While I may be a slower writer than some, I suspect that I'm nowhere near the end of the bell curve. Like Yeats, who could spend hours "stitching and unstitching" a single line of poetry, or Ernest Hemingway, who drafted forty-seven different endings to his novel *A Farewell to Arms*, many of the writers I interviewed devote enormous amounts of time and attention to the unseen labor of getting their words exactly right.[4] For some, the hard work falls mostly at the front end of the writing process (thinking, planning, drafting); for others, it takes place mostly at the back end (editing, polishing, revising). And for those who work as I do—writing, deleting, tinkering, and rewriting in seemingly endless iterative loops—it begins the moment they dream up a new project and doesn't end until the final proofs go to press.

Only when I started talking with other academics about their writing processes did I become fully cognizant of the quirks and idiosyncrasies of my own—not to mention my own lack of formal training as a writer, beyond the content-based feedback that I received from my PhD supervisors. The first chapter in this section focuses on "Learning to Write" in all its messiness and complexity. Next, "The Craft of Writing" offers a behind-the-scenes look at the sometimes obsessive level of craft and care that even the most prolific writers typically bring to their work. (I say "typically" because, as with every other aspect of the writing process, artisanal habits vary widely among individuals.) Finally, "The Other Tongue" addresses a topic that I have come to regard as crucially important for anyone who cares about improving the institutional culture of academic writing: the particular challenges faced by L2 English speakers who write and publish in English.[5] I hope that L1 readers will not skip over this chapter, assuming that it has nothing to do with them. Rare indeed is the L1 academic today who has no L2 colleagues, students, or friends who could benefit from their understanding and support—not to mention their admiration and respect. And rarer still is the monolingual English-speaking scholar who will find nothing to learn from the remarkable multilingual writers profiled in this chapter. Their artisanship extends beyond academic writing and into the realm of language itself.

4

LEARNING TO WRITE

"How, where, and when did you learn to write in your discipline?" Many of the successful academics I interviewed admitted up front—whether proudly, defiantly, or regretfully—that they have never received any formal training whatsoever in this most crucial of academic skills:

> I've never been to a formal workshop on how to write. I'm not even sure I've been offered one. (*Miles Padgett, Physics, University of Glasgow*)

> I'm not sure how I learned to write. I was never taught it. (*Thomas Aastrup Rømer, Education, Aarhus University*)

> I never did learn to write. I just wrote. (*Donald A. Barr, Human Biology, Stanford University*)

The faculty, postdocs, and graduate students who filled out my data questionnaire responded with similar formulations:

> I had no formal training, which is ironic because I now teach academic writing in a research skills class for MA students. (*Associate professor of English, Canada*)

> No formal training, except one two-hour class in grant writing. (*Assistant professor and cancer researcher, United States*)

> Thrown in at the deep end. (*Research fellow in environmental health, New Zealand*)

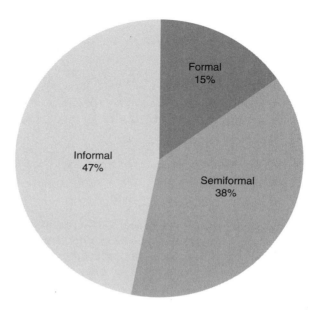

Figure 4. Types of learning reported in interviews and questionnaires in response to the question "How did you learn to write in your discipline?" (n = 1,323). *Semiformal* may include some informal learning; *formal* may include both informal and semiformal learning (see pages 215–216).

Overall, nearly half of the respondents in my two survey groups (47 percent) reported that they had learned to write more or less under their own steam, whether through trial and error, by drawing on past experience, or on the basis of advice and feedback from other people—processes that I will refer to throughout this chapter as "informal learning." More than a third (38 percent) said that, in addition to learning informally, they had also read books on academic writing or participated in occasional one-off events such as writing workshops, mentoring programs, or facilitated writing retreats ("semiformal learning.") Only 15 percent—about one out of every six respondents—have been educated as academic writers via an accredited course or its equivalent ("formal learning"). (See Figure 4.)

Let's take a moment to ponder the paradoxes of this situation. All academics, by definition, are deeply invested in higher education: they hold advanced degrees from and are employed by tertiary institutions such as universities, colleges, and research centers. Those institutions, in turn, operate according to the premise that students learn most effectively and efficiently when guided through a formal learning program built on educational units called "courses." (Local terminology may vary.) A course is *iterative* (the students and instructors meet more than once), *cohort based* (the participants learn with and from a group of peers), *expert facilitated* (the course is designed and led by acknowledged authorities who have studied the subject in depth), *research informed* (students are exposed to the latest findings in the field, not just to anecdotal knowledge), and complemented by a range of *learning activities* intended to deepen and accelerate both in-class and out-of-class learning: for example, readings, discussions, field trips, research and writing assignments, and group projects. Students receive *formative feedback* about their learning, and they demonstrate their mastery through *summative assessments* such as quizzes, tests, examinations, essays, projects, or presentations. In return, their achievements are recognized through some kind of *certification*, such as a letter of completion or a formal accreditation.

As cultural evolutionists Peter Richerson and Robert Boyd remind us, the default mode of learning in most human societies is to "imitate the common type"; we acquire new skills mainly by observing those around us and doing as they do.[1] A well-designed course moves students beyond the default by equipping them with the confidence and skills that they need to challenge preconceptions, try out new approaches, and create new knowledge. Yet many academics remain remarkably resistant to the notion that they, like their students, might benefit from expert-facilitated courses in writing, teaching, or other essential academic skills—an attitude that contrasts starkly with the disposition of their colleagues in fields such as medicine, law, or engineering, for whom ongoing professional development is not only expected but required.

To be a successful academic, it is not enough merely to have mastered the craft of writing intelligibly. You must also be creative enough to produce original research, persuasive enough to convey the significance of your findings to others, prolific enough to feed

"Polishing a gem that's already there"

KEITH DEVLIN

Human Sciences and Technologies Advanced Research Institute,
Stanford University (USA)

Mathematician Keith Devlin believes that successful writers are born, not made:

> If you find you've got a flair or a skill, you can refine and reflect and get better at it, but I'm not sure it can be taught. Writing is a mixture of a whole bunch of things including the desire and the pleasure in doing it. It's polishing a gem that's already there. I mean, anyone can play golf, but if you're Tiger Woods, you've got to be born Tiger Woods.

Yet Devlin's own success as a writer is clearly due to his thirst for learning as well as his innate ability. He honed his craft as a science writer by reflecting on other authors' writing and attending the occasional conference workshop, which, he says, "was as close as I ever got to sort of taking formal lessons or instruction in writing." Now he is often invited to run science-writing workshops for others:

> But quite frankly I learn at least as much as the so-called students in those classes. Thinking about their work, talking about what I see in their writing, seeing if I make the same mistakes myself—I'm constantly trying to improve, and arguably I am improving.

A prolific writer who once drafted a full-length book in just three weeks, Devlin typically begins with a mental map of the project—"calling it an outline is probably overstating it"—and starts writing as soon as he has a general sense of what he wants to say:

> I structure the earlier parts so that they build to the later parts, and most of that preparation is largely subconscious, just something floating in my brain.

He allows his ideas to marinate during hundred-mile bicycle rides:

> While I'm riding, the writing is sort of going on in my mind, semiconscious. It comes in and out of consciousness, but I'm sure that in those long periods of four, five, six hours on my own, the book is essentially writing itself.

Later, when he sits down to do the actual writing, "it just flows out. It's all somehow queued up in the brain and just pours out."

the tenure and promotion machine, confident enough to withstand the slings and arrows of peer review, strategic enough to pick your way safely through the treacherous terrain of academic politics, well organized enough to juggle multiple roles and commitments, and persistent enough to keep on writing and publishing no matter what. So how do academics gain this formidable set of skills, if not through formal training? For many of the colleagues I talked to, the process of learning to write started in early childhood:

> How did I learn to write? That's a puzzling question to me, because it's a bit like asking, "How did you learn to talk?" The answer is, "God, I don't remember ever not being able to talk!" (*Lee Shulman, Education, Stanford University*)

Some picked up ideas and interests from their parents:

> My father was an English teacher, and my family always played word games, did crosswords, liked poems—we played around with language, always had an interest in language, and that found its way into my writing. (*Bill Barton, Mathematics Education, University of Auckland*)

Or from their teachers:

> I had a terrific teaching assistant in an undergraduate history course. I still remember her grading one of my papers and saying, "In German, you can have a sentence that goes round and round until it lies down like a dog making a bed. But in English, you don't do that. You go from the beginning to the end." (*Janet Currie, Economics and Public Affairs, Princeton University*)

Or from their partners:

> My husband is a brilliant man but not an academic. He has six different trade tickets: machinery millwright, welder, pipefitter, steam engineer. He's a bright man and a curious man and will poke holes in my argument faster and sooner than any of my colleagues. (*Janelle Jenstad, English, University of Victoria*)

Or even from their grown-up children:

> My daughter has a master's in journalism. We worked on an article together, and she helped me manage the edits. Then at the

end she said, sort of like a mother, "Wasn't it good that we made the article stronger?" (*Mindy Fullilove, Clinical Psychiatry, Columbia University*)

Others have learned to write by transferring skills acquired in other jobs or careers, such as serving in the army:

I was taught to prepare written orders and commands or tactics in a very clear, concise way. (*Stephen Rowland, Higher Education, University College London*)

Or working as a tour guide:

The art of good storytelling and being able to keep people's interest has been very helpful. (*Lena Roos, Religious Studies, Uppsala University*)

Or volunteering in the community:

For years, I worked for the nuclear-freeze movement. Writing press releases and stuff like that, you had to use words that everybody would understand, and you had to get your point across in very few words. (*David Pace, History, Indiana University*)

Some academic writers have drawn on their experiences of writing in other genres, such as fiction:

I got an MFA in fiction writing, and the techniques I learned there have just been golden for me. It was the first time I ever got to focus on writing and be with people who really cared about every word, what the cadence was and characterization and how to tell stories and make them interesting. (*Deborah Kaple, Sociology, Princeton University*)

Or poetry:

My early explorations of nonsense poetry were very central to how I now see language and communication. (*Douglas Hofstadter, Cognitive Science, Indiana University*)

Or technical writing:

Before I moved into accounting, I was trained in engineering, where we learned to put together a manual or a description of something, which is really an organization of facts in a very specific order so

"Like a spontaneous voice talking to you"

ALISON GOPNIK

Department of Psychology, University of California Berkeley (USA)

Psychologist Alison Gopnik grew up in a family of readers and writers. Her father was an English professor, and her earliest experiences of writing and reading were literary:

> I was always writing in the literary-essayistic tradition, and as a young woman, I was a completely omnivorous reader, a sort of insane reader. I think that reading informs the way you write probably more than anything else you do.

As an undergraduate philosophy major and later a graduate student in psychology, she was exposed to a wide range of critical styles:

> In philosophy—a discipline that really values writing—there's this sort of analytic tradition that emphasizes clarity; the structure of what you're arguing has to be made clear in the writing. Then there's also this belletrist tradition, where you're allowed to use metaphors and figures of speech and do things that are more like literary writing. Scientific writing was a relatively late form of writing for me, and I always hated it—like beating my head against the wall.

Eventually she discovered that "it's not actually that hard to describe a scientific experiment in a fairly engaging way as a narrative." Now, in her scientific papers as well as in books and articles aimed at wider audiences, Gopnik strives for what she calls "a sort of American plain style, like the *New Yorker* style from the thirties." She has developed her writing style through email correspondence with colleagues ("Writing to somebody else is a very good way of learning your craft"), through conversations with family members ("I have two brothers who are professional writers"), through careful attention to audience and tone ("in *The Scientist in the Crib*, I wanted to avoid the kind of polemical, edgy, sarcastic voice that is common in popular books, so I went through and took out every single bit of snark and aggression"), and above all through sheer hard work:

> People often say to me, "Oh, I love your writing because it's just like you talking. It must be so easy." I feel like saying, "You have no idea!" If you looked at the first draft, you would see something that reads like a developmental psychology article. It's only after the hundredth draft that it sounds like a spontaneous voice talking to you.

that you can have clarity and understanding—which kind of parallels the kind of story line or structure that an academic paper demands. (*John Dumay, Accounting, Macquarie University*)

Or journalism:

I learned that the perfectionist voice has to be stifled really quickly, because you realize you have to hand the thing in. (*Lisa Surridge, English, University of Victoria*)

Some have learned from writing in other languages:

My doctoral thesis was written all in Māori, so that sort of gave me that stylistic expression and that language. But then writing the book in English meant I had to reorganize my structure and restructure the work. (*Poia Rewi, Māori, Pacific, and Indigenous Studies, University of Otago*)

Or from learning other languages:

We did a lot of grammar at school, as well as deconstructing sentences: indirect objects and direct objects and all that. (*Wim Vanderbauwhede, Computing Science, University of Glasgow*)

Or from translating other languages:

I had a really good Latin and Greek teacher who would insist that when we did a translation from Plato or Thucydides, we also had to communicate their tone. So I learned how to emphasize and deemphasize things without explicitly saying, "Now, this is important. This is not important." (*Massimo Morelli, Political Science and Economics, Columbia University*)

Some have learned to write from reading well-written academic books and articles:

I was very interested in how people expressed their ideas—not just the content but the writing itself and how people were persuasive and so on. I still have a file somewhere up there full of those articles. (*Tony Harland, Higher Education, University of Otago*)

Or from reading badly written academic books and articles:

I learned to write by reading other anthropologists and ethnographers. But I often felt that the writing was very distant, sometimes boring, and sometimes very abstract. (*Ruth Behar, Anthropology, University of Michigan*)

Or from reading journalistic prose:

I learned from reading really good journalism and observing the tricks they use to ties things together neatly. (*Stefan Svallfors, Sociology, Umeå University*)

Or from reading fiction:

I read a lot of fiction, so sometimes I borrow techniques from fiction writers: varying paragraph structure or using a variety of sentence lengths for emphasis. (*Kalervo Gulson, Education, University of New South Wales*)

Or from reading poetry:

I went through a William Blake phase as a graduate student, and I like to think that my writing at least makes gestures to—well, beauty is such a big word—a grace that is not just academic, a gracefulness that is not just academic. (*Enda Duffy, English, University of California Santa Barbara*)

Finally, some academics have learned to write by teaching others:

Together with some colleagues, I run courses for PhD students on how to write a good dissertation. They could be training to be physicists, engineers, lawyers, legal researchers, etcetera. That has actually helped me to be a better writer myself. (*Agnes Lam, Applied English Studies, University of Hong Kong*)

Or by editing others:

Coediting a scholarly journal has really expanded my vocabulary for talking about other people's writing and my own writing (*Mary Elizabeth Leighton, English, University of Victoria*)

Or by writing with others:

Writing together forces you to make explicit the kinds of conversations and ideas that you only have internally or implicitly when you're writing by yourself. (*Eric Hayot, Comparative Literature, Pennsylvania State University*)

If they are very fortunate, they may have learned from a conscientious peer reviewer:

> It was the review process that helped shape my writing. I've kept that in mind when I'm writing a review for somebody else's work. (*Julie Stout, Psychology, Monash University*)

Or a meticulous editor:

> I learned a great deal from a copyeditor who would flag things and said to me, "Are you aware of the fact that you tend to use a gerund at the beginning of your sentences over and over again? Don't you think that is going to bore people to tears if every sentence has the same syntactic structure?" A lightbulb went on over my head: "Oh, these sentences should be varied in syntactic structure!" (*Susan Gubar, English, Indiana University*)

Or a generous mentor:

> When I was a beginning assistant professor, an older colleague offered to read my book manuscript. She read a few chapters and really looked at the style and said, "Think about what you're saying here. Think about how you are writing this." It was really helpful. (*Marjorie Howes, English, Boston College*)

A few of the academics I interviewed mentioned that they had learned to write from their doctoral supervisors. These, however, represented the exception, not the rule. Most focused on learning experiences that occurred outside their formal education, whether before, during, or after the PhD.

The benefits of informal learning processes such as constructivism (building on previous knowledge and experience), situated learning (acquiring new skills on the job and through professional communities of practice), and reflective practice (learning through trial, error, and self-reflection) have been well documented in the research literature on adult and higher education, and there is no doubt that such experiences can be highly beneficial to academic writers at any stage of their career.[2] The problem with informal learning, however, is that it tends to be ad hoc, sporadic, and serendipitous, which means that many people miss out. What if your parents weren't college professors or profes-

"From salt water into fresh water"

JAMES SHAPIRO

Department of English, Columbia University (USA)

As an undergraduate, Shakespearean scholar Jim Shapiro recalls,

> I loved to write, but I was a very bad writer. It took me a long time to become a good writer, by which I mean someone who understands when writing is good and when it isn't. I think many academics confuse good thinking with good writing.

He learned to write from an array of sources: from the undergraduate teacher who failed his first few essay assignments ("He set me on the path to much more rigorous writing"); from his journalist brother ("He said, 'Right now, there are too many characters in this book, so choose six'"); from trusted friends and colleagues ("I have six readers who have read drafts of everything I've written since 1980, and they're brutal and direct with me"); from other writers ("I urge my graduate students to subscribe to the *London Review of Books* and the *TLS* and to read these cover to cover"); and from "being in conversation with really smart people who understand writing in ways that I don't."

Shapiro's first book was a standard academic monograph, written, he says, "according to the formulas of the scholarship that I had read: four or five chapters, each thirty pages long, covering one or two works of literature." With his second book, he began "crossing over from salt water into fresh water," consciously pitching his prose to a general audience. In his third book, he adopted a more conversational voice. But only with his fourth book did he finally succeed in producing the kind of writing that he "had always aspired to":

> The manuscript was 130,000 words, and I did not submit it until I had trimmed it to 105,000. Sometimes you're cutting fat; sometimes you're cutting bone. But you have to cut.

Shapiro explains why he does most of his writing at work: "My energy while I'm writing is something no one else should have to experience: I walk, I make noises." Upon leaving campus, he shifts gears to focus on family:

> When my son was six, he asked me, "Dad, can you not write any more books? I can tell when you're talking to me but thinking about your book." I couldn't fool a six-year-old.

Times change, of course. "Now that my son is older," Shapiro sighs, "he just wants me to go away and write books."

sional journalists but Latino immigrants to New York who never finished primary school?

> In small spaces, people who can't read books may see them as a lot of clutter and dirt. They're dust collectors. So even keeping a few books in my room, that was a big deal for my mom. Put them in the closet, keep them out of sight. We're poor, but we're not dirty. (*Marysol Asencio, Sociology, University of Connecticut*)

What if your high school teachers actively discouraged you from writing?

> My professional formation as a writer began with a comment from a respected eleventh-grade English teacher: "Carl, you'll never be a writer." As a working-class kid, I respected my teachers, and so when they told me things like that, I believed them. (*Carl Leggo, Education, University of British Columbia*)

What if your thesis adviser provided only negative feedback?

> When I submitted the first draft of my thesis, my supervisor threw it back to me and said, "This is not a kids' book you're writing." He didn't tell me how to write, though. (*Kristina Lejon, Clinical Microbiology, Umeå University*)

What if the peer-review process, rather than inspiring you to become a better writer, left you feeling battered and risk averse?

> Early in my career, I sent a couple of papers to a plant ecology journal and got a couple of thumbs-down rejections. I can see now that the reviewers must have been in a bad mood; their arguments weren't very strong. But my reaction was to kill those papers. They are still in a drawer somewhere. (*Christer Nilsson, Ecology, Umeå University*)

Not all aspiring academics have been lucky enough to meet that thoughtful coauthor, that sympathetic mentor, that meticulous editor who was willing to offer constructive yet supportive advice on a manuscript draft.

Another risk of informal or semiformal learning is that it can lack rigor and range. If you learned to write from your PhD supervisor, chances are you were taught to write *like* your supervisor, rather than being exposed to a wide variety of disciplinary styles and techniques. If you learned to write through self-directed reading and reflection, you probably missed out on the kind of developmental feedback offered by supportive peers with your best interests at heart. And if you learned to write by trawling productivity websites or attending workshops on academic writing, the advice you received may have been based on anecdotal evidence and personal experience rather than empirical research. Successful academics who have never been formally trained as writers themselves are often eager to relay the "tricks of the trade" to younger colleagues, without realizing that what worked for them might not necessarily work for everyone.

How can we break the cycle? Ideally, all universities would provide their PhD students and faculty with access to iterative, cohort-based, expert-facilitated, research-based writing courses on topics ranging from grammar and style to academic productivity, publication strategies, and emotional resilience. But even in the absence of such formal learning opportunities, individual writers can advance their own sophistication and skill in a variety of ways. Self-improvement guru Stephen Covey tells the story of a man who is trying to cut down a tree with a very dull saw: "Why don't you sharpen the saw?" asks a passerby; "Because I don't have time," comes the reply. Covey recommends that you spend at least a few hours every week engaging in activities that will stretch and strengthen your mind, body, and spirit: read a challenging novel, sign up for a dance class, start learning a new language, engage a friend in conversation about a topic you don't know much about.[3] Similarly, there are many ways to "sharpen the saw" of your academic writing—starting with reading the next chapter of this book.

THINGS TO TRY

Reflect

How, where, when, and from whom did you learn to write in your discipline? How, where, when, and from whom might you learn more? Start by listing your own main sources of formal, semiformal, and informal learning: the people, books, courses, workshops, and other experiences that have contributed to your professional formation as a writer thus far. Next, identify the strengths and gaps in your education. In what areas have you engaged in a self-reflective process of questioning, challenge, and change, and where have you learned mainly through trial and error or by unconsciously imitating others? What steps might you take to hone the blades of your saw?

Emulate

In *The Sense of Style: A Thinking Person's Guide to Writing in the Twenty-First Century*, Steven Pinker advises writers to find examples of prose that they especially admire and then to reverse engineer them, identifying the authors' specific techniques and making them their own.[4] This approach can be expanded beyond artisanal habits to the behavioral, social, and emotional domains of writing. Do you have colleagues who publish more prolifically than most or who engage in fruitful collaborations or who seem more optimistic and enthusiastic about their academic work than others around them? Invite them out for a coffee and ask them how they do it.

Learn by teaching

One of the best ways to learn any new skill is by teaching it to others. You will be obliged to slow down and devote time to researching, analyzing, and reflecting on how to explain the principles and practices involved, and your own mastery will increase as a result. For example, instead of enrolling in a generic workshop on how to give better feedback on student essays, you could work with a colleague from your university's writing center to develop a seminar series for your whole department—thereby helping to sharpen other people's saws as well as your own.

Read a book

Books can support either your informal learning, your semiformal learning, or your formal learning as a writer, depending on which books you choose and how you make use of them. For informal learners, "Read a book!" could mean "Read a great academic book and pay attention to what's good about the writing" or "Read a terrible academic book and pay attention to what's bad about the writing" or even "Read a book of poetry or fiction and let the rhythms of the language seep into your unconscious." For semiformal learners, it could mean "Read a book that will teach you to write more productively" (such as the books listed at the end of Chapter 1) or "Read a book that will teach you to write more stylishly" (such as the books listed at the end of Chapter 6) or "Read a book that will teach you to write more collaboratively" (such as the books listed at the end of Chapter 9) or "Read a book that will teach you to write more confidently" (such as Roy Peter Clark's *Writing Tools* or Patricia Goodson's *Becoming an Academic Writer* or Peter Elbow's *Writing with Power* or Ralph Keyes's *The Courage to Write*). At the formal-learning end of the scale, it might mean "Read a book that will help you support your colleagues' academic writing" (such as Anne Ellen Geller and Michele Eodice's *Working with Faculty Writers*) or "Read a book that will help you support your PhD students' writing" (such as Barbara Kamler and Pat Thomson's *Helping Doctoral Students Write* or Susan Carter and Deborah Laurs's *Giving Feedback on Research Writing*) or "Read a book that will help support your undergraduate students' writing" (such as Barbara Walvoord's *Helping Students Write Well*). It may even mean "Read a book about how writing supports learning" (such as William Zinsser's *Writing to Learn*) or, more broadly, "Read a book about the cultural evolution of learning" (such as Kim Sterelny's *The Evolved Apprentice*), which will give you new insight into the nuances and complexities of learning to write.[5]

5

THE CRAFT OF WRITING

A PhD student approached me after a writing workshop to recount his tale of woe. "I write these messy, incoherent first drafts," he lamented. "They're absolutely awful! Then I have to work on them for hours and hours to bash them into shape. It's such a frustrating process, and so discouraging. My PhD adviser is a really good writer; she makes it all look so easy. I wish I were more like her." I didn't get a chance to interview the student's supervisor; but if I had, I can guess what she might have told me. Probably something like this: "I write these messy, incoherent first drafts—they're absolutely awful! Then I have to work on them for hours and hours to bash them into shape. Writing can be a hard and frustrating process, but for the most part, I really enjoy the challenge of honing and polishing my sentences until I get them just right." Same story, different spin.

Of all the myths surrounding academic writing, the fallacy of effortless productivity is among the most persistent. Many of the academics I interviewed told me that they find the craft of writing to be fascinating, pleasurable, even exhilarating:

> I see writing as an artisanal activity, like being a potter or a woodworker. The craft of putting words together—you do a whole range of things simultaneously—just strikes me as so interesting. (*Ludmilla Jordanova, History, Durham University*)

> There's a deep craft satisfaction in writing that comes before everything except family. (*Carlo Rotella, English, Boston College*)

Only a rare few, however, said that they "find writing easy"—and even then, mostly in the context that they "find *writing* easy" compared to other aspects of the process, such as the research, planning, and editing:

> When I'm really going, I just fly. It's what they call "flow." I love it. But I know that I'm going to have to go back later and take a third of the prose out. (*Stephen Ross, English, Victoria University*)

Others describe the writing process itself as extraordinarily taxing:

> It's mostly pain, let's be honest about it. It's grueling. Torture is too strong a word. But it's hard. It's draining. (*James Shapiro, English, Columbia University*)

The bottom line is that it takes most academics a long time—whether at the front end of the writing process, at the back end, or both—to produce high-quality work. Apprentice academics may regard the enormous effort involved as a symptom of their own inadequacy, especially if they have been led to believe that writing is supposed to be easy:

> When I first started on my PhD, I wrote a lot of stuff, because the books all say you should produce *x* amount of words a day. So I sat down every day and said, "Right, I'm going to write two thousand words today." And I did that for three or four months and ended up with thousands and thousands of words. But they weren't connected, they weren't going anywhere. Afterwards I had to go back and spend months organizing what I'd written: cutting it down, creating coherent chapters. (*Ewan Pohe, Māori Studies, Victoria University of Wellington*)

Experienced writers, on the other hand, understand that messiness and frustration come with the territory:

> It doesn't come out right the first time. You work it over and over—many drafts. That's the really discouraging, scary part of the process. It feels like it will never come together—and then it does. Just hanging in there through that development phase, that messy phase, is so important. (*Jennifer Meta Robinson, Anthropology, Indiana University*)

"This zigzag writing"

MARIALUISA ALIOTTA

School of Physics and Astronomy, University of Edinburgh (UK)

As a PhD student in Italy, nuclear astrophysicist Marialuisa Aliotta had a dissertation adviser "who was extremely meticulous about writing":

> I remember after handing in my first draft of my first chapter, I was looking forward to meeting with him and thinking he was going to say, "Well done," because I was kind of proud of it. It was a disaster! It was all marked in red pen, all crossed. But now with hindsight, I see that the guidance he offered was extremely valuable—he really taught me to write.

Later, as a full-time academic, she noticed that many of the graduate students in her program struggled with their writing, but they had no place to go for help:

> At this university, supervisors are supposed to not interfere in students' writing, because their thesis is supposed to be their own work. I thought, "How are these students supposed to learn? Just picking these things up by osmosis?"

She started a doctoral blog "as a way of giving some guidance to students" and eventually developed a three-day residential course that is now attended by postgraduate physics students from all over Scotland: "I take them through the process of writing something from scratch, going through the very basic steps." Her own articles, unsurprisingly, are carefully crafted from start to finish. She begins by gathering together all the relevant research publications:

> Sometimes I read through them chronologically because I like to see how ideas and things have progressed; other times I start from the latest paper to get an overall picture first. I underline or highlight key points using a paper annotation tool, which is a one-page double-sided document containing specific questions, like "What was the method used? What was the purpose of this study? What was the key finding?"

Next she prepares the structure of her paper, "because if you break the writing down into small chunks, it becomes a lot more manageable." Then, at last, she starts drafting:

> That's when things get difficult. I'm a bit of a perfectionist—maybe without the "bit"—so very often I find myself writing a sentence, rereading it, and saying, "Oh no, I'm deleting it," and then rewriting it. So it's this zigzag writing: I can spend hours polishing a sentence.

The PhD student at my workshop hadn't yet learned any of that. But what if his supervisor had told him about her own background and processes as an academic writer: her sources of learning, her struggles to improve, her day-to-day schedule, her history of rejections, her pleasure in the craft? Perhaps then he would have been able to see his own frustrations as normal and even necessary speed bumps on the road to successful writing.

When I asked the writers I interviewed to describe their daily writing habits—where, when, and how they write—many quickly tilted the conversation toward craft: that is, "how they write" in the sense of how they shape the words on the page, rather than "how they write" in the sense of how those words got there in the first place. From the cadence of a paragraph to the structure of a book, I learned, stylish academic writers sweat the details. They think about *elegance*:

> The ability to write elegantly in the style appropriate for a specific journal is essential in science. We spend ages crafting even very short articles before we send them off to journals like *Science* or *Nature*. (*Russell Gray, Director, Max Planck Institute for the Science of Human History*)

They think about *concision*:

> The quality I try for most in my writing is succinctness—some people waffle on so much—but it's bloody hard. I think it's one of the hardest forms of writing. (*Michael Corballis, Psychology, University of Auckland*)

They think about *structure*:

> I'm very much a structural thinker, so when I go for a run and think about my writing, I'm already hearing the shape of the essay. As I write, that doesn't usually change much at all: when I'm working on a section, I know that this is going to be the midsection or the second paragraph in. (*Margaret Breen, English, University of Connecticut*)

They think about *voice*:

> I think my writing is less often affected by other people's style than it used to be, and I've found a voice. It's not an easy voice.

It's a voice that takes a lot of pruning and editing, of course. Nothing you write is ever a first draft. (*Trudy Rudge, Nursing, University of Sydney*)

They think about *identity*:

The question I ask my students is, "How do you write your research up in First Nation studies in ways that don't reproduce those 'othering' discourses that have plagued anthropology or sociology or other disciplines for so long?" (*Dory Nason, First Nations Studies, University of British Columbia*)

They think about *clarity*:

In science, sentences should be logical and unambiguous. You're not writing literature, where ambiguity might be a good thing. There you might want two possible meanings on purpose. But in a scientific paper, you don't want that. You want a very clear meaning. (*Wim Vanderbauwhede, Computing Science, University of Glasgow*)

They think about *accessibility*:

I try to model my work after the very accessible style of writers such as Lionel Trilling and William Empson; it has a strong colloquial aspect to it, where they're not afraid to use the full resources of the language, and they don't try to write like some sort of neutered computer. (*Robert Miles, English, University of Victoria*)

They think about *vocabulary*:

In history, your audience often includes ordinary people who have a curiosity or passion for the past, which marks it out from academic disciplines where the more polysyllabic words and the more theoreticians you invoke in one sentence, the more illustrious you are, even if no one has any idea what the words mean. (*Michael Reilly, Māori, Pacific, and Indigenous Studies, University of Otago*)

They think about *syntax*:

I learned quite a lot from one of my coauthors. I would start off a sentence with "This shows that," and he would say, "Well,

"The smell of newly sawn wood"

ANTHONY GRAFTON

Department of History, Princeton University (USA)

Historian Tony Grafton credits several people with having taught him the craft of writing. One was his high school English teacher, "a very courtly, well-educated southern gentleman who had a passion for the English language":

> He would start each term with an announcement like, "Gentlemen, this term you will learn to write without the verb *to be*." Or "Gentlemen, this term you may use the verb *to be* but not the passive voice."

Another influential figure was his father, a professional journalist who could turn any piece of writing into "something half as long and twice as good":

> He used to say, "Are you a professor or a writer?" Professors hate being edited, and writers love it. I always really enjoyed it when Leon Wieseltier, the legendary editor of the *New Republic*, would read a draft of my work and go, "Well, this is great. You just need a new beginning and a new ending, and you have to do something about the middle."

Undergraduates today, Grafton notes, often lack "the grasp of the mechanics of grammar and syntax that used to be a standard possession of those in the college track":

> I've had so many bright students who weren't conscious of writing as an art or a craft. A lot of people—not just the young—write as if everyone in their readership is going to know exactly what they are working on.

A famously prolific writer himself—"If I'm on leave, I write in the morning from about eight to twelve thirty, and I try to hit thirty-three hundred to thirty-five hundred words or somewhere in that area"—he nonetheless finds writing to be an "infinitely postponable" activity: "The computer gives one endless things to fiddle with, and I'm always willing to pick up my Mavis Gallant and read a short story before I start writing." But once he gets started, he enjoys the process:

> I have the sense of doing a piece of work almost artisanally. I used to be a theater technician, so I feel as though I'm sawing and fitting and nailing and screwing and gluing so that things are neat and shipshape. The kind of pleasure that goes with that craftsmanship—if you only had the smell of newly sawn wood, it would be all there.

Miles, *what* shows that? What does the *this* refer to?" Now I find myself saying the same to all my PhD students, with great relish, when they start a sentence with "this." (*Miles Padgett, Physics, University of Glasgow*)

They think about *agency*:

I always use "I," because it's always my own views. I never write "one," and I don't let my students write like that. I want to see the agency. I don't allow the passive voice because it excludes agency. (*Martin Fellenz, Business, Trinity College Dublin*)

They think about *audience*:

A colleague of mine read one of my early papers and said, "You know this is very solid research, but it's boring." That was a really important experience—I thought academic writing was supposed to go on and on and on: "Now we have Table 24 and Equation 13." Now I work hard to make it interesting. (*Janet Currie, Economics and Public Affairs, Princeton University*)

They think about *telling a story*:

I have learned to work harder at writing stories. Now, I start more broadly, stepping back from the forest to see the trees, so to speak, to provide context and set up impact. (*Kurt Albertine, Pediatrics, University of Utah*)

They think about *"the big picture"*:

My job is to tell a story about what's going on in this particular field, how do we know this, and who has told us what the data are, and I tie all that into the big picture. It's kind of like putting together Legos into a shape or construction. (*Donald A. Barr, Human Biology, Stanford University*)

They even think about visual issues such as *typography*, *pagination*, and *layout*:

I seem to have a pretty good eye for layout, which is important when you're writing your own grant proposals: deciding the font, deciding the headings, deciding the figures and the tables so the page looks pleasing to the eye. (*Patricia Culligan, Engineering, Columbia University*)

Successful writers also attend closely to the *technologies* of writing: that is, to the physical and electronic tools they use in their shaping and crafting of language. These days, most academics do the bulk of their writing and editing on a computer:

> To me, writing is something you do at a keyboard. I like to fiddle with sentences as I'm writing them; if you do that on a typewriter or with a pen, the result is extremely messy. That gives you negative feedback, and it becomes depressing. On a screen, you can get the latest version and it looks tidy. (*Kwame Anthony Appiah, Philosophy, Princeton University*)

Some supplement standard word-processing programs with specialized desktop software such as Freemind or Scrivener (for mind mapping and nonlinear drafting, respectively) and online file storage and sharing services such as Google Drive or Dropbox. For many, however—especially those who came to word processing relatively late in their academic careers—there is still nothing quite like the feeling of pen on paper:

> For important work, I've always enjoyed using foolscap or yellow-lined paper. After I type it up on the computer, I make my changes on a printout of the original draft, and then when it gets too clogged up, I print off another triple-spaced copy and go from there. (*Daniel M. Albert, Opthalmology, University of Wisconsin*)

In *Lines: A Brief History*, anthropologist Tim Ingold reflects on how "the practice of inscription" narrows the gap between thought and expression:

> In typing and printing the intimate link between the manual gesture and the inscriptive trace is broken. The author conveys feeling by his choice of words, not by the expressiveness of his lines.[1]

Several of the writers in my interview cohort affirmed the cognitive and artisanal value of writing by hand:

> I sometimes like to write longhand if I am thinking about something difficult. I curl up on the bed or couch and then transfer it to the computer later. I find it useful because it slows you down. Sometimes I even copy things over longhand to make myself think about the sense of it. (*Marjorie Howes, English, Boston College*)

While academics with a natural flair for language may well have a better chance of becoming stylish writers than those who merely put in the hours—in the same way that elite athletes at the pinnacle of their sport draw on innate talent and an appropriate physique as well as intensive training—the fact remains that *all* successful academics work hard, one way or another, at the craft of writing. What's more, many of them relish rather than resist the effort and challenge involved:

> I hear the sound of the words as I write, and I care about that. I derive pleasure from polishing my work and hearing it; I take pleasure in getting the language right. (*Kevin Kenny, History, Boston College*)

Perhaps it's a matter of reframing what we mean by *success*:

> Success is a process, a mindful process. A lot of students make the mistake of comparing their beginning efforts with other people's final products, which is not a smart thing to do, since rarely do you start with something wonderful. And even if you did, it wouldn't be any fun. (*Ellen Langer, Psychology, Harvard University*)

Psychologist Carol Dweck distinguishes between people with "a fixed mindset," who believe that talent is a finite commodity, and those with a "growth mindset," who believe that our innate talents can and should be stretched, challenged, and changed. For fixed-mindset people, Dweck explains, "effort is a bad thing. It, like failure, means you're not smart or talented. If you were, you wouldn't need effort." For growth-mindset people, on the other hand, "effort is what makes you smart or talented."[2] Writers with a fixed mindset are likely to resist learning new skills, whereas those with a growth mindset never stop seeking out new ways of developing and testing the limits of their craft.

THINGS TO TRY

Think like an artisan

Craftspeople respect and cherish the materials and tools that they work with: the stonemason loves the stone and the chisel; the weaver loves the fiber and the loom; the sushi chef loves the raw

"A deep pleasure"

STEVEN PINKER

Department of Psychology, Harvard University (USA)

Cognitive psychologist Steven Pinker started as a "conventional academic" but always cared "about language, about style." He learned to write "by savoring examples of good writing and reverse engineering them":

> I was fortunate to be in a field that had at least two gorgeous writers: Roger Brown and George Miller. They were clear. They were witty. They were elegant. They were unpretentious. I pored over their sentences and asked myself, "Why do I enjoy that so much? What's the trick?"

After Pinker published his first two scholarly books, he was encouraged by an academic editor to write for a popular audience, a challenge that he likens to undergraduate teaching: "in both cases, you're writing for smart and curious people who just don't know the topic." Every book he publishes typically goes through six or seven drafts:

> I write a draft of the first chapter and then immediately go back and revise, because the first draft is inevitably messy and flawed. Then I go to the second chapter and do two passes, and so on with the other chapters. Then I send them out to specialists and also to certain readers. For example, I send them to my mother, who is smart, educated, and highly literate—she is my target reader, and she's willing to do it as I'm her son.

By the time he gets to the final chapter, months have passed since he wrote the first one: "So I can look at it and say, 'Who wrote this crap? Oh yeah, it was me.'" He reworks each chapter two more times—"Draft four cleans up draft three in the way that draft two cleaned up draft one"—and then reads the whole book straight through:

> So the goal of draft five is to make all the chapters consistent with each other and to make sure the book has a coherent narrative thread. Draft six cleans up whatever mess I've left from draft five. Then, of course, it comes back from the copy-editor, so I always put it through another draft then.

Long after publication, Pinker sometimes experiences a "surprising feeling":

> of picking up the book to look for something and then being captivated by my own writing, and reading page after page, and thinking, "Wow, did I write that?" That is a deep pleasure.

fish and the knife. To cultivate your identity as an artisan of language, start by writing down all the things you love about writing, from the feeling of words in your mouth to the sound of a tapping keyboard. If your list is a short one, look for ways of expanding it: for example, by reading a book on the pleasures of writing or by talking to colleagues whose writing is a pleasure to read. What is their attitude toward the hard work of writing? How did they learn and develop their craft?

Get some new gear

Some academics love high-tech tools such as grunty computers and whizzy new software. Others prefer more old-fashioned pleasures; for example, I still enjoy writing with a fountain pen in a notebook, and whenever I get a new computer, the first thing I do is set up the color scheme and wallpaper. Whatever your favorite writing tools, it's worth investing in some new ones from time to time—not only for the sake of increasing your writing efficiency and stretching your skills but also because acquiring new gear can be fun. This exercise need not be expensive: paper is cheap; many computer programs and apps can be downloaded for free.

Dare to grow

Take a few minutes to examine your own attitudes and beliefs about writing. Do you have a *fixed mindset* ("I've always been a good writer"; "I'll never be a good writer") or a *growth mindset* ("I like to stretch my writing muscles by trying out new kinds of writing"; "I can get better if I work at it")? How do you feel about other aspects of academic labor: your intellectual abilities, your teaching skills, your leadership potential? Writers with a fixed mindset tend to avoid risk; they focus mainly on what they already do well. Those with a growth mindset constantly seek out new challenges, not only in the areas where they already feel competent but also wherever they see opportunities for new learning.

Read a book

Every writer, it seems, has a favorite book on the craft of writing. For general advice on writing style, it's still hard to beat the classics: Strunk and White's *The Elements of Style*; Ernest Gowers's

The Complete Plain Words; Joseph Williams's *Style*; William Zinsser's *On Writing Well*. Alternatively, you can study the nuances of sentence-level writing with Bruce Ross-Larson's *Stunning Sentences*, Stanley Fish's *How to Write a Sentence*, or Claire Cook's *Line by Line*; you can explore the delights of revision with Joseph Harris's *Rewriting*, Richard Lanham's *Revising Prose*, or Jay Woodruff's *A Piece of Work: Five Writers Discuss Their Revisions*; or you can home in on specific disciplinary styles with books such as Eric Hayot's *The Elements of Academic Style: Writing for the Humanities*, Stephen Pyne's *Voice and Vision: A Guide to Writing History*, Bryan Garner's *Legal Writing in Plain English*, Howard Becker's *Writing for Social Scientists*, Michael Billig's *Learn to Write Badly: How to Succeed in the Social Sciences*, Robert Goldbort's *Writing for Science*, Anne Greene's *Writing Science in Plain English*, Harold Rabinowitz and Suzanne Vogel's *Manual of Scientific Style*, or Joshua Schimel's *Writing Science*. For books on the particularities and pleasures of English grammar, syntax, and punctuation, see the "Read a Book" section at the end of Chapter 10. (Yes, believe it or not, grammar books appear in the chapter on pleasure!)[3]

6

THE OTHER TONGUE

When asked to describe their experiences of writing in English, a group of Danish doctoral students got creative. "Writing in English is like a bad hair day," one observed. "You can leave the house, but you're not really comfortable with the situation." Others said that writing in English feels like making an Italian pizza for Italians ("The result is almost always edible, but I am embarrassingly aware that the Italians can make it better themselves"); like driving without a global positioning system ("Without GPS, sometimes you may have to take a detour"); like riding a rusty bicycle ("You can keep your balance, but you'll never win the Tour de France"); or like walking in high heels ("Sometimes it goes smoothly and well, but other times it's unsightly and wobbly.")[1]

For better or for worse, English has become the primary language of international research scholarship—which means a lot of bad hair days, rusty bicycles, and wobbly shoes for academics worldwide. The L2 colleagues I interviewed were quick to list the disadvantages they face when compelled to write and publish in English. Linguistic subtleties get trampled:

> I feel really handicapped when I write and speak in English. Being a lawyer, I'm used to arguing: I find words easily, and I have so many nuances. That's lost to me when I speak and write in English. (*Ann-Sofie Henriksson, Teaching and Learning Development, Uppsala University*)

Vocabulary gets muddled:

We have a problem in Sweden with Swenglish—mixed languages—and that's very common in academia. We have proper Swedish words, so why don't we use them? (*Christer Nilsson, Ecology, Umeå University*)

And familiar words fly out the window:

Several years ago, I was invited to give a seminar in Italy, so I naturally decided to speak in Italian. I was struggling to find the words. At some point, I said *nitrogeno*, meaning *nitrogen*, but in Italian you say *azoto*. I thought, "*Nitrogeno*?! That doesn't sound right!" But I couldn't figure out what the Italian word was. (*Marialuisa Aliotta, Physics and Astronomy, University of Edinburgh*)

For the most part, however, the L2 colleagues I spoke to (25 percent of my overall interview sample) proved more likely to dwell on the positives than the negatives. Writing in English, they told me, encourages precision and concision:

It forces me to be much more concise and precise and to write shorter sentences. When I choose a word, I have to think about it very carefully. (*Claudia Bernardi, Languages and Cultures, Victoria University of Wellington*)

A firm grounding in foreign languages and grammar can even put them at an advantage over native English speakers:

The current generation of British PhD students didn't have grammar at school, and as a result, they make lots of mistakes, which I have to catch. This is very ironic—here I am, the nonnative speaker, but my grammar is better. (*Wim Vanderbauwhede, Computing Science, University of Glasgow*)

When asked to recommend specific strategies for mastering written English, L2 academics offer (predictably?) varied and even contradictory advice:

First they have to get the basic grammar correct. If they cannot parse sentences, then they won't be able to figure out which is the main verb, and if they cannot figure out which is the main verb, then they get into all kinds of problems. (*Agnes Lam, Applied English Studies, University of Hong Kong*)

"Something universal about languages"

SUN KWOK

Department of Physics, University of Hong Kong (China)

Astronomer Sun Kwok grew up attending Chinese-language schools in Hong Kong, where literature and writing were among his favorite subjects. Many years later, having become an international expert on planetary nebulae, he started publishing articles in astronomy magazines such as *Sky and Telescope* and *Amateur Astronomy*. Before long, he found himself in demand as a popular science writer:

> Many amateurs look at planetary nebulae, which are bright enough to be seen by an amateur telescope, yet they usually don't know much about what they are and their role in stellar evolution. I'm happy that I have the chance to relate the latest goings-on in research to people who are interested but may not have the technical background to read the scientific literature.

His 2001 book *Cosmic Butterflies*, lavishly illustrated with photographs from the Hubble Space Telescope, found a wide and enthusiastic readership:

> I was invited by quite a few North American amateur astronomy societies, and I also spoke at two major conventions. I got to meet the readers and hear their reactions and how much they enjoyed the book.

Writing for a wider public gives him "a lot of satisfaction," Kwok says, "totally different from the satisfaction of doing science; it's a different kind of reward." Although popular science writing places him in the role of a teacher, he has discovered that the learning flowed both ways:

> When you write for the layman, you put yourself in a totally different mindset; you really think about the research. The process of looking for a simple explanation actually helps me to understand the subject better.

Writing in English rather than Chinese has never been a major issue:

> After I submitted my first magazine article, the editor wrote back right away and said, "This is magnificent writing." That gave me a huge amount of confidence, because I'd never written for the wider public before. I have often seen with people of Chinese origin that if their Chinese writing is good, their English writing is also good. It's something universal about languages: I can organize things, I can express things in a clear way—all this helps.

It's not the grammar which makes the difference. If you make a mistake or a comma is wrong, of course that matters—but it's the clarity of thinking which is really important. (*Fabrizio Gilardi, Political Science, University of Zurich*)

Nonetheless, one consistent theme emerged from my interviews. Learning to write sophisticated academic English is not just a matter of reading a textbook or enrolling in a language course. Like any other artisanal skill, the art of communicating fluently and elegantly in a foreign tongue requires, at the top end of achievement, thousands of hours of practice—and there are no shortcuts.

To be sure, if you grew up in a country where schoolchildren learn English from an early age, where British and American television shows are subtitled rather than dubbed, and where most people speak a language closely related to English—for example Denmark, Sweden, or the Netherlands—you will naturally have a significant head start compared to someone from, say, Indonesia or Thailand, where the educational, cultural, and linguistic divide yawns much wider. Likewise, academics with a multilingual family background and an innate talent for languages will no doubt express themselves more confidently in English than will L2 colleagues who struggle to wrap their tongues around every new word or phrase. But when it comes to writing stylistically nuanced English, no one gets a free ride—except, of course, for the millions of Britons, Americans, Canadians, Australians, New Zealanders, South Africans, and other native English speakers born in countries or into families where their own local lingo just happens to be the lingua franca of international academe. Having won the global language lottery, we bemoan our lot as academic writers—"My supervisor is so demanding!" "Those peer reviewers were so unfair!"—without realizing just how fortunate we are.

Fluent L2 English speakers typically muster a wide range of strategies to help them improve and extend their English. Martin Fellenz, a German academic who teaches business studies in Ireland, recalls that he spoke "woeful" schoolboy English until he picked up an English-language thriller while doing his military service; he found the vocabulary to be so straightforward, the plot so gripping, that he could make his way through it even

"A matter of the writerly code"

ANN BLAIR

Department of History, Harvard University (USA)

Historian Ann Blair grew up in an English-speaking household in Geneva, where she attended a French-speaking school. As an undergraduate student in the United States, she had to learn how to write and think in academic English rather than translating in her head from French, which, she says, "obviously dragged my English down":

> The challenging differences aren't linguistic as much as a matter of the writerly code: how you're supposed to structure an essay and move through it and conclude.

Later, while doing doctoral research in France, she was taken under the wing of a French literary scholar:

> I showed him an article that I was writing in English, and he ripped it to shreds on a basic level of clarity of expression and grammatical accuracy—finding all kinds of little problems—even though he always spoke to me in French and was very self-conscious about his mastery of English. That really got me thinking: how can this guy who is unwilling to open his mouth in English have such good criticisms of how I use my native language?

Blair realized that her mentor's professional experience as a writer trumped his command of spoken English: "When it comes to rigor and precision of expression and grammatical agreement and how you build a sentence, those things carry over very nicely from French." Her intensive interaction with him—"an hour-long session where he basically pointed out all the places where the subject was not really the subject of the verb I was using or was inappropriate"—also alerted her to the value of one-on-one feedback, which in turn has influenced her work as a teacher:

> People are often aware once you point it out to them that they've broken various rules of proper language. I'm very big on getting the words to say what you want them to say and not assuming that the reader will read your mind.

Blair allows herself to be "draconian about concision and precision in student writing" only because she applies those same precepts to her own writing as well: "no wordiness, no roundabout expressions, no impersonals or passives or malapropisms." Over time, she says, "writing doesn't necessarily get easier, but I think I write better."

without a dictionary. From that moment forward, he resolved to read only novels published in English, a decision that paid off several years later when he won a PhD scholarship to the United States: "Within three weeks, four weeks, everything I knew about English from reading novels became active, and I started speaking and writing it as well." He advises L2 English speakers to immerse themselves in English-language media:

> It doesn't matter what medium you use. It could be TV. It could be books on tape. It could be reading. It doesn't matter. That's how you get to know what is right and wrong. I don't speak English by rules. I speak it out of an intuitive understanding of where the words should go. (*Martin Fellenz, Business, Trinity College Dublin*)

Likewise, French-Canadian zoologist Robert Poulin urges L2 colleagues to consume English novels in their leisure time—"Why read a translation of the Harry Potter books when you could read the original?"—and to spend time in an English-speaking environment. "But most of them don't," he notes:

> They'll go to a conference, where they'll meet with other people who speak their own language, and this is the group they go out to dinner with. They struggle through their talk, and those fifteen minutes when they speak English—that's about the only English they speak. (*Robert Poulin, Zoology, University of Otago*)

Poulin's attitude is one of resigned pragmatism rather than resistance or resentment. "English is now the international language not just of science but of everything—diplomacy and commerce and so on," he says. "If you're ambitious and want to make it as a scientist, you have to sort this out early on. It will not come easy."

Behavioral habits such as reading British novels or watching American movies can help L2 scholars improve their artisanal skills as speakers and writers of academic English. However, given the powerful interpersonal dimensions of language, social habits such as cultivating a network of English-speaking friends, collaborating with English-speaking coauthors, and seeking help from English-speaking colleagues can lead to even more lasting and satisfying gains. Some L2 scholars, such as Malaysian linguist Mei Fung Yong, have benefited from the generosity of a supervisor or mentor:

When I was doing my PhD in New Zealand, my supervisor spent a couple of weekends with me in her office, looking through my work paragraph by paragraph and talking about signposting and clarity in writing to make the text reader-friendly. (*Mei Fung Yong, Applied Linguistics, Universiti Putra Malaysia*)

Others, such as French-Canadian sociologist Michèle Lamont, have hired professional editors to help them hone and polish their prose, an experience that Lamont says she would recommend to any academic who wants to become a better writer, "not just those who are nonnative English speakers":

I always thought I wrote very well, but the editor made me much more aware of how to put yourself in the shoes of someone who's not an expert. (*Michèle Lamont, Sociology, Harvard University*)

Swedish immunologist Kristina Lejon spent several years in a research group that included an L1 researcher who helped them get their academic English up to publication standards:

But now when we're getting manuscripts ready for submission to English-speaking journals, we have to send them out for English correction. We make some common mistakes that we try to learn from; but it's harder when you have to use a central organization, because they don't always know your field so well. (*Kristina Lejon, Clinical Microbiology, Umeå University*)

A potential downside of cross-lingual collaboration is that L1 academics may assume a position of false superiority based purely on their command of English. One Swedish academic described to me the frustrations of working in a department where two senior colleagues are native English speakers:

They have this attitude that "we are so good at writing in English, we know how to write it better than you," which at one point actually caused me to go off and publish some academic articles in Swedish, just to prove that I'm better than them at something. In fact, I'm not that bad in English. But still there's always this power struggle: "We know English better than you. Don't dare to point too high." (*Name withheld*)

An attitude of mutual respect and empathy can go a long way toward mitigating such tensions. For colleagues in a multilingual research group, it's worth undertaking a frank and respectful inventory of the strengths and weaknesses that each coauthor brings to the table; for example, you might end up agreeing that an L2 speaker in your group is the most lucid and persuasive writer but that an L1 speaker should be assigned to do final editorial sweep before the manuscript gets sent out for review. Meanwhile, at the gatekeeping end of the publication process, editors can do their part to resist the sometimes brutal hegemony of academic English:

> As an editor, I'm always thinking I don't want to change this person's voice to be mine. I just edited a memoir by a guy who is Russian. I have left a lot of the strangeness in it, because that's its charm. I think you have to remember that different voices make the journal. (*Margery Fee, English, University of British Columbia*)

Attention to the social dynamics of writing in English exposes, inevitably, its complex emotional dynamics as well. Some of the L2 academics I interviewed addressed that tension through spatial metaphors that confounded predictable dualisms of alienation versus belonging. Writing in English, they said, can provide a safe haven amid stormy political seas:

> I come from an Urdu-speaking Muslim minority but lived in a Hindi-speaking area and attended an English-medium school. Every time I composed something in Hindi but put in something that was actually Urdu, it was crossed out. I didn't always know what I was doing wrong. English was neutral territory. I knew what its rules were. (*Tabish Khair, English, Aarhus University*)

It can launch a journey of discovery:

> I'm a migrant who comes from Sri Lanka. Having had to learn a different culture and write in a different language than my native language, writing to me is something like that journey as well, because you're picking up some things that may not necessarily be coming to you even in words. (*Shanthi Ameratunga, Population Health, University of Auckland*)

Conversely, L2 speakers may draw on ideas and images from languages that sit closer to their emotional core than English:

"There's definitely a learning curve"

MASSIMO MORELLI

Department of Economics, Columbia University (USA)

Imagine that you are a native Italian speaker who writes and lectures in English about complex economic and political issues. Now add an additional challenge: you are blind. For Massimo Morelli, a professor of economics at Columbia University, it's all about "learning by doing." He mastered spoken English during an undergraduate exchange to Michigan—"at school in Italy, they only teach you the grammar"—before enrolling for a PhD at Harvard:

> Some of the professors were speaking very fast, and my understanding of English wasn't very good then. So I had to record their lectures and then listen again at home to make my notes comprehensible. I made a lot of spelling mistakes (and still do now) when I typed, so there would be lots of stories about emails to department chairs where the spelling mistakes led to really funny interpretations.

The affordances of technology shaped Morelli's research trajectory. Having relied mostly on oral communication through his school years—"listening to books on tape and making recordings of the lectures, then taking notes in Braille and rereading and relistening"—he initially gravitated toward the study of history, sociology, law, and political science. Then, in 1993, the first computerized Braille board became available, and he was able to access software that allowed him to work with mathematical formulae:

> At that time, the PDF files of academic papers were not as easy to find as they are now, and I always needed someone to go with me to the library to check out books and read them to me. Therefore, a PhD in history looked like something quite difficult to do quickly and productively and competitively with sighted students. I found it easier and more rewarding to switch to scientific writing.

However, Morelli is not one to stay in his comfort zone for long. Having established himself as an economist, he started publishing articles in political science journals—"you have to be much more long-handed, long-winded"—and now writes about the European economy for Italian newspapers:

> It was quite interesting to see the reaction of the editors to sentences that in the context of an academic paper look perfectly clear, but when you're writing for a newspaper, they want a different level of clarification. So there's definitely a learning curve there.

If I find that I'm getting too academic, if the work is getting a bit cold, and if I think it's missing some emotion, then I'll grab a Māori phrase, a Māori proverb, and I'll drop that inside the academic writing and let that allow me to pull over some of my Māori history, narratives, beliefs, and concepts and embed that in the academic writing. (*Poia Rewi, Māori, Pacific, and Indigenous Studies, University of Otago*)

Such metaphors of added value—the safe haven, the intrepid journey, the warm emotional core—offer a compelling counternarrative to the dominant discourse of English-speaking academe, where second-language speakers are often implicitly regarded as second-class citizens. Far from portraying their own L2 status as a deficit, the writers I spoke to show how the behavioral, artisanal, social, and emotional resources that they bring to their work from other languages can enrich the sometimes barren terrain of academic English.

THINGS TO TRY

Swap services

All academics possess knowledge and skills from which other people could benefit. Conversely, all academics could benefit from other people's knowledge and skills. So why not offer or solicit support in English-language writing in exchange for services such as critical feedback, tuition in another language, or even cooking lessons? Whether you are an L1 or L2 English speaker, such arrangements may have benefits that go far beyond language learning alone; and asking for favors becomes so much easier when you have something to give in return.

Pay it forward

If you don't need language lessons or cooking classes, consider "paying it forward": that is, performing a good deed with no expectation of reciprocity. The hour or two that you devote to giving constructive, thoughtful, one-on-one English-language support to an L2 colleague or student can have positive resonances in that person's life and work far beyond what you can imagine. In turn, the beneficiary of your generosity may later feel inspired to undertake similar acts of academic altruism.

Find your emotional language

If you speak more than one language fluently, take some time to reflect on and analyze your emotional relationship to each—for example, by writing down all the emotion words that you associate with each language or by freewriting in each language for ten minutes and comparing the two experiences. How do your differing emotions about each language inflect or impinge on your academic identity? Can you find creative ways of building on the positive emotions and ameliorating the negative ones?

Read a book

If you are an L2 English speaker, any book will do: children's stories, spy novels, poetry. As long as it's in English, it will help you improve your fluency as a writer. You may also want to seek out how-to books aimed specifically at L2 students and academics: for example, Stephen Bailey's *Academic Writing: A Handbook for International Students*, Caroline Brandt's *Read, Research and Write: Academic Skills for ESL Students in Higher Education*, Ernest Hall and Carrie Jung's *Reflecting on Writing: Composing in English for ESL Students*, Sheryl Holt's *Success with Graduate and Scholarly Writing: A Guide for Non-native Writers of English*, or Hilary Glasman-Deal's *Science Research Writing for Non-native Speakers of English*. (Just don't let your own academic writing be unduly influenced by their bland, workmanlike titles!) For supervisors, a number of edited collections offer varied, context-specific advice on working with L2 students: for example, Valerie Matarese's *Supporting Research Writing: Roles and Challenges in Multilingual Settings*, Norman Evans, Neil Anderson, and William Eggington's *ESL Readers and Writers in Higher Education*, and Donna Johnson and Duane Roen's *Richness in Writing: Empowering ESL Students*. And finally, L1 and L2 writers alike may benefit from the theoretical, critical, and political perspectives offered in volumes such as John Flowerdew and Matthew Peacock's *Research Perspectives on English for Academic*

Purposes, Claire Kramsch's *The Multilingual Subject*, Theresa Lillis and Mary Jane Curry's *Academic Writing in a Global Context*, Ramona Tang's *Academic Writing in a Second or Foreign Language*, and Vaughan Rapatahana and Pauline Bunce's lively coedited essay collection, *English Language as Hydra*.[2]

PART THREE

SOCIAL HABITS

He aha te mea nui i te ao? He tāngata, he tāngata, he tāngata.

What is the most important thing in the world? People, people, people.

—Māori proverb

I'm writing this paragraph while sitting at an outdoor café table next to my friend and colleague Selina, who is still wearing her exercise clothes after a kickboxing session at the gym. We decided to meet here because I've never been to this particular café before; it's owned by Anna, a friend of Selina's, who stopped by our table a few minutes ago to set down a platter of bread and a saucer of freshly pressed olive oil from her own orchard. An hour from now, she will bring us lunch. In the meantime, I have set my "pomodoro" timer, which is ticking away silently at the top right-hand corner of my computer screen, gradually changing from green to yellow to red as the end of our writing session approaches. (For more on the pomodoro principle, see Chapter 9, "Writing among Others"). I have adjusted my timer from its default setting— twenty-five minutes followed by a five-minute break—to fifty minutes, to accommodate a longer run of writing followed by a longer break. Before we started writing, Selina and I spent half an hour or so talking about our current writing projects: the structural dilemmas we're struggling with, the conceptual break-throughs we've made, all our usual mélange of self-doubt, satis-faction, frustration, and delight. After the timer rings, each of us will choose one new sentence to read aloud (and Selina will cackle with laughter when I read her this one). Then we'll break for a plate of Anna's homemade meatloaf, a small glass of local rosé—and more conversation about writing.

The concept of writing as a social activity is a relatively new one for me, no doubt because my own habits in this area have been so underdeveloped. Throughout most of my academic career, my BASE has looked more like a triangle than a square: long and strong on the behavioral, artisanal, and emotional axes but alarm-ingly stunted on the social side. Trained as a literary scholar, I have always been a solo researcher who publishes mostly single-authored books and articles—not because I dislike working with other people (I am a highly collaborative teacher and colleague) but due to a slew of personal, historical, and situational factors: writing on my own suits my temperament and style; I've never found a writing partner with whom I've truly "clicked"; in the English and Comparative Literature departments where I have studied or taught over the years, most of my colleagues have been just like me, writing behind closed doors, publishing on their own, braving with fierce independence the rigors of peer review and the humiliation of rejection.

Writing this book has challenged me to pull down the "Keep Out" signs I had unconsciously erected around my own writing practice. The writing traditions I know best—poetry, fiction, lit-erary scholarship—fetishize the romantic ideal of the lone au-thor: the poet or novelist scribbling in a garret; the industrious scholar toiling in the bowels of the library. This ideal is largely affirmed rather than challenged by collections such as Mason Currey's *Daily Rituals* (a compendium of the daily rituals of 161 authors, composers, painters, choreographers, playwrights, poets, philosophers, sculptors, filmmakers, and scientists from the eigh-teenth century to the present); Gary Olson and Lynn Worsham's *Critical Intellectuals on Writing* (in-depth interviews with twenty-seven eminent scholars); Robert Boynton's *The New New Jour-*

nalism (extended interviews with leading American long-form reporters); Mark Kramer and Wendy Call's *Telling True Stories* (inspirational advice from prominent American nonfiction writers and journalists); Hilton Obenzinger's *How We Write* (interviews with Stanford University faculty and other writers about their writing); the famous *Paris Review* interviews (a still-growing archive of several hundred interviews with famous writers, artists, and intellectuals dating back to 1953); Rachel Toor's "Scholars Talk Writing" column in the *Chronicle of Higher Education*; and Noah Carney's "How I Write" column in *The Daily Beast*.[1] Virtually every profile or interview in these various collections—I counted more than 850 in all—focuses on a single named individual, with an emphasis on that person's distinctive routines and creative habits and with minimal reference to the other people who have nurtured, enabled, or otherwise contributed to his or her artistic practice.

Most of the interviews that I conducted for this book, likewise, conform to a single-author template. Even on the few occasions when I undertook joint interviews with coauthoring pairs or writing groups, my interview rubric consisted mostly of questions designed to tease out the details of individual writers' behaviors, skills, and emotions: how they write, how they learned to write, how they feel about their writing. In hindsight, I wish I had more explicitly probed the social dynamics of writing—for example, by asking questions such as "How do other people contribute to your writing practice?" or "Who are some of the people who have most influenced or inspired you?" But in a way I didn't need to. The writers I interviewed were quick to tell me about the teachers from whom they have learned to write, the audiences for whom they write, the colleagues among whom they write, the students whose writing they nurture, and the coauthors who have driven them to hilarity or despair. Even the habitual solo authors like myself—humanities scholars trained to churn out books and articles in monkish isolation—spoke eloquently of the mentors who have inspired them, the peer reviewers who have riled them, and the loyal friends, family, and colleagues who have read and critiqued their drafts.

In fact, every single interview question that I posed—whether focused on behavior, craft, or emotions—addressed the social dynamics of writing one way or another. Writing for publication is, after all, a deeply human act: we write to communicate our research findings *to* other people; we learn to write *from* other people; our writing habits are enabled and inflected *by* other people. Even risk-taking and resilience become meaningless concepts when considered outside the context of social interaction. Writing is risky only when other people can deride you for what you've written; resilience is required only when other people have the power to knock you back.

Each of the three chapters in this section spotlights a differently configured set of social habits. "Writing for Others" focuses on audience response, peer review, and the various ways in which writers learn from their readers. "Writing with Others" explores the complex interpersonal dynamics of coauthorship, cowriting, and other forms of collaborative writing and editing, surveying practices that fall along a continuum ranging from "You write the analysis, and I'll write the discussion" to "Let's sit down in front of the computer and write this paragraph together." Finally, "Writing among Others" attends to writing communities of various shapes, sizes, and functionalities, including writing groups, writing networks, and that peculiar form of intensive short-term community known as the writing retreat.

Fittingly, I drafted parts of this book while on retreat in the company of other writers. There was the weekend I spent at a beach house with a group of early-career academics; I shared meals with them, ran a writing workshop, conducted some interviews, and joined in a vicious late-night game of Boggle in which I, the visiting "writing expert," was put firmly in my place. There was a week-long retreat with three other academic women at an isolated house on a vineyard in New Zealand's South Island: having started off as near strangers, by the end of the week we were swapping personal stories, urging each other to physical daredevilry (diving into an icy pool, parasailing above a mountain lake), and making plans for a follow-up weekend a month later. And then there were my occasional writing sessions with my friend Selina, which often took on the character of a miniretreat; we varied our venues frequently and challenged each other to find increasingly exotic or unusual places to write. Selina won the competition on the day she persuaded her kickboxing coach to let us use the thatched wooden pergola that he had built in subtropical marshland behind his gym. We sat and wrote for several hours to a soundtrack of birdsong, falling rain, fingers tapping on keyboards, and occasional bursts of conversation or laughter.

These days I write for, with, and among others far more frequently than I used to. I have become more conscious of my target audiences and more ambitious about expanding my readership. Thanks to the examples of some of the inspiring academics I have interviewed, I have begun to experience the pleasures and challenges of truly collaborative cowriting, whereby two writers allow their words and ideas to cross-fertilize until their writing becomes something greater than the sum of its individual parts. I also routinely seek out colleagues willing to offer me the kind of early feedback that, like so many of the humanities-trained scholars I know, I once avoided and even feared. The social axis of my BASE has grown longer and stronger—and, along the way, its behavioral, artisanal, and emotional axes have lengthened and strengthened as well. With supportive friends and colleagues included in my writing practice, I write more often and more fluently. Every round of constructive feedback helps me hone my craft and reach out to my target audiences more effectively. And when I write in the company of others, my emotions tip much more readily toward pleasure, self-confidence, and joy.

7

WRITING FOR OTHERS

Why do academics write, and for whom? When I asked successful scholars to describe a piece of writing of which they are especially proud, some pointed to the conceptual, methodological, and artisanal qualities of the work itself:

> I'm pleased with my paper on chimpanzees and mirror recognition because I was able to articulate a difficult argument. (*Cecilia Heyes, Psychology, University of Oxford*)

> It held together nicely. (*Elizabeth Rose, Management Studies, Aalto University*)

Some foregrounded their own roles and identities as writers:

> It was written from the heart. (*Kristina Lejon, Clinical Microbiology, Umeå University*)

> There's a little bit of twinkle in the eye. (*Michèle Lamont, Sociology, Harvard University*)

A few mentioned their feeling of achievement upon having survived a difficult process:

> I'm proud of my thesis in the sense that it was very hard work to finish; it was something that was giving me nausea every day. (*Lena Roos, Religious Studies, Uppsala University*)

A striking number, however, dwelled mainly on their pleasure and pride in knowing that their work has made a difference to other people:

I'm proud of the comments I've got from colleagues saying, "Wow." As one of the reviewers said, "You said something that needed to be said." (*John Dumay, Accounting, Macquarie University*)

I have to satisfy my peers who will review my work, but the greatest pleasure I derived from my latest book was when I bumped into a neighbor on the way to school, walking with my youngest son. She said that when she finished reading chapter 2, she couldn't wait for chapter 3. (*Kevin Kenny, History, Boston College*)

These responses highlighted one of the most crucial yet least discussed aspects of academic writing and publication: the role that our readers play in shaping not only how and what we write but also how we feel about our writing.

The editors I spoke to were particularly adamant about the importance of paying attention to readers. "We don't just publish papers because the research is solid," noted Tim Appenzeller, a former magazine editor at *Nature*; "we publish them because the research is important in some broader sense, and we want the authors to make a case that it's important." Many academics, he added, "are not sympathetic to a wider audience; they are much more concerned with looking good to their immediate peers." And those peers can be hard to ignore. One of my interview subjects confessed to having a colleague with "a really horrible screechy voice":

When we were working on our book—especially the theoretical parts—I had her as a parrot screeching on my shoulder, even though she wasn't the person I wanted to write to. [*Name withheld*]

All too often, in fact, our imagined reader is what literary scholar Leah Price describes as "a stern critic who is weighing how original and how learned we are," rather than "someone who could enjoy and be entertained and amused and excited by our writing." Our real enemy, according to Price, "isn't disapproval or bad reviews or that imaginary critic who's poking holes in your argument":

The thing we should be afraid of is indifference or boredom: not making our argument interesting enough for someone even

"There's nothing quite like a narrative"

LEE SHULMAN

Graduate School of Education, Stanford University (USA)

As a young Yeshiva student, Lee Shulman landed a job helping to run religious services in a Jewish community center. Before long, he was delivering the sermons:

> I remember having to think hard about how to craft a fifteen- to twenty-minute talk that analyzes a piece of biblical or other religious text and then relates it to some real problem or issue in the world. That became a kind of story grammar, a kind of template.

Later, he brought a similar suite of techniques—storytelling, close analysis, and attention to real-world relevance—to his educational scholarship:

> I like looking at a really complicated, messy kind of problem and trying to clean it up by making a number of distinctions and helping people see the world through the lenses of those now distinguished categories. So I'll often begin by saying, "I'd like to tell you three stories." There's nothing quite like a narrative for reminding people of complexities and frustrations the world presents to them, often in quite funny ways.

His most influential articles have typically begun either as delivered talks or as something he "imagined saying":

> Even before a very large audience, I try to identify three or four people in the audience who are what my friend Howard Gardner calls "charismatic listeners." These are people in the audience who are smiling, who are at the same rhythm as the speaker, who are nodding, who are laughing at the right times. After a while, I'm talking to them.

Often Shulman agrees to "write up" a talk for publication, only to find himself procrastinating until the deadline looms: "So I am likely to finish writing a paper, even in my seventies now, staying up till three in the morning." Although he still regards academic writing as "a more difficult, painful, and challenging aspect of public speaking," he takes pride in his ability to communicate clearly and engagingly, whatever the medium:

> Late one night in Buenos Aires, a woman on the faculty of the university leaned over to me after my talk and said, "You know, Professor Shulman, if you taught here in Argentina, you would not be as respected as you are in the United States." "Why is that?" I asked. "Because you are far too easy to understand."

to care whether it has holes in it. (*Leah Price, English, Harvard University*)

In the introduction to his book *A Very Short, Fairly Interesting, and Reasonably Cheap Book about Studying Organisations*, author Christopher Grey gives voice to the anxieties that for a long time held him back from finishing the manuscript:

> Every time I tried to write something interesting I felt, as if it were at my shoulder, a hypothetical reviewer criticising: "the argument is confused"; "the author seems unaware of Joe Blogg's ground-breaking paper from last year"; "the author misunderstands Josephine Blogg's seminal book"; "theoretically naïve"; "lacking evidence"; or, worst of all, "Grey hasn't got a clue—as we have long suspected."[1]

Yet despite these anxieties, his book became an international success:

> A business journalist at *The Observer* called my book "indispensable and subversive." I think I'm going to have that carved on my tombstone. And then underneath it will say, "It turns out he wasn't indispensable." (*Christopher Grey, Organization Studies, Royal Holloway, University of London*)

Many of the academics I interviewed noted the challenges and rewards of targeting specific publications for specific audiences—for example, public policy makers:

> People think it's easy. Actually it's very hard to get policy makers' attention. And you can't always give easy answers. As an academic, you want to say, "Here is what I think, but there are all these qualifications. Here's why some aspects of this question are unanswerable." (*Janet Currie, Economics and Public Affairs, Princeton University*)

Or practicing nurses:

> I write for nurses who are studying and who are thoughtful about what's actually going on in nursing. I try to make contact with the deep humanity of what they do. (*Trudy Rudge, Nursing, University of Sydney*)

Or university administrators:

> I recently wrote a couple of courses for an online learning program
> for university leaders and managers. It reformed my writing con-
> siderably, as I had to move away from thinking about academic
> writing as being quite formal and quite distant from the reader.
> (*Shelda Debowski, academic leadership consultant, Australia*)

Or businesspeople:

> I wrote an article on bronchopulmonary dysplasia for *International
> Innovation*, in which I had to explain what I do to a new and dif-
> ferent audience—pharmaceutical CEOs, bankers, investors—folks
> whom I don't normally interact with. It was a great experience.
> (*Kurt Albertine, Pediatrics, University of Utah*)

Or students:

> I published an article in the *Huffington Post* about a new edition
> of Mary Shelley's *Frankenstein*, so that I could say to my students,
> "We're talking about this book in class, and I also wrote some-
> thing about it that you can read on the Internet." I wanted to
> model for them a literary scholar engaging with a critical public
> in real time. (*Victoria Rosner, English, Columbia University*)

But the gold standard of academic writing, for most, is the scholarly book or article that speaks to readers both within and beyond academe:

> The phrase I had in my mind as I wrote my book was that I wanted
> mathematicians to agree with it and my wife to understand it. (*Bill
> Barton, Mathematics Education, University of Auckland*)

Whether they tailor their writing for specific audiences or cast
a wider net, I found, virtually *all* successful academics put enormous amounts of craft and care into making their work accessible to their chosen readers. I heard versions of this message
from scientists:

> How I would write an article for submission to, say, *Nature* and
> *Science* is very different from how I would write if I wanted to
> submit it to a more specialist disciplinary journal. That's very

different from how I write a grant application, and again that's very different from writing a review-style article. (*Russell Gray, Director, Max Planck Institute for the Science of Human History*)

And from social scientists:

You have to adjust your style to address different audiences. If you only write in these strictly professional papers, work within academic borders, your writing will deteriorate over time; you're going to become more and more boring. (*Stefan Svallfors, Sociology, Umeå University*)

And from humanities scholars:

If what we do loses touch with the general audience, loses touch with our civilization, it's sort of pointless. If the whole fabric of the academic enterprise doesn't connect in any way with the literature, arts, and public life of the time, then I think we're not doing our job. (*Kwame Anthony Appiah, Philosophy, Princeton University*)

Indeed, many regard the ability to disseminate their research not merely as a useful skill but as an ethical imperative:

The taxpayer has just funded your research. The least you can do is tell them what you did. (*Miles Padgett, Physics, University of Glasgow*)

But writing for others is not just a one-way street. The very act of reaching out to new audiences can yield unexpected rewards:

I think writing for a general audience actually improves my research because I can capture the attention of students better as well as write better proposals. It forces you to step back and reconsider a lot of dearly held assumptions. (*Mark Moldwin, Space Sciences and Applied Physics, University of Michigan*)

Some authors may even acquire new perspectives on their subject matter. When historian Michael Reilly published two collections of nineteenth-century historical texts by people from the island of Mangaia in the South Pacific, he discovered that his own scholarly contributions—the learned commentary, the detailed historical analyses, the English translations—meant much

"The people we have studied talk back to us"

RUTH BEHAR

Department of Anthropology, University of Michigan (USA)

As a graduate student, anthropologist Ruth Behar "didn't even really think about audience." Like most students, she wrote to please her professors:

> But then I discovered that the professor I was trying most to please expected something less academic, more poetic and descriptive. I was trying to write neutrally in the standard academic way, keeping a certain distance from what I was writing about. But then I started introducing other kinds of feeling into the work—longing, rage.

The first time she presented a conference paper containing deeply personal material, Behar was so nervous that she broke out with fever blisters:

> I was in such a state of anxiety that I was going to present this in public to my fellow anthropologists. But people were very moved by it, and that was pretty much when I decided that I was going to be this vulnerable observer: I was going to find a way to merge ethnography with personal narrative.

It was a risky move professionally; however, her readers' responses over the years have convinced her that she made the right decision:

> Students write to me saying, "I went into anthropology because I read your work," or "I'm still in academia because I read *The Vulnerable Observer*," or whatever. So I know that the work I do reaches people. It reaches a lot of women. It reaches a lot of minority students who aren't sure if they want to be in the academy; they're looking for something that is going to allow them to write meaningfully.

Anthropologists, Behar observes, used to have no conception that their own research subjects might be among their future readers:

> They worked in peripheral areas and brought that knowledge back to the metropolis. But now the people we have studied talk back to us.

Recently she returned to the small village in Spain where she conducted her PhD research thirty years ago:

> I literally went from seeing people working with traditional tools on the land to seeing all of these tools behind glass in an ethnographic museum. The people there are very excited because I have returned a piece of their history to them.

less to many readers than did the original texts, which until then had been inaccessible to general readers:

> Mangaians have told me that they didn't worry about reading any of the English; they just read all the vernacular texts through from end to end. That's fine with me; it's quite nice that there are all these different reading strategies going on. (*Michael Reilly, Māori, Pacific, and Indigenous Studies, University of Otago*)

Likewise, when cultural anthropologist Jennifer Meta Robinson started researching a scholarly book on farmers' markets, she quickly came to realize that "life is a text" with multiple authors, readers, and interpretations:

> My audience now includes the people I am interviewing: farmers, growers, customers. At the same time I am trying to speak beyond that audience to people who have wider influence: policy makers, educators, community organizers. (*Jennifer Meta Robinson, Anthropology, Indiana University*)

A number of the writers I interviewed have become so deeply committed to telling their readers' stories—and their own—that they have deliberately crossed the line between research and activism. Political scientist Sarah Maddison wades into political issues that few other academics are willing to broach:

> I think of my books on aboriginal politics in Australia as a political intervention: I write to deliberately stir the pot. (*Sarah Maddison, Social and Political Sciences, University of Melbourne*)

Physician Donald Barr's most influential article chronicles the day he decided to slow down and "listen—really listen" to an elderly patient:

> She talked for twenty-two minutes, even though the nurses were tapping their watches. I diagnosed terminal lung cancer at that visit, and yet when she left, she said that was the best visit she ever had with a doctor, because I was the only one who had ever listened. So I simply described that encounter in about 250 words, and that article is still widely reprinted and taught in many places across the country. (*Donald A. Barr, Human Biology, Stanford University*)

And literary scholar Susan Gubar has transformed her own experiences with ovarian cancer into health advocacy for the benefit of others. "There are more than a thousand books about breast cancer," she told me, "and those illness narratives have played a major role in getting money for research":

> But no one has ever been able to do that for ovarian cancer because its symptoms are so disgusting and its treatments are so painful and dreadful. So I wrote a book calling for new detection techniques and different ways of dealing with the disease and protesting the protocols that are so dehumanizing for patients. Someone had to do it, and I'm very glad that I was given enough time to complete the book. (*Susan Gubar, English, Indiana University*)

A vast body of scholarly literature explores the practical, theoretical, and rhetorical challenges involved in writing for different kinds of audiences, both real and imagined: academic and nonacademic; addressed and invoked; rhetorical, universal, ideal, and implied.[2] Who are the readers for whom we are really writing, and how will we know when we have reached them? How can we reconcile what we want to say with what we think our readers and reviewers want to hear? These are complex questions that many academics have never been trained to address or indeed been encouraged to consider closely. Undergraduate students typically learn to write only for the teachers who will be grading their assignments: for example, in a 2014 study of more than two thousand undergraduate writing assignments from a variety of disciplines at US universities, Dan Melzer found that students were asked to write for general audiences only 7 percent of the time and to their own peers only 6 percent of the time.[3] The situation shifts only marginally in graduate school; unless doctoral students are pursuing a PhD by publication, most write for an audience of just a few people, namely, their dissertation adviser and the members of their examining committee. Even published academics may find it difficult to imagine real people—interested colleagues rather than pejorative judges—sitting at the other end of their sentences. Literary scholar Janelle Jenstad confessed that it took her many years to stop "writing up" to an audience that she felt was judging her:

"A vehicle for their voices"

MARYSOL ASENCIO
Department of Sociology, University of Connecticut (USA)

Marysol Asencio had an "epiphanic moment" right in the middle of our interview, when she realized that writing has always felt to her "like a luxury and a privilege" rather than "real work." Coming from a working-class background, she found it difficult to explain to her family—and to herself— that writing is a legitimate part of an academic's workload, just like teaching and service:

> If you've been taught that writing is not necessarily worth-while and doesn't symbolize real work, then when you're asked to do eighty committees, you do eighty committees, rather than saying, "On Monday morning, I carve out my writing time" or "I can't touch Friday; that's my writing day."

Asencio confessed that she did most of her scholarly writing on weekends and in the evenings, treating writing "as a sort of secret thing": "because I have doubts as to whether it's legitimate, whether I'm selfish, whether it's lazy or egotistical." Her political activism has contributed to her sense of guilt: "There's the whole issue of how activists look at academics: 'You could be out there occupying Wall Street 24/7. Why are you choosing to write?'" Over time, however, she has come to see writing itself as a form of activism:

> My work is with marginalized people, queer people, people of color, immigrants, and the poor—not the typical majority or core population. I write about people who are not in the literature; I am a vehicle for their voices.

She has also realized that "someone like me has a right to be part of the conversation":

> You always feel illegitimate. In many ways, academia can feel like it is made for white, middle-class males. The more you are not a white, middle-class male yourself, the more you can feel not welcomed. But I have something to contribute. I have something to contribute exactly because of where I came from.

Growing up in an environment where girls were expected to marry young and start a family, Asencio longed to "get away from traditional gender roles and expectations and be ex-panded physically, mentally, emotionally":

> I think that I saw very early on that education did that for me. Even though I grew up in a small, little apartment, books opened up worlds.

Only now that I'm post-tenure do I finally feel that I'm writing for peers. I'm sharing information with people who are going to be excited about it in the same way that I'm excited when I read an article that changes how I thought about something or that I can use in the classroom. (*Janelle Jenstad, English, University of Victoria*)

So how can academics learn to write more effectively for their target audiences, whether general or discipline specific? Most of the advice offered by the writers I interviewed echoes principles addressed elsewhere in this book. Sharpen your writing skills:

Many academics just don't have basic writing skills. At some point, as an editor, you get irritated with people who have every sentence backwards. It's totally fixable. (*Sam Elworthy, Director, Auckland University Press*)

Strive for clarity:

So many academics get so caught up in show-offy, jargon-filled fads and trends. Gradually they become immune to the goal of clear communication and to the joy of beautiful, simple, evocative, concrete language. (*Douglas Hofstadter, Cognitive Science, Indiana University*)

Avoid condescension:

They oversimplify, and to use a phrase that comes up all the time, they "dumb down." That's just fatal, because it betrays entirely the wrong idea. The person you're writing for doesn't necessarily know what you know—they may not use the sort of methodological apparatuses that you're used to or the jargon—but that doesn't mean they're dumb. (*Elizabeth Knoll, former Senior Editor at Large, Harvard University Press*)

Solicit feedback from people you can count on:

Show your writing to someone you can trust to give you really powerful, positive, but also critical feedback—I think that's about the best thing you can do in your writing. Do that in a really safe relationship with somebody who you know has really got your interests at heart. (*Alison Jones, Education, University of Auckland*)

Learn what specific audiences are looking for:

> Sitting on National Science Foundation review panels and reading other people's proposals—understanding what's selling the idea, where the holes are, and hearing the other people in the room—that has been an amazing training for me. (*Patricia Culligan, Engineering, Columbia University*)

Pay attention to the comments of anonymous peer reviewers, but don't let one or two negative reviews derail you:

> I had a pretty negative report on my first book from a reader who I felt had really not understood it. I was quite crushed, but I didn't think, "Oh my God, I have to change everything because one reader doesn't like this." I got advice from colleagues who said I could push back a bit. (*Marjorie Howes, English, Boston College*)

Above all, let your readers see your passion for your subject:

> One way to find one's voice is to show one's enthusiasm for what one is writing about. I'm very interested in how you can write about what you love in a way that that love is conveyed. (*Ludmilla Jordanova, History, Durham University*)

Good writing, after all, will always find appreciative readers. Psychologist Steven Pinker recalls being seduced by a book review from far outside his own field:

> The author of the book wrote, "It is often said that a camel is a horse designed by a committee—a quote that does grave injustice to a splendid creature and all too much honor to the creative power of committees." The book reverse engineered the camel—the joints, the feet, the water storage—and though I ordinarily wouldn't read a book on animal engineering, I knew from the review that it was written with such flair that I just had to buy it. (*Steven Pinker, Psychology, Harvard University*)

Pinker's conclusion? "There is no field in which you can't be stylish." Likewise, there is no topic that cannot be made accessible and interesting to many different kinds of readers.

THINGS TO TRY

Find your "charismatic listeners"

Write down the names of all the people who have given you encouraging feedback on your writing over the past few years: the partner or parent who took a fine-toothed yet gentle comb to the first draft of your manuscript, the old friend from graduate school who saw your newly published article in a peer-reviewed journal and emailed to congratulate you, the overseas scholar who approached you after a conference presentation to suggest a future collaboration. Could any of these people become a "critical friend," someone from whom you can solicit honest but reliably supportive feedback? Most academics already get more than their share of critical feedback, so you might as well pack a few cheerleaders into your corner.

Cross-train

All academics must vary their writing style from time to time: a scientific-journal article looks quite different from an encyclopedia entry, which in turn bears little resemblance to a grant proposal or a promotion application. Rather than regarding activities such as lecturing, blogging, and community engagement as time-sucking distractions from your research, try reconceptualizing them as muscle-building tonics instead. The more you cross-train by writing across genres as part of your everyday academic work, the better prepared you will be to adapt to new audiences when you write for publication.

Write a letter, not a diary

The following exercise is adapted from Gillie Bolton and Stephen Rowland's book *Inspirational Writing for Academic Publication*. First, write a letter to your imagined readers, asking them what they want from your writing. Next, write their reply. Finally, produce a summary of your research that takes into account your imagined readers' questions and objections. This third piece of writing might end up becoming the introduction to your article or book.[4]

Read a book

You can't always judge a book by its cover, but you can often gauge its academic register by its pronoun usage. Self-help books for scholars who aspire to write for nonacademic audiences speak directly to *you* about how to speak directly to others. Examples of this genre include William Germano's *Getting It Published*, Kathleen Kendall-Tackett's *How to Write for a General Audience*, Lynn Nygaard's *Writing for Scholars*, Laurel Richardson's *Writing Strategies*, Ann Curthoys and Ann McGrath's *How to Write History That People Want to Read*, and Dennis Meredith's *Explaining Research*. (Robert Nash takes a slightly different tack in *Liberating Scholarly Writing*, which focuses on the value of weaving personal narrative into research writing; but even in this *I*-dominated book, *you* are the author's interlocutor.) In scholarly books *about* writing for others, by contrast, third-person pronouns dominate. Whether in single-authored studies such as Gerald Graff's *Clueless in Academe*, Marjorie Garber's *Academic Instincts*, or Sarah Perrault's *Communicating Popular Science* or in edited collections such as Angelika Bammer and Ruth-Ellen Boetcher Joeres's *The Future of Scholarly Writing* or Jonathan Culler and Kevin Lamb's *Just Being Difficult?*, academics who critique the impersonal, jargon-driven nature of academic discourse mostly stop short of addressing *you*.[5]

8

WRITING WITH OTHERS

The academic universe can be divided into two types of writers: those who write and publish with other people and those who write alone. Scientists are mostly collaborative writers; humanities scholars are mostly loners; and social scientists tend to be either one or the other, depending on their discipline and disposition.

Except, of course, that things are rarely that simple. Scientists may end up doing most of their writing and editing while seated in front of a computer screen alone. Humanists may write and publish with other people in a variety of situations and genres. Social scientists may find themselves inhabiting a range of different roles across an academic career: solo author, lead author, contributing author, supervisor, editor, mentor. And academics in any field may cross and confound disciplinary norms: for example, distinguished scientists such as Richard Dawkins, Stephen Hawking, and Stephen Jay Gould have forged powerful authorial identities as humanities-style single authors, while philosophers, literary scholars, and historians such as Douglas Hofstadter and Daniel Dennett, Sandra Gilbert and Susan Gubar, and Tony Grafton and Joanne Weinberg have ventured beyond the familiar confines of single authorship.

Even academics who publish and theorize on collaborative writing often struggle to define it.[1] Writing and publishing with others is a complex and highly nuanced activity that can take on many different forms, from coattribution (whereby multiple researchers' names appear on a single publication, whether or not they have all actually been involved in the writing process) to coauthorship (whereby two or more authors contribute to the writing and editing of a single piece) to cowriting (whereby two or more people literally sit down and compose sentences together). My interview subjects noted the collaborative dimensions of other scholarly practices as well—for example, editing:

> It's important to make it clear that this is a collaboration and that you as an editor are trying to be a surrogate reader and trying to identify the places where a reader might be confused or lose a thread or feel bored or puzzled, and help the author past those things. (*Tim Appenzeller, former Chief Magazine Editor, Nature*)

Or human-subject research:

> I've been adopting a very formal method of collaboration with the people I'm interviewing: after the interview, I write down their stories and send them the text, and they can leave in or out whatever they want. So the research is really cocreated. (*Mindy Fullilove, Clinical Psychiatry, Columbia University*)

Or even peer review:

> People don't like a critic much. But I try to be extremely courteous as I raise questions about issues and to make sure that it's not personal and to have a collaborative style of writing, like "We want to get to the bottom of this. Maybe something that we've overlooked so far is . . ." (*Cecilia Heyes, Psychology, University of Oxford*)

In fact, it would be virtually impossible to find a piece of published scholarly writing that has involved the intellectual input of only one person.

However we define "writing with others," most academics would agree that it requires mastery of a range of interpersonal skills: how to communicate with other people across conceptual, linguistic, and disciplinary boundaries; how to negotiate authorship and attribution; how to respond to situations of power imbalance; how to get along. Like so many of the other core capabilities on which academics' career success depends, however, collaboration is seldom taught or even explicitly discussed as part of most academics' professional formation. Undergraduates in preprofessional fields such as engineering, business, and law are

"A very different side of my brain"

SHANTHI AMERATUNGA

School of Population Health, University of Auckland (New Zealand)

Epidemiologist Shanthi Ameratunga practiced as a hospital pediatrician for many years before becoming a research scholar and teacher: "I wrote notes in medical charts but did very little academic writing." Then she enrolled in an intensive master of public health program—"It was baptism by fire"—and later a PhD:

> My supervisor was very good at providing constructive feedback. He writes in a style that's actually quite similar to mine—or vice versa?—so we've learned off each other; he comes to me often with his own writing. He has a way of making things quite succinct but colorful.

Now, as a senior academic, Ameratunga spends most of her research time mentoring emerging scientists and "living vicariously" through their publications:

> I've got ten PhD students at the moment, and lot of other quite junior colleagues that I work with in Fiji, Sri Lanka, and New Zealand—all of whom I encourage to write. So that means I've become much more an editor and a reviewer of other people's work rather than having the time to really indulge in my own writing.

Typically she spends several hours a day reading, commenting, and providing feedback for others:

> Last year, I was an author on forty peer-reviewed scientific journal articles, but only one of them was a bespoke first-author paper; that was a major review I was commissioned to write. All of the others were first-author papers led by my students or junior colleagues working on projects I lead. I absolutely adore and am proud of this role. The excitement of emerging researchers with their first-author papers is infectious. But supporting them, asking them to do iterative pieces, getting all those into publication takes a lot of time.

Ameratunga admits to sometimes feeling "disappointment, sadness, and frustration" about how much of her time is given over to collaborative writing:

> It has a very different flavor to it academically, and I have to draw on a very different side of my brain to find the enjoyment for it. I would love to be able to write stories and poems and things, and I would like to do much more writing for a general audience. I need to give myself the license to write by myself again.

increasingly required to undertake group projects that simulate the kinds of collaborative problem-solving situations they may face after they graduate; doctoral education, by contrast, remains stubbornly focused on individual achievement. At most universities worldwide, the single-authored entity known as the PhD dissertation bears at best a tenuous resemblance to any genre of writing that the apprentice academic will be expected to produce later in his or her academic career.

And yet there is so much to learn. The academics I interviewed described an array of collaborative challenges that they have faced in their work as writers. There are language issues:

> I've got German and Israeli collaborators I recently wrote with. My goodness me, that was just a nightmare. They're molecular biologists, so they wanted everything supertechnical. I think I removed probably half the acronyms, but the end result was still pretty inaccessible. (*Russell Gray, Director, Max Planck Institute for the Science of Human History*)

And disciplinary issues:

> When I was writing about neoliberalism in politics, I invited an economist to join our research group. He said to me, "What do you know about economics and politics? You're in higher education," and he declined to be in the group. (*Tony Harland, Higher Education, University of Otago*)

And gender issues:

> I think on average the men in economics don't have the same facility with language as the women. Of course, many men are brilliant writers; but some make errors and are apt to use words in not quite the right way. So I usually end up doing the writing. But my male coauthors would probably hate that I said this! (*Janet Currie, Economics and Public Affairs, Princeton University*)

And conceptual issues:

> There are a few articles where I'm not happy with the way certain things were explained—but you wouldn't say "Take my name off!" just because you don't like the way your coauthors wrote a couple of sentences. (*Robert Poulin, Zoology, University of Otago*)

And hierarchical issues:

> One time I was trying to build up some early-career people and get them a chance to be profiled, but they hung back and waited for me to lead. In the end, I wrote most of the paper, and they insisted I should be named as the first author; so my efforts to be a sponsor and a minor contributor didn't come together quite so well. (*Shelda Debowski, academic leadership consultant, Australia*)

And power issues:

> I've been accused of being very controlling because I tend to write the framework of a grant proposal myself and then send it out without giving my coauthors as much time to respond as they would like. But recently I was involved with a proposal team where the principal investigator farmed out all the sections for everyone to write, and then we all got very frustrated because we just kept getting asked for different things. (*Patricia Culligan, Engineering, Columbia University*)

And stylistic issues:

> Collaboration is good for science, but it can be bad for the quality of the writing. It's very, very hard to have five people doing drafts and end up with something that's good. So I'll say to my collaborators, "Just send me bullet points or notes so that I don't have to redo someone else's writing," and then I write it the way I want it. (*Alison Gopnik, Psychology, University of California at Berkeley*)

Despite these challenges and caveats—and the occasional horror story of coauthoring relationships gone awry—most of the academics I spoke to emphasized the positive aspects of collaborative writing. When two or more people work together to produce a single piece of writing, core assumptions get clarified:

> Collaboration helps us justify our writing and to present our claims in a clearer way. (*Mei Fung Yong, Applied Linguistics, Universiti Putra Malaysia*)

Mental blocks get smashed:

> When you get stuck, then you don't have to wrestle your way through it. You can pass it over to someone else. (*Jennifer Meta Robinson, Anthropology, Indiana University*)

"A win-win all round"

SARAH MADDISON

School of Social and Political Sciences, University of Melbourne (Australia)

Political scientist Sarah Maddison considers herself to be "a bit of a bower bird" when it comes to what interests her, ranging across research areas including gender politics, public policy, and indigenous political culture without feeling constrained to adopt "any one disciplinary set of tools." She has published three single-authored books as well as a number of collaborative works: "coedited collections, a textbook, book chapters, articles, special issues." One of her earliest coauthoring ventures proved so painful that she still ranks it among "the most traumatic experiences" of her life:

> It was truly awful. By the time we had finished, if I hadn't already been committed to another couple of collaborations, I don't think I would have ever collaborated again.

However, the experience taught her some useful lessons:

> I learned that you do need to be careful. The next time I found myself in a collaborative project where I felt the workload wasn't evenly shared, I negotiated a bigger chunk of the royalties, which kept me from feeling bitter about doing more than 50 percent of the work.

Having started university as a twenty-five-year-old single mother, Maddison understands the benefits of collaboration for those who are seeking to climb the academic ladder quickly. She actively seeks out opportunities to mentor PhD students and early-career colleagues:

> For example, if you're invited to write a book chapter or journal article, most editors are quite open to you saying, "Yes, I would like to do that, but could I bring a PhD student of mine in to collaborate with me?" So I've done that a couple of times, and that's been really nice—a win-win all round.

She has also worked to facilitate fruitful collaborations between academic and nonacademic writers:

> For a book I coedited called *Unsettling the Settler State*, we asked indigenous governance practitioners who were not experienced writers to partner with a nonindigenous collaborator to produce a chapter. That was quite challenging at times. But at the book launch, an indigenous writer in the audience said she felt we had provided a template or model for ways in which indigenous voices could access mainstream academic publishing. I'm very proud of that.

Conceptual gaps get plugged:

> The collaborative process is essential for good writing; it brings together different perspectives and allows identification of holes that should be filled before submission. The outcome is a better product than if I wrote in a vacuum. (*Kurt Albertine, Pediatrics, University of Utah*)

Collegial relationships get strengthened:

> Collaborating on a grant proposal helps to create a good bond between the people who collaborate, which has value even if you don't get the grant. (*Wim Vanderbauwhede, Computer Science, University of Glasgow*)

Stylistic horizons get expanded:

> I co-authored a long paper with a brilliant linguist named Alan Prince. He was a colorful, almost outrageously flamboyant writer. Just by mixing my prose with his, I learned a lot. (*Steven Pinker, Psychology, Harvard University*)

And sentences get polished to a high gleam:

> There were four of us writing the article together. We'd go to one of the group member's houses, project it on the wall, and literally go over every line, discussing, arguing. Eventually we won an award for the article; we were told that there was a universal sense of how well written it was. (*David Pace, History, Indiana University*)

In a best-case scenario, collaboration enables researchers to tightrope-walk into unfamiliar territory even while providing a safety net of peer encouragement and support. Mathematician Keith Devlin was drawn into the "soft, soft" science of ethnomethodology by a social scientist colleague who helped him break out of his "hard science" shell:

> It was such an interesting process. We ended up writing what is probably the book I'm most pleased with from an academic perspective, because we took risks; we didn't follow a well-trod map. (*Keith Devlin, Human Sciences and Technologies, Stanford University*)

Similarly, literary scholar Margery Fee discovered a whole new research area when she accepted a colleague's invitation to work on a collaborative project about food:

> I decided to write about a scientific theory called the "thrifty gene hypothesis." I read a huge number of scientific papers and analyzed them for assumptions about racial difference and whether this hypothesis actually panned out, which it didn't. That felt very risky, because science studies was not my original field at all. Now I'm teaching it! (*Margery Fee, English, University of British Columbia*)

For historian Tony Grafton, writing with others always entails an element of intellectual and emotional risk, "because you have to be willing to chasten your own style and accept other people's criticism at a very intimate level." Yet the risk, he says, is worth taking:

> Recently I wrote a book with a dear friend, a very different kind of scholar from me. We didn't know if the project would work at all, yet we had the most amazing time doing it. And we've had some book reviews that really indicated that the reviewers saw the joy and the exuberance of the enterprise. (*Anthony Grafton, History, Princeton University*)

Grafton's account of the collaborative process as a perilous yet joyful process echoes the language of challenge and delight that I heard from many other successful academics. Writing studies scholar Andrea Lunsford, who has copublished extensively with her colleague Lisa Ede, noted that collaborative scholarship "is still a kind of anathema" in the humanities:

> Many people told us we would not succeed professionally if we persisted in this perverse practice of writing collaboratively. When Lisa came up for tenure, her chair wrote to me and said, "I want you to write a letter, and you have to say how many lines you wrote and how many lines Lisa wrote," which was impossible. (*Andrea Lunsford, English, Stanford University*)

Despite such frustrations and challenges, Lunsford's accounts of her scholarly collaborations are peppered with the vocabulary of pleasure: "It's very pleasurable because it's social" (on writing

"Two people, two pencils, and two pads"

SUSAN GUBAR

Department of English, Indiana University (USA)

In the late 1970s, Susan Gubar and her colleague Sandra Gilbert decided to write a book together, because the topic they were tackling seemed both too immense and too revolutionary for one author alone:

> We were aware of working on something that was very new. Books on women's literature and women's literary history were just starting to come out while we were in the process of composition. It seemed like such a huge undertaking, vaguely unprecedented and unnervingly fearful—that was one of the reasons we felt always that we needed to hold each other's hands.

The Madwoman in the Attic went on to become a classic work of feminist literary criticism, and the duo henceforth known as "Gilbert and Gubar" not only continued to coauthor books but also coedited the monumental *Norton Anthology of Women's Literature*:

> But we never got a grant for that first book. I think one of the main reasons was that funding agencies in the humanities were not used to funding collaborative work.

Gubar's "holding hands" metaphor invokes the comforts of the collaborative process, which provides solace and support for adventurous scholars who would otherwise be left to explore new territory on their own. Because joint authorship is so rare in literary studies, she and Gilbert were keenly aware that their nontraditional approach would likely be considered suspect by colleagues:

> So if we published something separately, it would be under Sandra's name or under my name. And at the beginning of the book, we make a very clear distinction over who had drafted which chapters and which had been written together so that when I came up for tenure, nobody could say, "Well, she [Sandra] wrote the whole book."

The first three chapters of *Madwoman*, Gubar notes, "were written in the same room with two people, two pencils, and two pads":

> There were differences of opinion. Sandra liked the word "moreover" much more than I did. There were differences of opinion, but for the most part, they could be ironed out.

with Ede); "It was sheer fun" (on writing with John Ruszkiewicz); "We were a little giddy; we just got carried away with ourselves" (on writing with Bob Connors).

Literary scholar Margaret Breen compares collaborative scholarship to a festive gathering:

> My aunt and uncle always threw wonderful parties. They would invite a variety of people. They had incredibly good food. Everyone felt welcomed and at home and at ease. What I realized a few years ago was that in terms of editing books—bringing together lots of different people and perspectives in a collection of scholarly essays—I'm like Tante Margit and Uncle Irwin. (*Margaret Breen, English, University of Connecticut*)

Like a great party, a successful collaboration repays all the planning, effort, and diplomacy that go into making it work. When two or more people "click" over a piece of writing, their ideas are amplified, their pleasure is increased, and the intellectual impact of their thinking becomes greater than the sum of its parts.

THINGS TO TRY

Compare your BASE assumptions

When you write collaboratively with other people—whatever your definition of "collaboration" may be—it's important to establish early and often that you and your coauthors are all on the same page, so to speak. Books on the logistics of collaborative writing and publication can guide you through standard issues of attribution and authorship and help you draw up an advance contract to be agreed on and signed by all. But what about all those other, less easily defined, questions that coauthors must grapple with? For example, what are your daily or weekly work patterns? Are you willing to take stylistic risks? What methods of giving and receiving feedback do you find most effective (or least stressful)? A premeeting at which you and your coauthors talk through your BASE assumptions about writing—in all its complex behavioral, artisanal, social, and emotional dimensions—may be one of the best investments in time that you will ever make.

Colocate

If you've never done it before, try cowriting a short piece with a colleague: that is, literally writing and editing every sentence while sitting in the same room together. Even if you decide never to repeat the experience, the process will teach you a good deal about each other's thought processes and artisanal habits. And if your styles and personalities turn out to be compatible, you may discover an unexpected new joy in collaboration.

Throw a party

Editing a multiauthored book or a special issue of a journal can be a frustrating chore akin to the proverbial herding of cats. But if you reconceive the task as throwing a party, the whole concept becomes more fun. Who's in charge of the hors d'oeuvres? Who will provide the disco lights and streamers? If you can bring your coauthors together physically and throw a few real parties along the way, all the better.

Read a book

Fittingly, books on collaborative scholarship are almost always the products of scholarly collaboration. In some cases, the editors have decided to "throw a party" by bringing together individual essays that discuss the theoretical implications and practical challenges of collaborative writing: see, for example, James S. Leonard, Christine E. Wharton, Robert Murray, and Jeanette Harris's *Author-ity and Textuality: Current Views of Collaborative Writing*, Jane Speedy and Jonathan Wyatt's *Collaborative Writing as Inquiry*, and Bruce Speck, Teresa R. Johnson, Catherine P. Dice, and Leon B. Heaton's *Collaborative Writing*, a comprehensive annotated bibliography of research articles on collaborative writing published between 1970 and 1997. In other cases, such as Lisa Ede and Andrea Lunsford's career-spanning *Singular Texts/Plural Authors* (1990) and *Writing Together* (2011), two or more coauthors enact the collaborative processes that they narrate and theorize. (On the title page of *Singular Texts/Plural Authors*, the authors' names have been printed twice: once as AndreaLunsfordLisaEde and once as LisaEdeAndreaLunsford.) Often the very titles of collaborative books invoke a sense of shared adventure, as in Ernest Lockridge and Laurel Richardson's *Travels with Ernest: Crossing the Literary/Sociological Divide* (a genre-busting blend of scholarly prose and creative nonfiction) or Ken Gale and Jonathan Wyatt's *Between the Two: A Nomadic Inquiry into Collaborative Writing and Subjectivity* (an extended exploration of intersubjectivity that draws heavily on the works of Gilles Deleuze and Félix Guattari, another famous coauthoring pair). Books *about* scholarly collaboration may also inspire you to read some works *of* collaborative scholarship, such as Douglas Hofstadter and Daniel Dennett's *The Mind's I*, Sandra Gilbert and Susan Gubar's *The Madwoman in the Attic*, or Anthony Grafton and Joanne Weinberg's *"I Have Always Loved the Holy Tongue."*[2]

9

WRITING AMONG OTHERS

When we write *for* others, we engage in conversation with our readers. When we write *with* others, we work with colleagues toward a common product. And when we write *among* others, we create a community of writers. This chapter explores three varieties of writing communities, which I refer to as *writing groups*, *writing retreats*, and *writing networks*, although the demarcation lines among them easily blur. For example, the members of a writing group (two or more people who meet regularly to discuss or advance their writing) could decide to go on a week-long writing retreat (a time- and space-bound gathering devoted to intensive writing and conversations about writing); or a subset of the members of a writing network (a loosely bound group of colleagues who support each other's writing in various informal ways) could decide to form a writing group and/or to organize a writing retreat. My aim here is not to define a specific set of practices but quite the opposite: to offer a sampling of the infinite variety of ways in which writing communities can support and nurture the work of individual writers.

Academics who want to establish a writing group can choose from a smorgasbord of possibilities:

- *Size.* Will the group be large or small? Impersonal or intimate? Consistently populated or variable in size? (For example, a large group of participants could decide to meet in rotating pods of three to four people each.)

- *Frequency.* Will the group members meet on a regular basis (e.g., monthly, fortnightly, weekly) or only as and when needed?

- *Duration.* How long will each group meeting be? Will the duration of the meetings be consistent or variable?

- *Longevity.* Will the group convene only for a set period of time (for example, until a specific project is finished) or indefinitely?

- *Venue.* Will participants meet face-to-face, online, or both? On campus or off campus? Always in the same place or in different venues each time?

- *Composition.* Will the writing group be discipline based or interdisciplinary? Expert facilitated or peer facilitated? Autocratic or democratic? Inclusive or exclusive? Will it consist mainly of friends, strangers, or both? Faculty, students, or both? Academics, nonacademics, or both?

- *Organization.* Will the writing group be institutionally sponsored? Run by a group of peers? Managed by a single energetic individual? (Who will have responsibility for "holding the baby"?)

- *Process.* Will the group's meetings be *formative* (participants give and receive feedback on work in progress)? *Reflective* (participants discuss the challenges of the writing process)? *Motivational* (participants hold each other accountable for achieving specified writing goals)? *Supportive* (participants help each other cope with criticism and self-doubt)? *Inspirational* (participants cheer each other on)? *Creative* (participants undertake writing or brainstorming exercises together)? *Productivity focused* (participants come together in the same physical or virtual space to make progress on their own work)? Some combination of the above?

- *Purpose.* Is the group mainly intended to provide participants with *behavioral support* (finding time for writing, keeping on track with writing goals)? *Artisanal support*

"Like a sandstorm in the desert"

MINDY FULLILOVE

Department of Clinical Psychiatry, Columbia University (USA)

Mindy Fullilove cowrote her first book with her father, a union organizer, when she was still in college:

> That was a book for people who were interested in African American communities and community building. It was a working-class text, written for the people of our town.

After earning her medical degree, she began to write and publish on the psychology of place and the role of cities in mental health. More recently, Fullilove helped her ninety-one-year-old mother publish a collection of autobiographical stories:

> She had the most fabulous book launch anyone could ever have, and it turned out that she was secretly a writer all her life. This book just popped out of her like an overdue baby.

Fullilove's own writing is fueled by "collaboration, confusion, and epiphany":

> When I was working on my most recent book, I had a two-month-long brainstorm that was like a sandstorm in the desert. It was mystical, transcendental. All the information was moving around in my head, and then I felt like I could see the sand pouring out of me, like in the movies where all of a sudden some magic happens and everything goes up in the air and whirls around and then it all comes down, perfect.

Fullilove has belonged since 1996 to a weekly writing group that has "nurtured six published books and four more in progress, as well as twenty-six dissertations and countless papers and presentations":

> The mechanics are simple: we meet once a week, and people sign up to send something out on the date they set. And then the next week people come and discuss it. If nobody has handed anything out, we talk about ideas. Sometimes we just work on sentences.

Her writing group has helped her develop the courage to take intellectual risks and the resilience to deal with rejection:

> I'd take my negative reviews to the writing group, and everybody would just strategize. Adolf Chris, the founder of our writing group, is wonderful at walking us through rejection. I got very good training from him on how to decipher what people were saying, how to respond back. Up until then, I was just emotional about it.

(reading and editing each other's work, discussing craft)? *Social support* (forging relationships, building community)? *Emotional support* (providing encouragement, making the writing process more enjoyable)? Support in other areas, such as building institutional knowledge, exploring methodological issues, or strategizing about publication venues?

Whatever the group's function and ethos, the word *support* is crucial here. Academics have plenty of opportunities to receive formative feedback on their writing, whether by attending research seminars at their own institutions or by presenting papers at disciplinary conferences. All too often, however, such occasions can feel more gladiatorial than generative: instead of building each other up with thoughtful but encouraging critique, participants engage in the time-honored academic sport of puffing out their own chests while stomping on everyone around them. A genuinely supportive writing group demonstrates a collective concern for the growth, development, and well-being of every member, fostering the kinds of alchemical transformations that can be forged only in a crucible of trust.

Many of the academics I interviewed have been involved with writing groups of one kind or another, whether as participants, facilitators, or both. Nursing scholar Kathy Nelson joined an institutionally sponsored group for early career academics:

> At the start of the year, we all had to have public goals, and my goal was to have seven articles. Everybody kind of laughed. But then I was assigned a mentor who asked me for a list of what I was writing, and it turned out there were twenty articles I'd started, ranging from 90 percent finished to more like 5 percent. So I meet with her every month and negotiate my priorities, and I report my progress back to the group. (*Kathy Nelson, Nursing and Midwifery, Victoria University of Wellington*)

Historian Ludmilla Jordanova organized a writing group focused on craft:

> The first writing group I organized for PhD students was supposed to meet for eight weeks but ended up meeting for nine

months. I would get the students to look at Raymond Williams's *Keywords*, and I would say, "What are the keywords of your thesis? Can you talk to us about the history of those keywords?" So they would begin to get a sense of how the bones, the very skeleton of their work, functions. At another session, they all brought the table of contents of their thesis. We had a wonderful time. (*Ludmilla Jordanova, History, Durham University*)

Literary scholar Janelle Jenstad meets with a colleague for mutual cheerleading and frank feedback:

We commit to meeting once a week, even for ten minutes, to remind ourselves that we are researchers. We give each other pep talks: "You don't have to be on this committee. How's your beheading piece going? What about that critical introduction you were working on?" We're not afraid to offer each other trenchant critiques. Honestly, it's so great when my "writing buddy" succeeds. I'm genuinely happy when she gets something published— as happy as when I get something published. (*Janelle Jenstad, English, University of Victoria*)

Whether large or small, university-sponsored or homegrown, crisply professional or casually conversational, what nearly all successful writing groups have in common is a shared sense of generosity, pleasure, and even fun: "Everybody laughed" (Nelson); "We had a wonderful time" (Jordanova); "It's so great; I'm genuinely happy" (Jenstad).

"Write on site" and "shut up and write" gatherings offer a low-stakes, low-commitment alternative to formal writing groups. At a typical "write on site" event, participants meet for a few hours in a café, library, or seminar room to write silently in the company of others. "Shut up and write" sessions provide a somewhat more structured alternative to this format: participants chat informally for a few minutes or do a quick introductory round— "Here's what I'm planning to work on today" or "Here's what I hope to achieve in this session"—before diving into an intensive "pomodoro" lasting for an agreed period of time, usually around twenty-five minutes. (The "Pomodoro Technique," developed by author Francesco Cirillo, is named for the tomato-shaped egg timer that Cirillo originally used to time his creative writing sessions.)[1] The potential variations on these two models are endless. Some universities even sponsor write-on-site "boot camps," encouraging academics and PhD students with lagging projects or looming deadlines to leave behind their usual workspaces and write in a quiet venue elsewhere on campus, with meals and snacks provided.

Writing retreats take the "write on site" model to a higher level of intensity, physically uplifting participants from the distractions of everyday life and cloistering them in an atmosphere of scholarly sanctuary. Residential retreats may be as brief as a single overnight stay or as long as several weeks in duration; they may take place close to home or a day's travel away; they may be institutionally supported or organized ad hoc; their demographic composition may be homogeneous (for example, female PhD students from a single academic department) or heterogeneous (male and female, students and faculty, multidisciplinary, even multi-institutional). However, it is worth noting that the most successful writing retreats—those that engender loyalty, return bookings, and rave reviews from participants—do generally have a few key ingredients in common. First, they provide a break from routine, so that the participants return to "ordinary life" feeling refreshed, renewed, and reenergized. Second, they are institutionally sponsored at least to some degree—whether financially, organizationally, or both—so that those who attend feel that their academic labor is being recognized and supported. Third and most importantly, they foster productivity and pleasure in equal measure, providing participants with "air and light and time and space" that they can internalize and carry back with them to their everyday lives. If the writing retreat itself should happen to take place *in* such an environment—a venue with comfortable bedrooms, inviting writing spaces, and beautiful surroundings—its benefits, both tangible and emotional, are likely to be magnified.

In recent years, a body of scholarly literature has verified what just about every academic who has ever participated in a well-run residential retreat already knows: its effects on a participant's individual writing practice can be galvanizing, even transformative.[2] The benefits appear to be especially powerful for academic women, who, if statistics reported in the literature are anything to go by, are attracted to communal professional-development events in signif-

"Building bridges across disciplines"

RUSSELL GRAY

Director, Max Planck Institute for the Science of Human History (Germany)

As an interdisciplinary scholar whose work spans areas including psychology, ornithology, linguistics, animal cognition, philosophy of biology, and the evolution of human and animal behavior, Russell Gray is mystified by tribal behaviors that narrow rather than widen academic inquiry:

> For example, one thing that a lot of humanities people seem do a lot of is to mark who they are affiliated to and who they are affiliated against. I'm always amazed at just how much work goes into that.

For an evolutionary biologist, he admits, addressing an audience of linguists can sometimes feel "like speaking a foreign language you have acquired as an adult":

> No matter how hard you try, you're almost certainly fairly rapidly going to be marked as an outsider, because you're just not quite expressing things in the way people who have been trained in this for twenty years might.

Gray is "increasingly at pains to minimize those differences and find ways of building bridges across disciplines." For example, he has organized several residential workshops for international scholars who have come together to share data, methodologies, and ideas around an interdisciplinary research project. The more memorable the venue, the more successful the event. At a week-long workshop in New Zealand, the visitors—many of whom had escaped the Northern Hemisphere winter for the Auckland summer—indulged in swimming, beachcombing, kayaking, and stand-up paddle-boarding between sessions. One evening, however, something went wrong with the dinner arrangements:

> We were renting a house with a big deck. So I went to the grocery store and bought a bunch of steak and salmon filets and some salad and bread and lots of good New Zealand wine, and we had a barbecue. It turned out to be the best meal of the conference.

Meticulous organization is essential to a successful workshop, Gray concludes, but serendipity can play a valuable role as well: "There's a special camaraderie that develops when you all have to improvise to solve a crisis."

icantly greater numbers than men. Higher-education researchers Barbara Grant and Sally Knowles have noted some of the particular advantages of writing retreats run by and for women: a safe space; a meditative, labyrinthine mode; a time away from the demands of domesticity and children. (Some women even write in their pajamas.)[3] But male academics, too, may long for such a productive haven:

> We have so-called research retreats which tend to be extended staff meetings, really; it's just management talking about research. But to actually go away somewhere where you have the chance to not have email or these other concerns and just to spend a couple of days writing collaboratively, I think that would be fantastic. (*Matthew Clarke, Education, University of New South Wales*)

Academics who take part in writing groups and writing retreats are often exposed through those group activities to new writing networks: informal or semiformal alliances among writers who support each other's work in various ways, whether through collaboration, mentorship, interdisciplinary exchanges, or friendship. Writing networks are often associated with specific disciplinary communities:

> Feeling part of a community is very helpful to my writing. The discipline of history is huge, but there is a subcommunity of people who are operating within the same frame of reference on similar topics as me. And so I try to envision them as my audience when writing, and I assume a tacit favorable reception from that ideal abstract readership which is rooted in a concrete community of real individuals. (*Ann Blair, History, Harvard University*)

Or with academic organizations and conferences:

> I was one of the first people to use Foucault in nursing research, which was seen as a bit radical at the time. It put me outside the nursing discipline—but it also widened me out and sent me out in other directions, so that I've now built up a pretty strong network of colleagues from other disciplines with similar interests. And we run a conference every two years that draws people from Iceland and Canada and Australia and the UK. (*Trudy Rudge, Nursing, University of Sydney*)

"Without bodies being present"

INGER MEWBURN

Director of Research Training, Australia National University (Australia)

Trained as an architect, Inger Mewburn was taught to write "by architects who themselves couldn't write." She found academic writing to be "extremely painful" until she discovered the writing-advice section of the library:

> I became obsessively interested in refining my craft, discovering new heuristics: really simple little techniques like "use a verb in every sentence you write in your notes" or things that people have told me walking across the crossing at the traffic lights.

Her love of "talking shop" led her to start her popular *Thesis Whisperer* blog (www.thesiswhisperer.com):

> Blogging gives you confidence, and you take more risks. The audience is listening, and they give you instant feedback. So now I'm trying to actively encourage other people to blog, and I'm mentoring other bloggers and publishing articles about academic writing practices in blogging.

Mewburn is particularly interested in the kind of "affiliation work" that occurs in the margins of academe—"the invisible articulation work that holds academia together, but we never give it recognition":

> For example, I've got a Tumblr blog called *Refreshments Will Be Provided* where people post and comment on photos of food served at academic events. And I recently published an article on "PhD student whingeing": my conversational analysis showed that the students who whine the most are not always in trouble; they're using their complaints as a form of bonding.

A self-described "cloud bridger," she is constantly experimenting with new forms of networking. Not only does she organize weekly shut-up-and-write sessions in a local café—"it's easily the most productive morning of my week"—but she also instigates them spontaneously on Twitter:

> I'll tweet, "I'm really having a hard time. I need to punch this thing out. I'm going to do a twenty-five-minute pomodoro. Who's with me?" Other people will come back, "Okay, I'm in." "I'm in." "Okay, go. Go!" You know there's someone watching, but they're sitting in Canada or South Africa or wherever. That sense of "someone else is doing it, therefore I should be doing it too" is really powerful, and it can be re-created without bodies being present or cups of coffee or whatever.

Or with online forums:

> On a website called www.russianhistoryblog.org, they did a special online event dedicated to my latest book, *Gulag Boss*. They organized it and asked seven other specialists to comment on the book, all on a certain day, and there were lots and lots of responses from other readers. It was a fantastic thing—the instant feedback about what people found valuable. (*Deborah Kaple, Sociology, Princeton University*)

But new writing networks can spring up whenever or wherever two or more colleagues share ideas about academic writing: for example, when the neighbor you play squash with tells you about the great new time-management software he recently installed on his laptop or at the conference where a star researcher in your field offers to write a reference in support of your next grant proposal.

Writing groups, writing retreats, and writing networks are all examples of what Jean Lave and Étienne Wenger call *communities of practice*: loose confederacies of colleagues who gain mastery of a craft or trade by sharing information, experiences, and ideas.[4] At their best, writing communities do much more than merely help early-career academics acquire specialized knowledge and skills; they also offer intangible benefits such as professional affirmation, emotional succor, and support for intellectual risk taking. Indeed, far from mandating conformity, a flourishing writing community can inspire creativity and embolden individuals to follow their own instincts rather than bowing to disciplinary convention. Paradoxically, writing among others can give you the courage to stand out from the crowd.

THINGS TO TRY

Start a writing group

"I'd really like to be in a writing group," faculty and PhD students sometimes tell me. "Do you run one that I could join?" Their assumption, apparently, is that all writing groups are organized and facilitated by writing experts who lead everyone else to mastery. Such expert-facilitated groups do exist and are well worth looking out for, whether in your department, your university, or the wider community. But if you can't find an existing writing group—or if the ones you do know about don't appeal to you—consider forming your own. All you need are three ingredients: a defined purpose, a dollop of commitment, and at least one other person to join you.

Retreat in the company of others

Solo writing retreats—occasions when you withdraw from the world to write in isolation for a few precious days or weeks—work beautifully for some academics, especially those with abundant self-discipline and a tolerant partner or family. But time away on your own, however productive, can never duplicate the complex and sometimes mysterious dynamics of an intensive retreat in the company of others. Residential retreats need not be facilitated by experts (although many are) or professionally organized (although it can be a wonderful luxury to have the logistics of food, transportation, and cleaning taken care of by someone else). A weekend in a rented beach house with three or four colleagues may prove just as generative as a large, institutionally sponsored retreat.

Chart your networks

On a large piece of paper or a whiteboard, write down all the different professional networks, both formal and informal, to which you belong: the departments or institutes with which you are affiliated; the disciplinary conferences you regularly attend; the colleagues you chat with about university politics at the grocery store. Which of those networks currently support your writing practice, and how? How might you make better use of your networks to nourish your own work and nurture the writing of others?

Read a book

Whether you want to start your own writing group, organize a writing retreat, or strengthen your writing networks, there is a book out there to help you. Judy Reeves's *Writing Alone, Writing Together* and Pat Schneider's *Writing Alone and with Others* explore the benefits of writing groups from a participant's perspective;

Julie Phillips's *The Writers' Group Handbook* and Barbara Grant's *Academic Writing Retreats* provide you with a facilitator's view; and Rowena Murray's *Writing in Social Spaces* addresses the social aspects of academic writing more broadly. You might also consider sharing books *about* writing communities *with* your writing community, thereby transforming your writing group into a reading group (as described in DeNel Sedo's collection *Reading Communities from Salons to Cyberspace*.) For readers seeking a critical perspective on writing communities, books such as Andrew Abbott's *Chaos of Disciplines*, Anna Duszak's *Cultures and Styles of Academic Discourse*, Ken Hyland's *Disciplinary Discourses*, Michèle Lamont's *How Professors Think*, Steven Mailloux's *Disciplinary Identities*, and Tony Becher and Paul Trowler's classic *Academic Tribes and Territories* may prompt conversations about the crucial difference between belonging to a supportive academic writing community and being "disciplined" into academic writing.[5]

PART FOUR

EMOTIONAL HABITS

If you here require a practical rule of me, I will present you with this: Whenever you feel an impulse to perpetrate a piece of exceptionally fine writing, obey it—whole-heartedly—and delete it before sending your manuscript to press. *Murder your darlings.*

—Arthur Quiller-Couch, "On Style," 1914

If you want a golden rule that will fit everything, this is it: Have nothing in your houses that you do not know to be useful or believe to be beautiful.

—William Morris, "The Beauty of Life," 1919

If editing is akin to infanticide, what other acts of violence and sacrifice does our writing demand of us? Arthur Quiller-Couch's murderous metaphor has been quoted, misquoted, and misattributed by numerous authors, but seldom with any commentary to the effect that its morbid view of the writer's craft might cause far worse damage than the demise of a few overblown sentences. What if we were to replace Quiller-Couch's "practical rule" for writing with William Morris's "golden rule" for living, which teaches us that practicality and beauty can be soul mates rather than enemies? What happens when we invite positive emotions and language into our writing practice—and encourage them to make themselves at home?[1]

I drafted much of this book during a half-year sabbatical when I was granted a semester of research leave free from teaching and administrative duties. By that stage, I had completed most of the research and data analysis, planned the overall structure of the book, and sketched out a few sample chapters. However, I was significantly behind schedule on the actual writing of the book and not entirely happy with what I had written so far. Drastic steps were called for. To rev things up and overcome my nagging anxiety that I might fail to finish the book by the date agreed with my publisher, I mapped out a rigidly structured writing routine for the next five months: I would write every weekday morning for at least five hours; I would spend my afternoons reading, editing, and attending to email; I would churn out at least one thousand words a day; I would complete a new draft chapter every week or two.

I should have known better. I hit the ground running on day one, like a marathoner determined to set a steady pace from the very beginning of a long race—and, like any marathoner who takes to the road without adequate conditioning and training, I soon crashed and burned. By the end of day two, I knew that I couldn't possibly produce a thousand words per day; six and a half hours of writing time had netted me only about six hundred. By the end of day three, my back and neck had seized up from too many hours spent hunched in front of the computer. Although I did manage to pump out a new draft chapter by the end of that first week, I was a physical and emotional wreck by the time I got there.

"You should be enjoying your sabbatical," a wise colleague counseled me. "It's supposed to be a time of renewal, a time to slow down and take pleasure in intellectual activity. God *rested* on the seventh day, remember?" I tried to imagine what would happen if I used my sabbatical as a time for reading and reflection, rather than waking up every morning feeling pressured to write. While the idea certainly held a certain appeal—a truly stress-free sabbatical would be a beautiful thing indeed—I knew that a relaxed research leave was not for me, at least not this time around. The pressure that I felt to finish the book was motivated above all by my own desire to accomplish something concrete and meaningful during my time away. *I* wanted to finish the book; *I* wanted to run the marathon.

"Shift your focus from productivity to pleasure," my colleague had advised. The breakthrough moment came when I realized that, for me, productivity *is* pleasure: the trick was not to exchange one for the other but to find creative ways of combining the two. What aspects of my work give me the most pleasure, I asked myself, and what pleasurable activities can I integrate into my work to support my productivity? I made a list: I love color, conversation, solitary walks, the sea; I enjoy sifting through data, plotting out chapters, writing author profiles, charting my progress; I relish experimentation, beauty, change. On the other hand, I become physically tense when I sit in front of the computer for too long and emotionally tense when the words snarl and stall (which tends to happen, unsurprisingly, when I sit in front of the computer for too long).

So I began to play with more organic, nonlinear ways of writing, paying close attention to my rhythms and moods at different times of the day. Some days I stayed at home and worked on a single chapter all morning. More often, however, I varied my tasks to suit my disposition: a fifty-minute pomodoro, a two-hour editing session, a half day of reading and note taking. If I felt myself losing momentum, I would allow myself the luxury of composing a new author profile, a reliably rewarding task (and what a relief it was to showcase someone else's words rather than having to manufacture my own!) Alternatively, I might carry my laptop to the library for a shift of posture and a change of scene; or I'd head out on a long walk, using my cellphone to record voice memos to myself; or I'd use colorful scrapbook paper and sticky notes to help me visualize structural patterns and connections; or I'd meet a friend for a cup of coffee or a glass of wine, either as a break from work or as an inspiration to work. The more pleasurable the activity, I found, the more likely it was to initiate a new spate of productive writing within the next day or two. Instead of marching through the manuscript in linear fashion as I had done for much of my previous book, I allowed this one to grow organically, like coral: a new paragraph or profile here, a "Things to Try" section there.

Along the way, I also made a conscious decision to recode potentially disabling emotions as positive opportunities for growth and discovery. If I, a scholar with a generally positive attitude toward writing and a track record of publication, was struggling to write my book, what must such a task feel like to an early-career academic belabored by isolation and inexperience or even to a senior colleague embarking on a single-authored book for the first time? My own experiences prompted me to reflect on the emotional challenges faced by so many of my academic colleagues when they write.

Among the most serious of those challenges, I came to realize, is the self-doubt that can arise when we undertake any kind of intellectual risk: a new writing style, a foray into unfamiliar disciplinary terrain. Writing this book has often felt risky; before I started, I had never designed a research questionnaire, interviewed a human subject, coded an interview transcript, or acquired more than a passing knowledge of the qualitative methodologies that "real" social scientists (or so I imagine) imbibe during their PhD studies like mother's milk. On the other hand, I have taken such risks before: for my previous book, I assembled and analyzed a data set of more than one thousand academic articles, despite having no previous experience with quantitative data or linguistic corpus analysis. Not only did the skies fail to fall, but several reviewers went so far as to praise my "innovative" methodology.

I write now with the knowledge that even if my imagined worst-case scenario were to come to pass—if reviewers were to pillory my writing style, trash my methodology, and unmask me as the intellectual imposter that I, like so many of the colleagues I have interviewed, still sometimes secretly feel myself to be—I have deep emotional reserves on which to draw. My self-confidence as a writer and scholar is fed by many replenishing springs: by my own passion for my research, by the encouraging feedback of the people about whom and for whom I write, by the love and support of my family and closest friends, and by the strategies for redemptive "re-storying" that I have learned while working on this book. Indeed, my choice of metaphors in this paragraph—

deep reserves, replenishing springs—exemplifies how figurative language inflects the stories we tell about ourselves and our writing. I could just as well have written that my fear of criticism *saps* my confidence, *drains* my energy, and *dries up* my courage—metaphors of depletion that risk becoming self-fulfilling prophecies.

Following William Morris's "golden rule" for living rather than Arthur Quiller-Couch's "practical rule" for self-inflicted violence, the three chapters in this section are furnished with material designed both to edify and to delight. "The Pleasure Principle" maps the emotional landscape of academic writing, tracing the dynamic relationship between positivity and productivity. "Risk and Resilience" explores the emotional dynamics of risk taking and the strategies that successful academics draw on to recover their equilibrium when things go wrong. The section rounds off with "Metaphors to Write By," a meditation on metaphorical imaginings of all kinds: on mountains of self-doubt and valleys of shit; on playing music, playing by the rules, and playing chicken; on dry subjects and wells of pleasure; and on the transformation of "murdered darlings" into words and ideas that we can still cherish as our own.

10

THE PLEASURE PRINCIPLE

When the participants in my two survey groups were asked to describe the main emotions that they associate with their academic writing, they found themselves at no loss for words. Overall, more than two-thirds of the respondents in both cohorts (72 percent interviews, 69 percent questionnaires) reported a mix of positive and negative emotions, an indication that emotional ambivalence about writing is the norm rather than the exception for most academics. This "mixed emotions" statistic held remarkably stable across a range of demographic categories, including gender (69 percent female, 67 percent male), academic role (71 percent faculty, 74 percent postdocs, 67 percent graduate students), and language background (71 percent L1 English speakers, 64 percent L2 English speakers).

At the margins of the data, however, a somewhat more complex picture emerged. Whereas the interview subjects were significantly more likely to report purely positive emotions than purely negative ones (17 percent positive only, 11 percent negative only), the questionnaire respondents showed the opposite pattern (13 percent positive only, 17 percent negative only). Moreover, the distribution of positive-only and negative-only responses varied markedly across demographic groups. Particularly startling was the substantial "emotion gap" exhibited by female PhD students, who proved three times more likely to report wholly negative emotions than wholly positive ones (see Figure 5). If the expression of purely positive or purely negative emotions can be taken as a proxy for a writer's unusually high or low

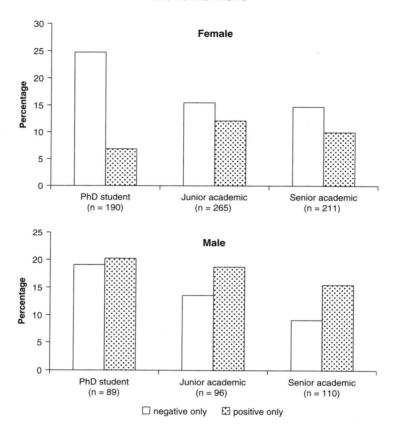

Figure 5. Percentages of female and male questionnaire respondents who reported positive-only or negative-only emotions (n = 961; graph shows data from PhD students and junior/senior faculty only).

self-confidence, then the well-documented social phenomenon that journalists Katty Kay and Claire Shipman dub "the confidence code"—the tendency of highly confident people, especially men, to overestimate their own abilities and of under-confident people, especially women, to underestimate them—may well be at work here.[1] Only after academic women have finished their PhDs and moved into academic positions does this emotion gap begin to narrow, although the prevalence of negative-only over

Figure 6. Top forty emotion words for questionnaires (n = 1,223); word size is proportionate to frequency.

positive-only emotions persists until retirement age. Male academics, by contrast, report higher percentages of positive-only emotions and lower percentages of negative-only emotions right across the board.

Many of the questionnaire respondents communicated their vexed relationship to writing by invoking extremist vocabulary (*guilt, despair, self-loathing, hate*), by bolding or underlining words ("I have to **force** myself to write. This makes me **really sad**"), or by inserting interjections that hint at emotional responses too powerful to be captured in ordinary language ("Aaah," "Ummm," "Aaargh," "Yikes"). Overall, they expressed a wider range and a higher percentage of negative emotion words than the interview subjects, with *frustration* and all its variants (*frustrate, frustrated, frustrating*) occurring nearly twice as often as the next most frequently cited emotion word, *anxiety* (see Figure 6).

The interview subjects also reported their fair share of self-doubt and existential angst. However, although negative words such as *frustration, anxiety, hard*, and *pain* made a strong showing in their responses, *pleasure* and *enjoy* topped the frequency list (see Figure 7). This difference in emotional affect corroborated an impression that I developed early on in the interview process and that grew ever stronger as my research progressed: successful writers, by and large, draw pleasure from their writing and infuse their writing processes with pleasure; struggling writers, on

Figure 7. Top forty emotion words for interviews (n = 100); word size is proportionate to frequency.

the other hand, often labor under debilitating burdens of anxiety, stress, and self-doubt. A key theme that emerged from my conversations with successful academics is that they write not just because they have to but because they want to; the driving force behind their writing is not externally mandated discipline but self-discipline motivated by desire. Some respond best to creative stimuli such as beauty, color, and laughter. Others find satisfaction and even pleasure in self-control and order, like Paul Silvia with his Spartan workspace and progress-plotting spreadsheets; or in moderation and routine, like Robert Boice with his daily regimen of scheduled writing time; or in hyperproductivity, like Rowena Murray with her thousand-words-per-hour writing blasts. But very few, in my experience, would agree with Silvia's recommendation that "academic writing should be more routine, boring, and mundane than it is."[2]

Instead, the colleagues I interviewed highlighted their positive experiences as writers. Writing, they told me, inspires in them a sense of gratitude and privilege:

> The great thing about our work—and isn't it amazing—is that the taxpayer pays us to pursue a hobby. (*Miles Padgett, Physics, University of Glasgow*)

And passion:

> If you write on something you're passionate about, the emotions are already in there because it's something personal to you. That's the motivator. The passion comes through in your work and allows you to focus on writing for extended periods as opposed to being forced to write something you're not really comfortable with. (*Poia Rewi, Māori, Pacific, and Indigenous Studies, University of Otago*)

And satisfaction:

> Even when it's painful and awkward, and I'm fighting with editors and menaced by deadlines, I try to remember that it's a good thing that this is my job and that most people's jobs are less satisfying. (*Carlo Rotella, English, Boston College*)

And even joy:

> When I write, I hear these structures—they're sort of Beethoven-esque. I think of "Ode to Joy." Maybe it's akin to when you run and your endorphins kick in. (*Margaret Breen, English, University of Connecticut*)

Some find special pleasure in particular stages of the writing process, such as researching:

> I go to the library, and looking at all those books, I still think, "Wow, this is fantastic." I just love working with these materials, and I would hope that would come across in the final book. (*Ludmilla Jordanova, History, Durham University*)

Or composing:

> For me, writing is just the greatest pleasure in the profession. You get to not only think but to refine what you think. (*Susan Gubar, English, Indiana University*)

Or revising:

> There is a lot of pleasure for me in revision, because that's when I see what I've got on the page or on the screen, and I can start playing with it. I can move things around, change the vocabulary, and reorganize. (*Ruth Behar, Anthropology, University of Michigan*)

"Creative as a circus"

BRIAN BOYD

Department of English, University of Auckland (New Zealand)

As a young boy growing up in New Zealand, Brian Boyd sorted magazines at his parents' little corner store: "I just read everything that came my way, from schoolgirls' comics to war comics to multipart encyclopedias." His thirst for knowledge sometimes led him to "go into things more deeply than is strictly required"; he remembers writing a twenty-two-page report of a movie when he was five or six. Even today, Boyd regards "work-life balance" as a false opposition:

> I see my work as play, as creative, as everything I'm curious about, so anything I encounter outside the work can end up serving the work at some point—when I'm listening to music, going to an art gallery or traveling or reading outside my field.

He draws inspiration from a "wonderful" Jacques Tati movie in which the camera keeps moving back and forth between the circus acts and the audience:

> The audience is just as funny as the performance. It's glorious. Tati's whole point is that life itself can be as creative as a circus; there shouldn't be a separation between work and play.

A meticulous craftsperson, Boyd treats writing and editing as inseparable elements of a single creative process. In the past, his longhand drafts looked like "palimpsests with deletions and insertions and arrows and so on." Now, however, he does most of his writing and editing on a computer:

> At a very late stage, I'll usually work in single space. Then I'll go to double space. And then, after I've printed the text out and edited in double space, I'll have two windows open and take the double-space version and copy a paragraph at a time over to the blank window on the right to make it go single-spaced again. And I'll just look at one paragraph at a time intensely and see what I can crank up.

For this indefatigably prolific writer, lack of enthusiasm is seldom a problem:

> I remember the typist who typed up my PhD said my thesis read pretty weirdly because it was so enthusiastic. I guess I didn't have the usual subdued academic decorum. I think academic work is not worth doing if you don't show your passion. If you're writing about something that doesn't excite your passion, you should be doing something else.

Others move beyond conscious enjoyment to enter that condition of utter absorption described by psychologist Mihaly Csikszentmihalyi as *flow*:[3]

> Once my writing has gone into that phase where I feel like I know how it's going to work, I'm not sure I'm feeling anything at all. The beauty of it is that I'm right inside. I'm not reflecting on my own experiences. I'm kind of losing myself in it. Then at the end of each writing bout, there is this lovely feeling of accomplishment and almost exhilaration sometimes. (*Cecilia Heyes, Psychology, University of Oxford*)

Although the flow state is often described as a temporary suspension of emotion—"I'm not sure I'm feeling anything at all"— writers who have experienced it almost invariably report positive emotions after the fact: *beauty, accomplishment, exhilaration.*

This is not to say that all successful academics find writing pleasurable or that they find all writing pleasurable all the time. The writers I interviewed spoke candidly about their negative emotions as well:

> Writing my PhD was like pulling teeth out. Fear was one emotion I felt. Another was guilt: what have I done today? Where are the words on the page? There was also frustration sometimes and anger and despair. (*Ewan Pohe, Māori Studies, Victoria University of Wellington*)

Many admitted to moments of existential doubt:

> I love putting sentences together. That's my favorite part. But there have been intervals where I've worried that writing was pointless. The audiences have been so small that you're wondering what you've been doing. (*Lesley Wheeler, English, Washington and Lee University*)

And professional doubt:

> Writing can be a bloody struggle, and sometimes I think, "What am I doing? Why am I kidding myself? Am I really an academic, or was that PhD from the back of a cornflakes packet?" (*Michael Reilly, Māori, Pacific, and Indigenous Studies, University of Otago*)

For Douglas Hofstadter—whose interests and expertise run the disciplinary gamut from mathematics, physics, and cognitive psychology to languages, comparative literature, and music—writing and invention have always been joyful experiences. As a teenager, he often played a "droll story-writing game" with family and friends: "We all played with great gusto, and we would always erupt into enormous bursts of laughter when we were finished." Later, Hofstadter fell "deeply in love with number theory" and became "intoxicated by the endless beauty of mathematics in general":

> Ever since I was a young boy, I had loved the mysteries of the invisible particles that constitute the fabric of the universe. When I was about eight years old, in fact, my big dream had been to become a zero-mass, spin-one-half neutrino.

While pursuing his PhD in physics, he read a book that revived his "earlier but long-dormant love for the twisty, paradoxical phenomena of mathematical logic":

> For the first time in many years, I began thinking about these beloved old matters very passionately, and it occurred to me that I might be able to teach a course, maybe even write a book, on these ideas that were churning like crazy in my mind.

One day, "in the white heat" of his "new passion," Hofstadter penned the thirty-page letter to a friend—"it was literally written with pen and ink"—that eventually developed into the manuscript of his genre-busting, Pulitzer Prize–winning book *Gödel, Escher, Bach: an Eternal Golden Braid*. He banged out an early draft on a little Hermès typewriter in a cramped student apartment: "This was all really heady stuff to me, completely new and absolutely exhilarating." Expressions of pleasure, challenge, and good fortune suffuse his account of the book's genesis and his subsequent academic career:

> Fantastic new ideas were blossoming in my mind. . . . I was truly lucky. . . . I loved that challenge. . . . A fabulous number of crazy coincidences and wordplay discoveries seemed to come out of nowhere—bolts from the blue. . . . I didn't think for a moment about taking risks. . . . I was simply doing something I was extremely excited about. . . . You can always figure out ways to work within constraints. Doing so is great fun, and it can lead to something beautiful. And beauty is what I live for. Yes, no doubt: beauty is really what I live for.

And social doubt:

> I still hear the voice of my high school English teacher telling me that I'll never be a writer. I often feel like I've gotten away with something. (*Carl Leggo, Education, University of British Columbia*)

And self-doubt:

> Academic writing is my most ambitious encounter with my dreams for myself, and that's why it's terrifying. (*Eric Hayot, Comparative Literature, Pennsylvania State University*)

All the same, I couldn't help noticing how often these same writers tempered their descriptions of negative emotions with the vocabulary of pleasure. In the interview transcripts, *hate* walks hand in hand with *love*:

> I love to write, and I hate to write. Writing is something I consider painful and difficult. On the other hand, I love the pleasure I get out of crafting a really neat sentence, of telling a really compelling story. (*Lee Shulman, Education, Stanford University*)

Pain partners with *exhilaration*:

> Sometimes the most trivial things have taken me an incredible amount of time—just fitting the ideas together, rethinking the order, making sure I could articulate what was on my mind in the best possible way. So it's painful but at the same time exhilarating. (*Eric Mazur, Physics, Harvard University*)

Hell cohabits with *heaven*:

> Writing is kind of heaven and hell, because there's a lot of anxiety, a lot of pain and suffering—but then there's also this euphoria when you're actually able to get these words down on paper, and you look at them and say, "Wow. Did I write that?" (*Stefan Svallfors, Sociology, Umeå University*)

Agony flows into *fun*:

> It's complete bloody agony to start out with, at least for me. So I'm miserable and convinced that I'm a fraud and not ever going to be able to write anything ever again every time I start writing something new. Then when it gets to the last phases, then it gets

to be flow, and it gets to be really satisfying and fun. (*Alison Gopnik, Psychology, University of California Berkeley*)

And *guilt* gives way to *joy*:

> The strongest emotion I feel is guilt and regret that I'm not writing and not publishing and not completing things. But when I'm writing—when the bug has bitten me—then it's just a really joyful experience. (*Martin Fellenz, Business, Trinity College Dublin*)

Even *frustration*—that most persistent and ubiquitous of negative emotions—was described by many of the academics I spoke with as a natural and even necessary part of the writing process. They admitted to sometimes feeling tongue-tied:

> Writing feels great if it comes across okay, but it can also be very frustrating. It's sort of knowing what you want to say but trying to find the words. It gets harder as you get older too, I have to tell you. (*Michael Corballis, Psychology, University of Auckland*)

And underproductive:

> The negative emotions are simply frustrations that I'm not getting any more done and that there are too many things else that I have to do or that I'm not concentrating enough. (*David Pace, History, Indiana University*)

And self-critical:

> You can get quite happy about what you've done, or you get frustrated that you can't do it, get depressed that you can't get it out on the page, get cross with yourself. (*Trudy Rudge, Nursing, University of Sydney*)

But wherever frustration sloped across the stage, a *but* clause nearly always waited in the wings nearby:

> There's an element of frustration when it doesn't quite work, but when it does, I find that extremely exhilarating. It's a source of happiness, certainly a source of contentment when I'm writing and when it flows. (*Christopher Grey, Organization Studies, Royal Holloway, University of London*)

Indeed, the words *frustrating*, *frustrated*, and *frustration* so often accompanied narratives of accomplishment and even ecstasy— *exhilaration, happiness, contentment, flow*—that I began to wonder whether, at least for some writers, frustration is a prerequisite for elation. Perhaps the pleasure of the breakthrough, the intensity of the flow, would lose some of its emotional force if writing were easy all the time.

As Alice Brand lamented more than two and a half decades ago, the role of positive emotions in academic writing is not just an underexplored topic but a repressed one:

> Still threaded through contemporary psychology are assumptions about an intellect unaffected by emotion or about emotion as a complex disturbance, an interruption or defect in otherwise lawful, goal-directed mental processes. It is no wonder that anxiety, apprehension, and blocking immediately come to mind when writing specialists think of emotion.[4]

Brand's 1989 book *The Psychology of Writing* remains, alongside Ronald Kellogg's 1994 book of the same title, one of the few major research-based studies to address the constructive interplay of cognition and emotion in the work of successful writers.[5] By and large, the academic-productivity literature either ignores positive emotional affect altogether or pathologizes positive emotions, as when Boice disputes the "romantic" belief that "the most original and esteemed writers necessarily work in great, long binges with euphoria and its inspiration" or when Silvia interprets aroused emotional states such as *excitement* and *enthusiasm* not as core ingredients of a successful writing practice but as warning signs: "If your collaborator is a binge writer, be skeptical of assurances about writing the paper quickly or expressions of excitement about the research. Enthusiasm isn't commitment."[6] Nearly half of my interview subjects (46 percent) spontaneously used the word *fun* to describe some aspect of their academic work; yet, according to Silvia, "writing about research isn't fun. Writing is frustrating, complicated, and un-fun."[7]

In recent years, behavioral and cognitive psychologists have demonstrated that creativity, productivity, intrinsic motivation, and even luck can be influenced and enhanced through positive

"Laughing a lot"

MARY ELIZABETH LEIGHTON and LISA SURRIDGE

Department of English, University of Victoria (Canada)

Before literary scholars Lisa Surridge and Mary Elizabeth Leighton started writing and publishing collaboratively, they both experienced academic writing as an emotional burden: "I found it hard to face writing" (Surridge); "My early writing experiences were characterized by a kind of crushing perfectionism" (Leighton). These days, Surridge says, "we have a lot of fun writing":

> We end up laughing a lot, and I think that's because when you're doing excellent writing together, you are pushing yourself to the limit of what you can engage with intellectually. That process is fun and sometimes almost hilarious.

Even the physical mechanics of cowriting can generate shared mirth: "I will type something—and I'm a very bad typist," explains Leighton—"which is a source of great glee to us as we write together," interjects Surridge—"and so that does introduce humor," Leighton concludes, "but for me, having my hands on the keyboard is part of being able to write." However, their collaboration is not all fun and games. Both women "ruthlessly" block out shared writing time each week, Surridge explains, and stick to their schedule no matter what:

> So, for example, yesterday Mary Elizabeth's son had violent stomach flu—diarrhea and vomiting—and I was quite tired too because my mother-in-law had just had her ninetieth birthday at my house, and I had been partied under the table by the ninety-year-olds. We had agreed that we were going to meet at two o'clock to write, but we couldn't because Mary was home with Jacob, who was barfing in the toilet. So we got on the phone. I emailed Mary the document. She was on the computer. We started writing over the phone and just saying, "Okay, where do we go with this? What do we want to say?"

Leighton's husband, a sociologist, insists that he associates no particular emotions with academic writing: "He says, 'It's just routine. I do it every day. I set up my life so that I can write.'" For Surridge and Leighton, collaborative writing has a similarly neutralizing effect: "It takes anxiety off the board" (Leighton); "We never suffer; we've found ways of taking the worry out of it" (Surridge). But much more than that, their intellectual partnership fosters friendship and nurtures joy, which in turn motivates their writing. Our interview was filled with laughter as they told of hours spent together wrestling with ideas in front of a computer, lunchtime walks through the park, conference trips to Paris, and other stories of shared productivity and pleasure.

thoughts and actions.[8] Positive psychologist Barbara Fredrickson has shown in a variety of experiments that negative emotions discourage innovation and suppress resilience, whereas positive emotions encourage exploratory actions that help create a wider repertoire of skills and deeper reserves of confidence—a virtuous circle that Fredrickson calls "broaden-and-build."[9] In a study with intriguing implications for academic writers, Fredrickson and her colleague Christine Branigan tested a sample of 104 college students who had been randomly assigned to watch two short videos, each designed to invoke one of five emotions: amusement (penguins at play), serenity (soothing nature scenes), anger (innocent people being treated unfairly), fear (a mountain-climbing accident), or neutrality (a screen saver showing falling sticks). When the students were asked to make a list of all the things that they felt like doing immediately after watching the video, those who had been artificially induced to experience pleasurable emotions (amusement or serenity) exhibited a broader "thought-action repertoire" than did participants in the other three groups: that is, they wrote longer lists and came up with a wider range of positive actions than those in the other three groups.[10] This research suggests that academics who harbor strong negative emotions about writing might benefit from undertaking prewriting activities designed to shift their mood and kick-start a new "broaden-and-build" cycle of performance and pleasure—for example, by engaging in physical exercise:

> When I was doing my PhD, I would often go for a swim, and after swimming I'd go to a restaurant or bar and sit and do a bit of reading and writing. This was all very nice, because writing became part of my happy life. (*James Garraway, Higher Education, Cape Peninsula University of Technology*)

Or creative writing:

> Sometimes I write a poem to get myself into the writing mood. I sit at my desk, think of something, write a poem or a draft of a poem, and then I tell myself, "Okay, now you've done something that is very relaxing; it's time to do more serious stuff. Sit down and write your academic papers." (*Agnes Lam, Applied English Studies, University of Hong Kong*)

Or pleasurable domestic tasks:

> I like to be doing something all the time. So if I'm not doing work, I'm doing laundry, or I'm singing, or I'm baking. A lot of people get stressed out because they have all kinds of things hanging over them all the time. But for me it's like, "I'm doing this now," and everything else is just gone. (*Kristina Lejon, Clinical Microbiology, Umeå University*)

Or any other activity that puts them in a positive and creative frame of mind: gardening or listening to music or watching talking guinea pigs on YouTube.

For many academic writers, of course, such positivity-inducing steps are unnecessary. Their relationship to writing is already an affirmational one, and their occasional bouts of frustration are caused mostly by a thwarted desire to write more:

> I don't experience much in the way of anxiety or displeasure when I come to write, but it's frustrating when you have to go back to teaching and you haven't finished a piece of writing. (*Robert Miles, English, University of Victoria*)

But what about the many aspiring authors—especially PhD students, untenured or adjunct faculty, and other members of the "precariate" that makes up so much of the academic workforce today—who suffer from crippling negative emotions that in turn impede their writing? In the short run, the "unblocking" techniques recommended by Boice and his followers may prove an effective remedy: remove emotion from the equation; adhere to a daily writing schedule; just write. In the long run, however, the road to productivity will be a long and tedious one unless you can find meaningful ways to pave it with pleasure.

THINGS TO TRY

Learn from the past

Recall a time and place in your life when you felt especially productive as a writer—or especially creative or intellectually engaged or articulate or passionate or even just *happy*. Identify the physical, emotional, and intellectual circumstances that enabled your positive experience. Can you build some of these same circumstances into your everyday writing life? For example, if you once drafted an entire article during a long plane flight, can you find a daily or weekly workplace that re-creates the narrow, concentrated, nowhere-else-to-go-for-the-next-few-hours environment of an airplane? If you have fond memories of writing poetry in a handmade notebook with a fountain pen, can you incorporate those tactile pleasures into your academic writing by using a pen and notebook for brainstorming or mind mapping?

Get frustrated

Frustration is a normal and natural part of the writing process. Can you turn frustration into a friend—or at least into something other than a paralyzing foe? For example, you could personify your frustration by drawing a cartoon or finding an image to tape to your computer. (What does your version of frustration look like—a bandit, a baby, a buffoon? What food keeps your frustration going? What threats, bribes, or narcotics might put it to sleep or shoo it away?) Or you could visualize frustration as a surmountable obstacle: a dam to burst through (the thicker the wall, the more powerful the flood), a mountain to climb (the higher the summit, the better the view).

Find your happy penguins

If playful penguins and soothing nature videos don't get you in the mood to write, what does? A conversation with a friend about why your research excites and interests you? A run, a swim, a walk in the park, some quiet time in the garden?

Read a book

The words *writing* and *pleasure* are all too seldom found together in books by or for academics. There are some notable exceptions, of course; James Axtell's *The Pleasures of Academe* offers a frankly joyous celebration of academic life; Kim Stafford's *The Muses among Us* enumerates "the pleasures of the writer's craft"; Roland Barthes's 1973 classic *The Pleasure of the Text* illuminates the role of both *plaisir* (pleasure, enjoyment) and *jouissance* (ecstasy, transcendence) in the experiences of readers and writers. (Also not to be missed are Barthes's musings on his "almost obsessive relation to writing instruments" in *The Grain of the Voice*). Overall, however, most academic writing guides convey the message that, if you want to enjoy writing, you'd better go and do it somewhere outside the university. Contrast this shut-up-and-eat-your-vegetables approach with the many books by novelists, journalists, and poets on the pleasures of language and word craft: for example, Ray Bradbury's *Zen in the Art of Writing*, Bill Bryson's *Mother Tongue*, or Anthony Burgess's *A Mouthful of Air*. If you really want to have some fun, visit the grammar and punctuation section of your local bookstore. Who could resist books with titles as playful and inviting as Roy Clark's *The Glamour of Grammar: A Guide to the Magic and Mystery of Practical English*, Karen Gordon's *The Deluxe Transitive Vampire: The Ultimate Handbook of Grammar for the Innocent, the Eager, and the Doomed*, Constance Hale's *Sin and Syntax: How to Craft Wicked Good Prose*, or Lynne Truss's *Eats, Shoots & Leaves: The Zero Tolerance Approach to Punctuation*? Enjoy![11]

11

RISK AND RESILIENCE

Academics are expected to create new knowledge and expand the boundaries of the known world. Yet many of the institutional factors that shape our research careers—from the scholarly conventions that mold our thought and expression to the peer-review processes that determine our grant funding and tenure prospects—seem calculated to "discipline" us into timidity and conformity instead. So how do successful academic writers become risk takers rather than rule followers? How do they learn to bounce back from criticism and rejection? And to what extent can their academic survival and even success be attributed to their emotional habits rather than to sheer good luck?

Not all of the colleagues I interviewed would classify themselves as academic risk takers. Most, however, were able to identify at least a few occasions when they have pushed against stylistic or disciplinary boundaries in their writing and publication. When asked whether there is an optimal time for taking such risks, some were adamant that early-career academics need to "prove themselves" first:

> Before Picasso started doing cubist paintings, he did conventional, descriptive paintings. To break the rules, you have to know how to play by the rules. (*Fabrizio Gilardi, Political Science, University of Zurich*)

They warned of the hazards of sticking one's neck out too soon:

> The most important thing is to get the job security. If you're going to go out on a limb as an untenured faculty member and it blows

up in your face, that can be the end of your career. If you're going to go out on a limb as a tenured faculty member and it blows up in your face, who cares? (*Stephen Ross, English, University of Victoria*)

Others, however, disputed the notion that only tenured faculty can or should take academic risks:

It's not like you've been kissed and turned into a prince when you've been a frog all along. If you have wriggled in a kind of academic way for the seven or eight years leading to tenure and have not made any effort to change that style, it's probably impossible to do so at that point. So the fantasy that you're allowed to be free and express yourself more freely when you receive tenure is just that—a fantasy. (*James Shapiro, English, Columbia University*)

Indeed, many of the senior colleagues I interviewed noted that they have been risk takers all along:

I've taken risks my entire writing career. I've gone in different directions and done risky things the whole time. (*Keith Devlin, Human Sciences and Technologies, Stanford University*)

Often they felt they had no choice in the matter:

It happened really quite by accident. I meant to follow all the rules. The people I worked for said, "No, you can't do that. It's too risky." But I wasn't taking a risk. I was doing what I thought was honorable. (*Mindy Fullilove, Clinical Psychiatry, Columbia University*)

Howard Becker's classic book *Writing for Social Scientists* contains an entire chapter on risk, mostly written by his former graduate student Pamela Richards, who describes the emotional risks that academics face when they write for publication: "It means that I have to open myself to scrutiny. To do that requires that I trust myself, and it also means that I have to trust my colleagues."[1] In my interviews, I heard some shocking stories of colleagues who have betrayed that trust: the anonymous peer reviewer who dismissed an eager young scholar's research passion as "a fad"; the professor who phoned up a graduate student

"Squeeze it down and open it out"

CARLO ROTELLA

Department of English, Boston College (USA)

American studies scholar and journalist Carlo Rotella publishes in a range of genres, from newspaper columns to academic monographs: "I've done a scholarly book, a trade book for a university press, a trade book for a trade press, and the next one is going to be a trade book from a university press." Writing across genres, he believes, is "good for your writing chops":

> There's a certain way to play a slow blues and a certain way to play a prom jam; they're different. All that cross-training makes you better at recognizing what a genre is and how a genre works. I think of it as playing the accordion: squeeze it down and open it out.

A devotee of the "write every day" school of productivity— "I write from five to seven every morning, seven days a week; the blanker the page, the earlier in the day"—Rotella fits his other academic work around his writing, rather than vice versa:

> I steal minutes in the day for things that I can do in a more start-and-stop fashion, like preparing class and or any kind of stuff I have to do for administration. When I'm taking my daughter for her piano lesson, if I remember to bring my stuff, I can be working on preparing class.

He welcomes critical feedback, especially when provided by a professional copy editor with a meticulous eye for detail: "That kind of thing can change you forever and change what you think about what editing is." Indeed, one of the most useful skills that he has learned as a journalist is the ability to deal gracefully with rejection:

> Not only does it thicken your skin to be rejected, but there is a technique to being rejected well. In the academy, it's almost taken as a final judgment on your worth. On the trade side, it's really all about fit, and you learn about fit if you're paying attention.

Rotella dismisses the notion that young academics need to prove themselves as scholars before they turn to trade publishing:

> The idea of waiting until you are tenured and "safe" is becoming outmoded. There are lots of reasons, not just intellectual but also professional, to start writing across the whole range of possibilities.

at eleven p.m. on a Sunday night to announce, "I read the chapter you sent me, and I've got to tell you, I hate it."

From these conversations, I learned that the risks of writing and publication never really go away. One recently tenured academic told me an uplifting tale of risk taking rewarded:

> At one point when I wasn't publishing a lot, my dean said something to the effect that I shouldn't write about marginal populations, that I should work with more normative populations, and that would help me in my career. Then I got a big research grant, and the next year, when I was being introduced to graduate students by the same dean, my work that had previously been called "marginal" was now called "cutting edge." (*Name withheld*)

But that same colleague later asked me to anonymize the anecdote for this book, as publishing it with a name attached feels too risky even now.

A common theme in my interviews was the story of the naïve early-career researcher who has no idea how to respond constructively to the peer-review process. Without the benefit of experience or training, apprentice academics tend to read with their emotions rather than their intellect:

> I got the letter back from the editor, and he started with, "I'm sorry to have to tell you . . ." I was very upset at first, but it turned out that they just wanted some minor changes. (*Maja Elmgren, Teaching and Learning Development, Uppsala University*)

Or they interpret criticism as rejection:

> Junior scholars are precarious and sensitive. They will, to a surprising degree, take a "revise and resubmit" suggestion as a rejection. They are completely crestfallen. (*Kevin Kenny, History, Boston College*)

Or they respond to a negative review by sticking their article in a drawer and their head into the sand:

> I would literally take the article and put it in a file cabinet with the letter in shame. I didn't even want to go back to that article or that idea. I think I wasted a lot of time with these things in drawers. (*Marysol Asencio, Sociology, University of Connecticut*)

Some senior academics confessed to me that they still hate being criticized, especially when they feel the feedback is unjust:

> My first reaction is always to disagree with all the negative comments—"This guy got it wrong. He did not read it right. He misunderstood." Of course, in hindsight, three weeks later: "Oh, yeah. Maybe they were right about that." But the first reaction is always anger, disappointment. (*Robert Poulin, Zoology, University of Otago*)

Most, however, have developed strategies for recovering quickly and moving on:

> Rejection feels horrible, but the feeling has a shelf life. And you just develop your plan: "Well, this didn't get in here, so I'm going to do this to it and send it there." As soon as I have a plan for postrejection action, I feel a lot better. (*Victoria Rosner, English, Columbia University*)

Best of all is the sweet revenge that comes from proving the reviewers wrong:

> The first paper I ever wrote and submitted to a journal was rejected on the grounds that there was nothing new or interesting in the paper. So what did I do? I threw it out and wrote a book on the same subject. (*John Heilbron, History of Science, University of California Berkeley*)

Strikingly, more than half the tenured or tenure-track colleagues I interviewed used words such as *good luck*, *lucky*, or *fortunate* to describe their academic careers, as though their success were due to the generosity of smiling academic gods as much as to their own intellectual labor and perseverance:

> I used to experience a lot of fear about writing and anxiety. But now, I have a real sense of the privilege—and I know it sounds corny—of having the time to write and being paid to do it. I just think, "Whoa, I'm the luckiest person alive." (*Alison Jones, Education, University of Auckland*)

According to psychologist Richard Wiseman, self-described "lucky" people typically make their own luck by cultivating four characteristic habits of mind that maximize opportunity and help

"A risky thing to do"

JANET CURRIE

Center for Health and Well-Being, Princeton University (USA)

As a PhD student, economist Janet Currie worked in the same research field as her supervisor: "that's what everyone in my shop did." Eventually, however, she grew bored with the topic: "I had taken the safe approach." She decided to start researching child development within the paradigm of economics, which "was a risky thing to do at the time, because no one in economics was working on children's issues, and no one was particularly interested":

> Then Bill Clinton was elected president, and there was all this discussion about welfare reform. Suddenly everyone was interested in child development, and there was this big explosion of research in an area where I was already ahead and there wasn't anybody else doing it. So that was lucky, but it also happened because I was willing to take a risk and do something that I thought was important.

In 1996, Currie published an article on the long-term economic effects of Head Start, a program for disadvantaged children. Although her paper broke new methodological ground—"It pioneered a way of looking at the effects of such programs on children while controlling for other factors"—her conclusions about the cost-effectiveness of the program were widely misconstrued, much to her chagrin:

> I had people writing to me saying that people were going to use this study to cut off funding for Head Start for black kids. It was terrible. The Head Start people didn't speak to me for years; I was this evil ogre. But then, at a certain point, the Republicans wanted to cut Head Start entirely, and my paper was the only one showing there was any long-term benefit. So then all of a sudden I was the darling again.

Currie advises early-career academics to "listen to other people's advice, but that doesn't mean you should follow it":

> Being conservative and risk averse is stifling and probably counterproductive. You get assistant professors who aren't ever willing to say anything in faculty meetings or seminars because what if they annoy somebody? But then when they come up for tenure, they get no votes because nobody knows who they are.

them turn lemons into lemonade.[2] First, lucky people notice and act on chance opportunities in their life, creating strong social networks and holding themselves open to new experiences:

> I was lucky; I went to a grad school that was very open to risk taking and very open to freedom. That was at McGill back in the 1960s. I think they almost had a culture of risk taking, and my supervisor used to tell me, "Just have a go. It doesn't matter if they reject it." (*Michael Corballis, Psychology, University of Auckland*)

Second, they trust their intuition:

> I'm a big fan of following serendipitous encounters: you leave no stone unturned and follow all kinds of paths even if you don't really expect much there. Some of them of course don't pan out well, but occasionally, you really get rewarded. (*Ann Blair, History, Harvard University*)

Third, they persevere in the face of criticism and rejection:

> When I first started getting published in medicine, I was accused of being fluffy, Mickey Mouse. All kinds of awful criticisms were made of my work and my writing—"This isn't medical," "You can't publish this kind of thing as medical research." The more I received that criticism, the more absolutely determined I became to overcome it. (*Gillie Bolton, freelance writer in literature and medicine, United Kingdom*)

And fourth, they transform bad luck into good by seeing the positive side of unlucky events:

> I absolutely subscribe to the notion that any feedback is a blessing. I don't actually care how negative the feedback is; I just keep thinking, "Gosh, this could only strengthen my paper for the next place I'm going to send it to." (*Shanthi Ameratunga, Population Health, University of Auckland*)

These qualities of connectedness, self-confidence, perseverance, and positivity were abundantly evident in my conversations with successful academic writers and particularly with senior academics at the top of their game. However "lucky" they may have been to reach their current positions of influence and privilege,

"A difficult journey"

MARAEA HUNIA, PANIA MATTHEWS,

and PAULINE HARRIS

Victoria University of Wellington (New Zealand)

In a group interview, three early-career Māori researchers spoke to me about their passion for their subject matter, their struggle to navigate the sometimes baffling world of academe, and their determination to represent a Māori world-view through their scholarship, even when doing so feels risky. Hunia, a PhD student in education, described the contradictory messages she has received from senior academics about her use of personal narrative:

> When I did my MA, I was advised to put more of myself in there and say who I was. Then I came to this university, and one of the people who looked at my expression of research interest ripped it to shreds because it was "too personal." But I've learned that I can't really exclude myself. I'm a linguist, and I'm Māori. I'm an educator. I just have to trust in my own voice.

Matthews, a master's student in education, noted that indigenous scholars often find themselves caught between competing epistemologies:

> It's a difficult journey, because when you think of things in Māori and you're trying to fit them into this world, sometimes it clashes. I'm often swayed between including things that are important to me and things that are very technically based. It's important to me to keep that Māoriness in my thesis, because ultimately, at the end, I want to affect the way Māori learners receive education in the classroom. So who do I listen to when my advisers tell me to change something?

Harris, a postdoctoral fellow in chemical and physical sciences, discussed the particular challenges of integrating *matauranga Māori* (a knowledge system that embodies the Māori worldview) into her work as a scientist:

> Scientists tend to be "hard core" and not so open to doing publications in that area. But Aristotle and all those dudes—those ancient philosophers—they used to be so multidisciplinary. Now, if you try to be more rounded and more knowledgeable in multiple disciplines, people say, "What are you trying to do that for?" I get told that the stuff I'm interested in is something I should do later on, when I'm sixty or something. But no one's doing it now. Am I supposed to wait thirty years?

their emotional habits of pleasure, passion, risk taking, and resilience played a crucial role in helping them get there. In turn, they cultivate habits of gratitude and generosity that ensure their luck will get passed on to others.

THINGS TO TRY

Strategize

Some academics take risks with their writing because they simply can't imagine behaving otherwise; they follow their hearts, and damn the torpedoes. Others strike a more strategic balance between life-enhancing activities (academic work that they are truly passionate about) and career-advancing pursuits (academic work that will increase their visibility or prestige). The chart below will help you choreograph your own balancing act. Ideally, most of your research will already sit in the top-left quadrant of the chart. If it doesn't, consider how you might shift more items there from other sections of the grid, whether by extracting more value from the writing you *want* to do or by seeking more enjoyment from the writing you *must* do. This exercise can be expanded to other aspects of academic life as well: for example, how might you turn a routine administrative job (career-advancing but not life-enhancing) into a proactive leadership role that feeds your sense of personal fulfillment and professional purpose (career-advancing *and* life-enhancing)?

	Life-enhancing? YES	Life-enhancing? NO
Career-advancing? YES		
Career-advancing? NO		

Bounce

The harder you're thrown, the higher you'll bounce—unless, of course, you are a crystal ball, in which case you'll smash to smithereens. Writers with egos made of glass are unlikely to survive in academia for long. To build up your resilience, try orchestrating some practice falls onto padded ground: a mock conference presentation at which you ask a few friends to take on the role of challenging audience members; a writing-group meeting dedicated to helping you respond to a negative peer review.

Celebrate failure

It's easy and intuitive to acknowledge success; but habitual risk takers understand that failure, too, is worth celebrating. (In Albert Einstein's famous formulation, "Failure is success in progress").[3] Consider writing up a "CV of failures" to share with a few trusted friends, or look for other ways of rewarding risk taking even when it doesn't pay off.[4] A participant in a writing workshop once told me that she and her husband buy each other dinner whenever one of them has had an article or funding application rejected—a win-win proposition, she explained, as every submission, however risky, is guaranteed to result either in academic kudos or a nice meal out.

Read a book

Why take risks with your writing? Books by and for academic writers have explored this question from a variety of angles: for example, from the research scholar's perspective (Stanley Fish's *Versions of Academic Freedom*), the postgraduate student's perspective (Linda Cooper and Lucia Thesen's *Risk in Academic Writing*), and the beginning writer's perspective (Mark Edmundson's *Why Write? A Master Class on the Art of Writing and Why It Matters*). Jordan Rosenfeld's *Writer's Guide to Persistence* cultivates the professional resilience of fiction writers and journalists; Elizabeth Gilbert's *Big Magic* teaches artists and writers to embrace "creative living beyond fear"; Joni Cole's *Toxic Feedback* coaches writers of all stripes in the art of surviving criticism and critique; and Catherine Wald's *The Resilient Writer* soothes bruised egos with "tales of rejection and triumph from 23 top authors." Academics with a broader interest in risk and resilience might want to consult research-based popular psychology books on topics such as positivity (Barbara Fredrickson's *Positivity*), creativity (Scott Barry Kaufman and Carolyn Gregoire's *Wired to Create*), vulnerability (Brené Brown's *Rising Strong*), happiness (Emma Seppala's *The Happiness Track*), self-belief (Amy Cuddy's *Presence*), expertise (Anders Ericsson and Robert Pool's *Peak*), grit (Angela Duckworth's *Grit*), luck (Richard Wiseman's *The Luck Factor*), flow (Mihaly Csikszentmihalyi's *Flow*), and posttraumatic growth (Martin Seligman's *Flourish*). Published by research academics who have risen to professorial appointments at major universities despite (or perhaps because of?) their ability to write for nonacademic audiences, such crossover books offer powerful models not only of risk and resilience but also of public outreach, clear communication, and the potential of scholarly research to make an impact on the wider world.[5]

12

METAPHORS TO WRITE BY

Metaphors render abstract ideas concrete and memorable; in Shakespeare's words, they give "to airy nothing/A local habitation and a name."[1] Many of the academics I interviewed—scientists and social scientists as well as humanities scholars—wield metaphorical language deliberately and strategically:

> Even in technical scientific writing, elegant and minimal and powerful use of metaphor is really effective. (*Russell Gray, Director, Max Planck Institute for the Science of Human History*)

Metaphorical language is more than merely another tool in the artisanal writer's toolbox, an artistic flourish applied to embellish otherwise plain prose. In their classic book *Metaphors We Live By*, philosophers George Lakoff and Mark Johnson show how metaphorical concepts such as "argument is war" and "time is money" exercise a powerful "feedback effect" on our psyches, shaping how we think and act: "In all aspects of life . . . we define our reality in terms of metaphors and then proceed to act on the basis of the metaphors."[2] Indeed, this paragraph contains not only conspicuous metaphors such as *toolbox, artistic flourish*, and *embellish* but also not-so-obvious ones such as *show, exercise, feedback, shape, define*, and *contain*. Many of these belong to one of the most commonly occurring metaphorical gestalts identified by Lakoff and Johnson: "Meanings are objects; linguistic expressions are containers."[3] So accustomed are we to conceptualizing ideas as objects that we no longer even register such constructs as metaphors.

Unsurprisingly, the authors of popular how-to books and articles on academic writing tend to favor active, energetic metaphors of transformation, fulfillment, and progress when describing the writing process: for example, military metaphors (boot camps and battles), metaphors of religious devotion (congregations, missionaries, conversion narratives), food metaphors (snacking, bingeing, feasting), and transportation metaphors ("turbocharge your writing," "fly in your writercopter").[4] By contrast, struggling writers gravitate toward metaphors that emphasize the difficulties and frustrations they encounter when writing. Remember those Danish doctoral students who compared writing in English to walking in wobbly stiletto heels, riding a rusty bicycle, or having a bad hair day? Higher-education researchers Barbara Kamler and Pat Thomson asked PhD students to identify an image or metaphor that describes for them the task of writing a literature review; the results included "a myriad of ways in which the doctoral researcher is represented as being lost, drowning and confused," including one student who likened the task to "eating a live elephant" and another to "persuading an octopus into a jar."[5] Similarly, a doctoral student once told me, in a tone of frustration mixed with humor, that writing his dissertation feels "like trying to peel an onion layer by layer while it's rolling around on the floor and then reconstructing it layer by layer and then offering it to people and saying, 'Here, take a bite.'"

My interviews with successful academic writers yielded a wide and nuanced array of images that were neither relentlessly productivity-punching (like turbocharged engines and military boot camps) nor redolent of anxiety and loss of control (like a squirming octopus or a slippery onion). There were architectural and spatial metaphors: academic writing is like a home (Breen), a threshold (Elmgren), a cocoon (Hayot), an echo chamber (Ross), a bank with marble pillars or a ramshackle trailer on the edge of town (Pinker). There were travel metaphors: writing is like experiencing a sandstorm in the desert (Fullilove), going on a journey (Garraway), climbing a mountain (Reilly), parachuting into new territory (Grafton), wading through a valley of shit (Mewburn). There were artisanal metaphors: writing is like cutting wood or metal (Jenstad), throwing a pot (Jordanova), building a theater set (Grafton), painting a room (Heilbron), wearing a Madame Grès

"Playing around with language"

BILL BARTON

Department of Mathematics, University of Auckland (New Zealand)

When Bill Barton became a mathematics education researcher after years as a high school teacher, he learned to write in his new academic discipline mainly by imitating others: "For the first five to eight years of my academic life, I don't think I ever used *I*, just because I thought you didn't." But Barton admits that conformity "has never been a strong point" for him:

> So eventually I started really intellectualizing my writing and thinking about what it was that I wanted to do, rather than just flying by the seat of my pants.

Bit by bit, he began to question and challenge disciplinary conventions:

> I have a reasonably good bullshit detector, and I have a low tolerance for people carving themselves off into niches that other people can't access. Jargon is a way of doing that, so I have a low tolerance for jargon.

He also acquired the confidence to speak his mind:

> Now that I'm a senior academic and I do a lot of reviews, when I think someone is just writing garbage—or writing in a way that will not be understandable by the audience they're writing for—I will say that clearly and forcefully. And I've had editors come back and say, "Thank you, that needed to be said."

Having grown up in a family that relished language and wordplay, Barton eventually started "playing around with language" in his academic articles and presentations: "I found that often people respond to metaphor and wordplay in positive ways." Once, at a disciplinary conference in Poland, he gave a presentation that used a metaphor drawn from his love of gardening ("a good frame produces better tomatoes") to illustrate the challenges of undergraduate mathematics education:

> Afterwards I was sitting with the editors of the conference proceedings, and they said, "Oh, that talk was fantastic. We really liked your tomato metaphor." I said, "Hang on, I got told to tone it down and take it out for the published proceedings." They all turned to the editor who had made that recommendation; there was a discussion, and in the end, the one person who had rejected the metaphor got overruled. That was quite fun. I quite enjoyed that.

dress (Gopnik). There were sports and fitness metaphors: writing is like playing golf or tennis (Appiah), diving into the water (Lamont), getting back on a horse (Heyes), bungee jumping or tightrope walking (Grafton), cross-training (Rotella), heavy lifting (Miles), learning to play cricket (Gray). There were performance metaphors: writing is like watching a circus (Boyd), producing a screenplay (Shapiro), doing stage magic (Pinker). There were gambling metaphors: sending papers out is like buying lottery tickets (Gray); getting a grant is like winning the lottery (Padgett). There were engineering metaphors: constructing an argument is like putting together Lego (Barr); communicating across disciplines is like building bridges (Piekkari, Gray); writing for different audiences is like switching gears (Kwok). There were cooking metaphors: a research project resembles a restaurant kitchen (Vanderbauwhede); "cookie-cutter" articles all sound the same (Surridge); writing projects can sit on either the front burner (Devlin) or the back burner (Ameratunga). There were aquatic metaphors: writing for popular audiences is like swimming from salt water to fresh water (Shapiro); reading jargon-filled prose is like drowning "in a porridge of abstractions" (Boyd). There were musical metaphors: writing across genres is like playing in different styles (Rotella); bringing collaborators together is like conducting an orchestra (Breen); editing one's own prose is like producing a remix tape (Devlin). There were relationship metaphors: writing is like a conversation (Mewburn); a work in progress is a like a friend (Kaple); an early-career academic is like the institution's taken-for-granted wife (Asencio). There were metaphors of parenthood: letting go of a manuscript is like sending a child off to college (Devlin); being asked to identify your favorite piece of writing is like being asked to name your favorite child (Shulman, Reilly); producing a book late in life is like giving birth to an overdue baby (Fullilove). And there were some fanciful animal metaphors: collaborative writing is like herding cats (Piekkari); a tough supervisor is a dragon (Hunia); academe is full of *taniwha*, mythical creatures that require propitiation and are often associated with danger (Reilly); a scholar with wide-ranging interests is a bower bird (Maddison); being asked to make multiple revisions is like being "nibbled to death by ducks" (Lunsford).

Most of these metaphors are neither Pollyanna-ishly positive nor Eeyore-ishly negative; instead, they fall into an in-between zone of conceptual complexity and emotional ambivalence, showing both a sunny face and what educator Parker Palmer calls a "shadow side": that is, a negative aspect that deepens and illuminates the metaphor's positive dimension. In his book *The Courage to Teach*, Palmer invokes the metaphor of a sheepdog— "not the large, shaggy, loveable kind, but the all-business Border collies one sees working the flocks in sheep country"—to demonstrate how generative metaphors can reveal complex truths about a teacher's practice. He begins by elucidating the positive side of his metaphor: like a good teacher, Palmer explains, a sheepdog takes the sheep to a place where they can graze, protects them from predators, brings back strays, and moves the flock along to greener pastures when food gets scarce. Next, he addresses its shadow side:

> The shadow suggested by my metaphor seems obvious: I have a tendency to see my students as "sheep" in the invidious way that word can imply. I sometimes get angry about my students' apparent docility or mindlessness or the way they hang their heads down.[6]

Finally, he offers a personal case study—a meditation on how the sheepdog metaphor eventually led him to new insights about his handling of a difficult classroom situation—to show how generative metaphors can help us through "the hard times in our teaching" and remind us of our own core values. His image of himself as a nurturing-but-bossy sheepdog, Palmer writes, "returns me in imagination to the inner landscape of identity and integrity where my deepest guidance is to be found."[7]

Academics' metaphorical accounts of their writing process can be unpacked in a similar fashion. For example, two of my interviewees employed the metaphor of "playing chicken"—the dangerous game of driving at full speed toward an oncoming car or immobile obstacle and daring yourself not to swerve—to describe their habit of putting off work till the last minute:

> I used to have rather a traumatic experience with writer's block in college and graduate school. I would play chicken with myself.

"A chef mastering a recipe"

JOHN DUMAY

Department of Accounting and Corporate Governance,
Macquarie University (Australia)

When accounting lecturer John Dumay enrolled in a course on higher-education pedagogy, he and his colleagues were encouraged to become more self-reflective teachers: "We had to look at what we were doing as teachers, question why we were doing it, and ask ourselves, How can I change and improve it?" He decided to apply a similar mindset to his research writing:

> I had heard from reviewers that my writing tended to be very abstract, so I tried to change the style and write this really dynamic, personal, me-from-the-first-person kind of narrative.

His first journal article in the new style received an enthusiastic response—"the reviewers thought it was fantastic"—but then he hit a stumbling block:

> It was all ready to get published, and the editor came back to me and said, "Oh, you're writing in the first person. We only publish in the third person. You have to change this." I thought, "Are you kidding me?" It took me half a day to go back through it, making sure it was in the present tense and writing everything in the third person. Instead of "we," I would write "the researchers." But I didn't like that. I thought it constrained what I did.

The next time he submitted a paper to the same journal, he used personal pronouns again: "Again the paper got accepted, and this time, the editor didn't say boo. So maybe I pushed his buttons a little bit." Dumay compares academic writing to cooking and likens a scholar learning the craft to "a chef mastering a recipe":

> You can get the structure right, you can get the ingredients right, but it's actually how you combine those ingredients and the quality of those ingredients—the quality of the analysis, the quality of the data—that take it to the next level. We can all bake a chocolate cake if we have the right recipe, but only a few of us can bake an absolutely superb chocolate cake.

As a writer, Dumay now feels that he has now passed his apprenticeship but still has a lot to learn:

> Can I cook that pièce de résistance that's going to be a hit in the finest restaurant? I don't think I'm there yet, but I'm certainly working on it.

Part of me would keep me from sitting down and writing. Then just at the point when it was almost too late, I'd stay up all night finishing it. (*David Pace, History, Indiana University*)

I play chicken with my classes—because it's easy to let your research go during term time, but you know you won't walk into a class unprepared. (*Lisa Surridge, English, University of Victoria*)

Note the key difference between these two stories: while the first emphasizes a student's anxiety ("Will I finish this assignment in time?"), the second demonstrates a teacher's professional self-confidence ("I prioritize my writing time, because I know I will pull off my class preparation no matter what"). For the insecure student, playing chicken with writing is a nerve-wracking avoidance ploy; for the experienced academic, on the other hand, playing chicken with teaching is a canny and considered strategy for prioritizing writing. Together, the two sides of the metaphor offer a balanced view of the pros and cons of last-minute, deadline-driven behavior.

Literary scholar Mary Elizabeth Leighton (the writing partner of chicken-playing Lisa Surridge) offered a very different kind of metaphor when she emailed me a progress report several months after our interview:

Our new metaphor is *Spanxing*, as in those undergarments that squeeze you into a desired shape. We now talk about Spanxing our prose so that it's leaner, tighter, better and so that it doesn't wander into interesting analysis unrelated to our argument; we say things like, "OK, let's go get tea, then come back and Spanx this paragraph" and "Ugh, this paragraph we wrote yesterday really needs Spanxing." (*Mary Elizabeth Leighton, English, University of Victoria*)

Here, Surridge and Leighton have taken a potentially negative metaphor—the punishing diet, the pinching corset—and turned it into something playful. Without altogether denying its shadow side (scholarly sadomasochism, anyone?), they imbue the sometimes painful act of editing with a spirit of challenge and fun.

Anthropologist Daromir Rudnyckyj ran through a whole sequence of metaphors as he struggled to describe the process of writing his first book:

> Once you figure out what the map is, then it becomes easy. . . . The
> narrative arc became clear. . . . It's like filling in the pieces of a
> puzzle. . . . One editor told me to look for the "red thread." Once
> you find the red thread, you're figuring the way out of the maze.
> (*Daromir Rudnyckyj, Anthropology, University of Victoria*)

Each of these metaphors imposes a sense of order, direction, and
inevitability on an initially confusing and chaotic enterprise: the
map shows the way; the arc connects the beginning of the story
to the end; the puzzle pieces need only to be fitted into their or-
dained places. Most evocative of all is the image of the red thread,
which invokes the clew of red yarn gifted by Ariadne to Theseus
in Greek mythology to help him navigate his escape from the
Minotaur's maze. (Other cultural references include the invisible
red string that binds future lovers together in Chinese and Japa-
nese mythology; the crimson thread that runs through the ropes
on a British navy ship, first used figuratively by Wolfgang von
Goethe in his 1809 book *Elective Affinities*; the red string worn
by kabbalists to ward off the evil eye; and the "scarlet thread of
murder running through the colourless skein of life" in Arthur
Conan Doyle's *A Study in Scarlet*).[8] Although the red thread in
Rudnyckyj's account is clearly intended as a redemptive metaphor, I was reminded of another trope that occurred frequently
in my interviews:

> She just put red ink all over it and handed it to me across her
> desk. I swear it was just a sea of red. (*Tony Harland, Higher Edu-
> cation, University of Otago*)

> It looked like he had bled all over it. (*Elizabeth Rose, Manage-
> ment Studies, Aalto University*)

Like red ink trailing across a white page, the "red thread" in Rudnyckyj's metaphor hints that coherence and completion can be
achieved only through struggle: false leads, dead ends, bloody
traces. Without that initial sense of disorientation and confusion—
"How do I get out of here?"—there would be no labyrinth to navigate, no Minotaur to slay, no hero to emerge victorious from the
maze.

But what about metaphors that are all shadow, no light?
In among the colorful metaphorical mélange of my interview

transcripts—playing chicken, Spanxing, the red thread—there were disturbing images of physical abuse and humiliation that appear at first glance to elude redemption. Receiving a negative peer review, I was told, is like being wounded (Reilly), stung (Duffy, Albert, Surridge), thrashed (Gilardi), burned (Morelli), shocked (Corballis), beaten up (Grafton, Gopnik), crushed (Jones), whacked (Rewi), gutted (Poulin), knocked back (Boyd), trampled (Fee), and pissed on from a great height (Maddison). Not a single one of my hundred interview subjects used the optimistic phrase "bounce back" to describe how they respond to harsh criticism. On the other hand, at least half a dozen respondents invoked images of thick, thin, bruised, or irritated skin:

> It can be so bruising to ask people to read your stuff. (*Marjorie Howes, English, Boston College*)

> You begin to develop a bit of a thicker skin; it's the school of hard knocks. (*Michael Wride, Zoology, Trinity College Dublin*)

While the "the school of hard knocks" metaphor suggests that struggle and setbacks can lead to new learning, its accompanying image of "thicker skin" merely promises a dulling of pain. Becoming thick-skinned is at best a survival strategy, and its shadow side offers a warning: as our skin thickens, will our hearts harden as well?

In *The Redemptive Self*, a study of redemption narratives in American culture, psychologist Daniel McAdams reviews the research literature on the positive effects of "benefit-finding," a strategy deployed by psychologists to help patients move from a condition of posttraumatic stress to a paradigm of posttraumatic growth. McAdams analyzed the personal narratives of nearly two hundred midlife adults and college students and discovered that "the more redemptive the life story, the better a person's overall psychological well-being":

> Redemption stories are not simply happy stories; rather, they are stories of suffering and negativity that turn positive in the end. Without the negative emotions, there can be no redemption.[9]

McAdams's research helps to explain the recuperative process whereby resilient writers transform painful experiences of frus-

"A snowfall of words"

ELIZABETH KNOLL

Former Senior Editor at Large, Harvard University Press (USA)

As a PhD student in the history of science, Elizabeth Knoll found part-time work in the editorial office of a medical journal: "I got a view over the railings of disciplines other than my own." Later she became an acquisitions editor at Harvard University Press, where she developed a keen eye for "the big picture" of scholarly research:

> I look for work that is interesting, stimulating, original, provocative without just being crackpot, thoughtful without being solemn or unreadably earnest, ambitious without being grandiose, and most of all—and this is really important to me—sounding like it was written by an actual human being and not cranked out by some kind of machine for emitting academic prose.

Knoll's own use of language is refreshingly human—and chock full of metaphor. Academic writing, she says, is "a letter, not a diary: you're trying to say something to someone else, not just recording something for the sake of your own self." She prefers authors who are "trying hard to get the ball over the net" to those who are merely "in a performance of themselves." Many social scientists, she believes, "still feel in the presence of the natural scientists like the newly arrived middle class in the presence of the aristocracy in a nineteenth-century English novel":

> They feel that they themselves are not quite the real thing, and that's why they write like this. It's like with the Veneerings in Dickens's novel *Our Mutual Friend*: everything has to be superficially shiny, and there has to be too much of it.

Knoll is in favor of academic risk taking, so long as authors are "clear-eyed" about what the risks are: "There's a Spanish proverb that I just love, which goes, 'God says take what you want—and pay for it.'" Many academics, she believes, suffer not from overambition but from a crippling anxiety:

> They are overcautious. They take too long to get to the point, and they don't quite get to the point. They overexplain. They use too many examples. They repeat themselves. They are a little circuitous, and even if they have piled up an awful lot of evidence to make a point strongly—as strongly as they could—they muffle themselves with too many words. It's like the snowfall that obliterates all the features of the landscape. A snowfall of words that just cuts out any sound.

tration, anxiety, humiliation, and anger into stories not merely of survival but of growth. Many of the academics I interviewed told me that the trauma of a harsh critique has helped them become more empathetic reviewers:

> When I write peer reviews, I always try to start out saying something nice about the paper, like it's a good idea, or something positive. When you get one of these reports that doesn't say anything nice, then you don't even want to get out of bed in the morning. (*Janet Currie, Economics and Public Affairs, Princeton University*)

Perhaps our bleakest metaphors are the ones that lead us to our most important insights: the darker the shadow, the brighter the light. When successful senior colleagues talk about feeling beaten up, battered, bruised, and "pissed on from a great height"—images of helplessness and alienation in the face of malign thuggery—we as a profession need to sit up and pay attention. Can we redeem those metaphors by acknowledging and learning from their shadow side even while refusing to succumb to darkness? Humiliation, after all, is not the only route to kindness:

> When I was a young twerp just starting out, I wrote a savage review of a big guy who was a Cambridge classicist in my field. My book was published by Oxford, and the *Times Literary Supplement* gave it to that classicist to review. He wrote a first-page review in the *TLS* which was thoroughly laudatory. That may be why I lost all interest in polemics, because it was an act of such humaneness and generosity. (*Anthony Grafton, History, Princeton University*)

Writing this chapter has sent me back to look at my own use of figurative language in this book. Attending to the metaphorical "feedback effect" noted by Lakoff and Johnson, I have weeded out some of my more negative images and planted more positive ones in their place. For example, an early reader of the introduction to part 2 ("Artisanal Habits") pointed out that, within the space of just a few paragraphs, I had used the words *finicky, fuss, fiddle, tweak, fiddly, pathetically slow*, and *snail-paced* to describe my own compositional style. "But surely the way you work is also your strength," my reader gently reminded me; "Those of us who are true believers in slow writing would appreciate a more affirmative presentation of this way of working!" As a consequence of her intervention, I resolved to depict "fiddly" writing not as a nervous disease but as a worthy artisanal imperative. That decision in turn led me to replace many negatively inflected words with constructive verbs such as *adjust*, *tinker*, and *polish*.

I also took a fresh look at my positive metaphors to see what I might learn from their shadow side: for example, at the end Chapter 11, I supplemented a cheery image of "bouncing back" with a cautionary image of shattered crystal. A participant at a writing workshop once told me that she labels her folder of rejected sentences and paragraphs "I Still Love You," acknowledging the loss and guilt that authors can feel when they usher their fondest creations off the dance floor—all that care and attention we lavished on their ball gowns and tuxedoes!—even while refusing to buy into Arthur Quiller-Couch's macabre imagery of murdered darlings. Likewise, I have seeded this book with metaphors that foreground the creative aspects of the writer's craft: W. B. Yeats's image of the poet "stitching and unstitching" his verses until they come right; Ted Hughes's description of Sylvia Plath building tables and chairs and toys from discarded lines. Just as traumatized patients can learn to restore a strong sense of self by "re-storying" their lives, academic writers can rescue themselves from the quicksand of criticism and self-doubt by grabbing onto a lifeline of playfulness and pleasure.[10] Metaphors, after all, are the stories that we tell ourselves about our relationship to the world. By changing our metaphors, we can change our stories.

THINGS TO TRY

Re-story your metaphors

Generate some metaphors of challenge, frustration, and anxiety by completing the following sentences (or concoct your own variations):

- Getting started with a new writing project is like . . .
- Getting stuck is like . . .
- Working with an uncooperative or lazy collaborator is like . . .
- Sending off a paper for peer review is like . . .
- Receiving a negative review is like . . .

Now see if you can transform those negative metaphors into narratives of learning and development. A *blocked* writer could reimagine a conceptual barrier as a door gradually opening or a wall to fly over; a *flattening* review could become a springboard to new ideas.

Take a walk on the shadow side

Alternatively, try generating some positive writing metaphors and then putting them through Parker Palmer's "shadow side" process. First, unfold the positive aspects of the metaphor in as much detail as you can. (For example, you might picture your research as a garden and yourself as the gardener: planning, planting, sowing, tending, watering, weeding, fertilizing, and transplanting to ensure that every plant thrives.) Next, delve into the metaphor's shadow side. (A gardener often has to cut plants back in order to make them bloom; some die no matter where you put them; there's always another gardener in the neighborhood who has a bigger or better garden than yours; some days it feels as though you're doing nothing but pulling out weeds.) Finally, consider what the fully rounded, light-and-shadow metaphor can teach you about your own practice. Even a "shitty first draft" (in Anne Lamott's famous formulation) can eventually become a fertile field of ideas—or at least a wheelbarrow full of nutrient-rich compost.[11]

Get concrete

For a permanent exhibit at the Nobel Museum in Stockholm, former Nobel Prize recipients have donated personal objects that speak to their own scientific or humanitarian work. Some have presented items linked to a specific moment in their careers, such as geneticist Randy Shekman's first real microscope, purchased with his own savings at the age of twelve. Others have chosen objects with a more symbolic import, such as chemist Peter Agres's cross-country racing skis, which represent the challenges of scientific research and the role of physical activity in his intellectual growth. And many have donated objects with both metonymic and metaphorical qualities, such as the pink headscarf that youth activist Malala Yousafzai wore while addressing the United Nations General Assembly on her sixteenth birthday (a powerful symbol of one girl's courage in the face of religious oppression) or the bicycle that transported economist Amartya Sen around the Indian countryside to weigh babies for his research (a practical object with many symbolic resonances: economic inequality, social and intellectual mobility, scholarly persistence). What object would you choose to represent your research, and why?[12]

Read a book

If reading a book is like opening a door into another world, then reading a book about metaphor is like opening a door and discovering not just another world but a whole new galaxy. You can find metaphor books with a philosophical bent (such as Denis Donoghue's *Metaphor*) or a linguistic bent (such as Andrew Goatly's *The Language of Metaphors*) or a scientific bent (such as Alan Wall's *Myth, Metaphor, and Science*) or a pedagogical bent (Rick Wormeli's *Metaphors & Analogies: Power Tools for Teaching Any Subject*). You can find comprehensive single-authored tomes (such as L. David Ritchie's *Metaphor*) and multiauthored scholarly compendia (such as Raymond Gibbs's *The Cambridge Handbook of Metaphor and Thought*). You can find books for beginners (such as Murray Knowles and Rosamund Moon's *Introducing Metaphor*) and books for discipline-based specialists (such as J. Berenike Herrmann and Tony Berber Sardinha's *Metaphor in Specialist Discourse*). You can find books about why we use metaphor (such as Timothy Giles's *Motives for Metaphor in Scientific and Technical Communication*) and how we use metaphor (such as George Lakoff and Mark Johnson's *Metaphors We Live By*) and even when to avoid using certain metaphors (such as Lakoff's *Women, Fire and Dangerous Things*). One way or another, all of these books explore the expressive power of figurative language—a universe of almost infinite possibilities.[13]

Conclusion

Raising the Roof

By now you have probably started drafting architectural plans for your remodeled house of writing. Maybe you have already poured a new foundation and framed in the walls and windows. However, if we really want to change the culture of academic writing in a lasting and meaningful way, we must "raise the roof" not only on our individual habits but on our institutional *habitus* as well: that is, on the unexamined norms and attitudes that shape our personal and professional lives.[1] Whether in our own writing practice, in our interactions with students and colleagues, or in our roles as academic leaders, administrators, and gatekeepers, each of us has the capacity to bring a little more "air and light and time and space" into the writing lives of those around us.

Open the curtains
Successful academics who make their own vulnerabilities visible to others—for example, by showing their "shitty first drafts" to their students—help create a culture of transparency in which conversations about writing become a normal part of academic life rather than a rare occurrence. For graduate students and early-career academics, in particular, it can be comforting to learn that our teachers and mentors are as susceptible as we are to the demons of self-doubt, the perils of peer review, and the humiliation of rejection. Economist Janet Currie recounts the first time she received a negative referee report:

I showed it to one of my supervisors and told him I was very upset. He didn't say anything but just walked over to a file drawer and pulled out a report on one of his papers that was absolutely scathing; it was this horrible ad hominem attack that said something like, "Not only is this paper awful, but this person clearly doesn't know anything and has never known anything in any of his papers." (*Janet Currie, Economics and Public Affairs, Princeton University*)

Her supervisor offered some sage advice that Currie now passes on to her own students: "He said, don't bother sending the paper back to the same journal, but do send a letter to the editor saying, 'This and this and this that the referee says is wrong; you did not get a good-quality referee.' " By sharing her story with her graduate students and postdocs just as her supervisor shared his with her, Currie demystifies the peer-review process and helps prepare the academics of tomorrow to face their own future challenges as writers.

Widen the eaves

Sometimes just a small act of courage or dissent can make a big difference to others. Every time we push back against an editorial decision ("I'd like to retain the personal pronouns in my article rather than convert all my sentences to the passive voice, and here's why") or push forward a new idea ("I propose to organize a plenary conference session addressing this controversial new research area"), we not only expand the footprint of our own house of writing but also help reshape the contours of the field in which we work. Historian David Pace (Indiana University) recalls attending a summer program at the Carnegie Academy for the Scholarship of Teaching and Learning (SoTL), where the participants were encouraged to think of "one particular thing you could do in the next year to help the field of SoTL along." Pace arranged a lunch meeting with the editor of the *American Historical Review* "to sort of grease the skids: to let him know this is a legitimate field, so that if somebody were to submit an article in this area, he might consider publishing it." By the time the lunch was over, the editor had invited Pace to write a peer-reviewed article explaining the importance of SoTL to historians; that article, in turn, paved the way for others to submit articles in this emerging field. What started out as a modest gesture by a single scholar helped expand the discipline and provide a sheltering space for new forms of research.

Hand over the toolbox

It's one thing to allow your junior colleagues to shelter under the capacious roof of your own successful academic career; it's another to empower them to construct new dwellings of their own. Physicist Eric Mazur (Harvard University) grew tired of spending all his time editing and correcting other people's writing and helping them respond to negative peer reviews. Consequently, he developed a ten-page document for his research group that lays out parameters and protocols for every step of the publication process, from proposing a topic ("The prospective authors have to be able to convey the overall message of the paper in no more than a few sentences") to attributing authorship ("Every named author takes full and complete responsibility for everything that's in the paper") to providing high-quality feedback ("We typically assign two people—a more experienced person and one of the new people in the group—to critique the paper at various stages, because this is a great way to transfer knowledge"). The papers produced by Mazur's research group generally sail through the peer-review process, having already undergone rigorous internal vetting. And by the time his graduate students and postdocs depart for academic positions elsewhere, they have all been meticulously trained in how to plan, pitch, structure, write, edit, critique, and revise a successful research paper.

Plant shade trees

According to an ancient Greek proverb, "A society grows great when old men plant trees in whose shade they shall never sit." Likewise, an academic culture grows great when senior scholars perform acts of generosity for junior academics who may never know their names. Literary scholar and poet Lesley Wheeler (Washington and Lee University) remains "endlessly grateful" to the two anonymous readers whose thoughtful responses to her first book manuscript set her on the path to becoming a successful scholar: "They told me bluntly what was wrong with the book, but they also found the time to praise it; and that was enough encouragement." Having benefited from the welcoming shelter of shade trees planted by others, Wheeler has little patience for "cranky" referees who poison the air with mean-spirited reviews. She takes care to ensure that her own feedback to colleagues and students is always gracious and constructive: "The conscientiousness and generosity that I've seen directed at my work is something that I want to pay back."

Sow seeds

The phrase "Let a thousand flowers bloom" recalls the sinister legacy of Chairman Mao, whose policy of "letting a hundred flowers bloom and a hundred schools of thought contend" later resulted in a crackdown on artists and scientists whose schools of thought differed from his own.[2] Perhaps it's time to recuperate Mao's motto, seeding innovation across our academic communities and providing the kind of nurturing professional environment where good ideas can take root and flourish. When researchers at the University of Massachusetts tried out several different mentoring programs aimed at boosting the productivity of early-career researchers, they found that some of the most cost-effective interventions were self-determined, individualistic, and targeted to the applicants' needs rather than top-down, homogeneous, and one-size-fits-all.[3] Similarly, a 2013 analysis of Canadian science-funding programs showed that, dollar for dollar, small-scale researchers published more papers and had higher citation rates than large grant holders did.[4] Even modestly funded initiatives, it turns out, can have a measurable impact on research productivity. Equally importantly, they enrich and enliven the habitus of academic writing, giving rise to a more colorful and diverse landscape of ideas.

Invite the neighbors over

Individual initiatives can take on a life of their own when they become community events. When religious studies scholar Lena Roos read Paul Silvia's book *How to Write a Lot*, she was inspired to reform her writing habits and start writing a little bit every day. Soon she started talking about her efforts during coffee

Figure 8. Skrivarsekten snail-fountain-pen logo "Cochlea vincit omnes" (The snail conquers all); courtesy of Annika Sjöberg.

breaks at work, and several of her colleagues decided to develop daily writing plans of their own:

> Gradually we found ourselves talking more and more about writing, until people started referring to us as *skrivarsekten* (the writers' sect), which also became our official name when we constituted ourselves on Facebook. We are now in the process of forming interdisciplinary "cells" of four to five people which will meet approximately once a month for coffee or lunch, so that you can get feedback from people that you don't usually talk to. (*Lena Roos, Religious Studies, Uppsala University*)

The group even has its own logo, designed by one of the participants: a snail-cum-fountain-pen carrying its own house of writing on its back and adorned with the motto "*cochlea vincent omnes*" (The snail conquers all; see Figure 8). When I checked in again with Roos two years after our interview, she reported that the *skrivarsekten* Facebook page was still going strong: "People post their writing achievements—sometimes an article being finished, sometimes just having written half a page that day—and we talk about obstacles, strategies, writing plans, and so forth."

Writers dip in and out of the online group, and the face-to-face "cells" flourish, fade, and get resurrected again—the usual ebb and flow of interest and commitment that mark any healthy writing community.

Start a school

As I traveled from one university to another while researching this book, I began to notice a curious phenomenon. At the writing workshops that I offered for faculty and graduate students in English-speaking countries, few if any participants raised their hands when I asked how many of them had been formally trained to write and publish in their discipline ("formal training" having been defined as completion of an iterative, cohort based, expert facilitated course focused mainly on research writing and publication). In non-English speaking countries, by contrast, hands went up all over the room. I learned that doctoral students in countries such as Germany, Switzerland, and Sweden typically enroll in mandatory academic English courses, which in turn may address other writing-related issues such as work habits, variations in disciplinary styles, social networking, and peer review. What would it take for universities in English-speaking countries to follow the lead of their L2 counterparts and start systematically teaching their graduate students how to become successful academic writers? And how might we extend such formal learning opportunities to faculty, replacing the current "sink or swim" approach with the kind of ongoing on-the-job support and training that professionals in other fields regard as a normal and natural part of their career progression?

Build parks and playgrounds

A functioning community requires a well-developed infrastructure to link its inhabitants together and keep them safe: roads and bridges, streetlights and sewers, power stations and water-treatment plants. A *flourishing* community supplements the necessities of modern life with amenities designed to lift the spirit and feed the soul: parks and playgrounds, walkways and foot-bridges, street art and skateboard ramps, fountains and follies. Have you ever noticed how universities often respond to fiscal pressures by cutting down on departmental catering budgets first, as though breaking bread together were a frivolous perquisite of academic life rather than an essential human activity? Informal social gatherings need not cost a fortune; nor do the kinds of congenial physical surroundings designed to house them. Rather than blowing the budget on state-of-the-art institutional furniture, the Queensland University of Technology kitted out its slick new Science and Engineering Centre with vintage sofas and retro décor sourced from thrift shops and antique stores. The result? Cozy, character-filled seating clusters that invite students and faculty to sit down, start a conversation, and stay a while.

Dwell poetically

In his 1951 essay "Building Dwelling Thinking," philosopher Martin Heidegger reflects on the difference between *building* and *dwelling*:

> We attain to dwelling [*wohnen*] . . . only by means of building [*bauen*]. The latter, building, has the former, dwelling, as its goal. Still, not every building is a dwelling.[5]

In German as in English, humans inhabit (*bewohnen*) the habitual (*Gewohnte*)—a condition that we can escape, Heidegger suggests, only by reconceptualizing boundaries as horizons:

> A space [*Raum*] is something that has been made room for, something that is cleared and free, namely within a boundary, Greek *peras*. A boundary is not that at which something stops but, as the Greeks recognized, the boundary is that from which something *begins its presencing*. [T]he concept is that of *horismos*, that is, the horizon, the boundary.[6]

In another essay from the same year, Heidegger brings these ideas together in the notion of "dwelling poetically":

> Making is, in Greek, *poiesis*. . . . Poetry, as the authentic gauging of the dimension of dwelling, is the primal form of building.[7]

For the eighteenth-century poet Friedrich von Hölderlin, "dwelling poetically" (*dichterisch wohnen*) meant inhabiting an imaginative space beyond human convention. For the nineteenth-century poet Emily Dickinson, it meant replacing boundaries with horizons: "I Dwell in Possibility—/A fairer House than Prose."[8] For twenty-first-century poet and educator Carl Leggo, it means merging the critical gaze of the scholar-teacher with the creative sensibilities of the artist:

> Living poetically for me is about living as a critical pedagogue, living as a creative pedagogue. It's living with the balance of poetry, with the rhythms of poetry. (*Carl Leggo, Education, University of British Columbia*)

For the rest of us—members of that peculiar, prosaic species classified by Pierre Bourdieu as *homo academicus*[9]—dwelling poetically could mean gauging the dimensions of our own habits and mindfully inhabiting the rhythms of our writing lives: taking pride in a beautifully crafted sentence, lingering in the hallway for a friendly chat with a colleague, and working with our neighbors to rebuild our academic habitus into a place of possibilities.

Beyond the House
of Writing

Enlarge the place of your tent,
   stretch your tent curtains wide,
   do not hold back;
lengthen your cords,
   strengthen your stakes.

—Isaiah 54:2

I worked on several chapters of this book while living not in a conventional house but in a bus. Toward the end of my six-month sabbatical—the push-comes-to-shove, get-that-manuscript-out-the-door month—I left my home in New Zealand for the foggy coast of Northern California, where a yoga instructor named Blake rented me her hippie house-bus, which contained (among many other colorful and fascinating items) a big bed covered with bright cushions, a small kitchen, a comfortable sofa, a large collection of scented candles, a shelf full of New Age books, and a tiny wood-burning stove. The toilet and outdoor shower were located a short distance from the bus, and I was granted the run of Blake's organic vegetable garden, which as far as I could see did not harbor any of the medicinal plants for which this region of California (sometimes called the "Weed Coast") is best known.

I set up my standing desk at the back of the bus so that I could look down its entire length toward the driver's seat, which had been converted into a cozy, fake-fur-covered reading chair. The vehicle's elaborately decorated exterior resembled a field of green and golden bamboo topped by a lavender-blue sky, and above the big windows at the front of the bus, Blake had painted in huge cloud-like letters its metaphysical destination: OMWORD.

My three weeks on the bus—along with other experiences of place and displacement during my research leave—alerted me to the inadequacies of the "house of writing" metaphor on whose square, solid BASE I have erected this book. My architectural imagery, I realized, needs to be expanded to accommodate a much-wider range of real and imagined dwellings: not just conventional single-family houses but also tents, cottages, cabins, studios, garrets, caravans, towers, bungalows, whares, fales, buses, igloos, yurts, town houses, tree houses, lighthouses, penthouses, houseboats, motel rooms, hotel suites, caves, cloud-castles, and any other kind of abode that a fertile imagination can build. But are our disciplinary communities ready to tolerate such architectural variety, such a range of alternative lifestyle choices? In the Malvina Reynolds song "Little Boxes," made popular by Pete Seeger in the 1960s, the function of universities is to deposit their graduates into cookie-cutter houses and jobs: "little boxes made of ticky tacky" that "all look just the same."[1] How much has really changed in our professional neighborhoods since then?

On the shadow side of the house metaphor, we all know how many things can go wrong with even the most modest of domestic dreams: drains can block, roofs can leak, rents can rise, noisy neighbors can move in next door. Most insidious of all are the shadowy poltergeists that wreak secret havoc deep inside our most private spaces: *doubt* about our abilities and potential as writers (that's our old friend, Imposter Syndrome, taunting us from the rafters); *envy* of colleagues whose houses appear so much bigger, cleaner, and more perfect than our own (how often did that green-eyed monster blow your fuses while you were reading about the successful academic writers profiled in this book?); *guilt* that our own less-than-perfect habitations have dirty dishes piling up in the sink and dust bunnies breeding under the beds (even though our rational selves know that the perfection we perceive in other people's lives is often illusory—and would we really want to live in a show home anyway?). Even the four solid cornerstones of the BASE throw long shadows of their own: behavioral habits too finely tuned to productivity can throw our personal relationships out of key; artisanal habits of craft and care can lead to a crippling perfectionism; social habits of generosity can slow the upward trajectory of our careers; and emotional habits of pleasure and passion can bring the homeowners' association to our front door, delivering the news that fuchsia and chartreuse are not on the neighborhood's list of acceptable paint colors.

The light-and-shadow-play of the house metaphor throws into relief the paradox at the heart of this book. Building a productive writing practice can be hard, slow, frustrating work—yet successful academics find satisfaction and joy in that labor, nourished by the pleasures of the process and made stronger by its challenges. What does it matter that the task will never be finished or that our next-door neighbors have just installed a new hot tub that looks bigger than our own living room? In the end, the size, splendor, and exterior trappings of our individual homes matter less than the sense of well-being we feel when we are inside them. The grandest mansion can be cold and sterile; the smallest cottage can be intimate and inspiring; even a makeshift tent can house a party.

My own house of writing has changed a good deal in the five years since I first started working on this book. Aside from a semester of dedicated research leave, I had to fit most of my data collection and writing time around the everyday demands of an administrative and teaching workload that sometimes threatened to suck all the oxygen out of my writing practice. Along the way, like so many other academics I know, I developed chronic neck and shoulder pain from hunching over a keyboard for too many hours a day, either chipping away at my manuscript or, more often, zapping the endless barrage of emails that swarmed into my inbox. And then there were the other foundation-shaking events—the death of a family member, the sale of a beloved house, a skirmish with breast cancer—that sent cracks through my BASE and left me temporarily floored.

Yet now, as I write these final paragraphs, I am dancing—literally. Yes, it's true: I have developed a stand-up keyboarding technique that involves shimmying, twisting, and kick-stepping while I write, which in turn prevents me from locking my back and shoulders into a single fixed position. Looks silly (I don't do it in public), but the benefits have flowed through my body to my mind and back again, and my writing sessions have become active and energizing rather than physically painful. Would I have been inspired to try out such an unconventional writing method if I hadn't been writing a book about inspiring academic writers? Possibly not. Certainly I would not have had the confidence to confess my eccentricities in print. But why shouldn't academics dance while they write? Perhaps by admitting more freedom of movement into our own writing habits—"air and light and time and space" and a bit of pleasure and playfulness besides—we can transform the habitus of scholarly labor into a dynamic habitat where all writers can flourish.

Appendix

Notes

Bibliography

Acknowledgments

Index

Appendix

All statistics, graphics, and author quotations in this book are based on ethics-approved research undertaken in fifteen countries (Australia, Canada, Denmark, England, Finland, Germany, Hong Kong, Ireland, the Netherlands, New Zealand, Scotland, Sweden, Switzerland, Thailand, and the United States) between 2011 and 2015. During that period, I conducted in-depth interviews with 100 academic writers and editors and gathered anonymous questionnaire data from 1,223 more: a mix of academic faculty, research fellows, PhD students, and other writers employed in an academic context. The interviews and questionnaires were transcribed and coded by Louisa Shen, a research assistant working under my supervision, and were cross-checked for accuracy by a second research assistant, Sophie Van Waardenberg.

INTERVIEWS

Just over half of my interview subjects (55 percent) were recommended to me by discipline-based colleagues as "exemplary academic writers" who met at least one of the following criteria:

- Publishes writing of an exceptionally high quality, as evidenced by markers of peer esteem such as book prizes, research awards, and collegial recommendations.

- Publishes prolifically, at a substantially higher rate than most other researchers in the field.

- Subverts or challenges disciplinary conventions; takes risks as a writer.

- Publishes innovative prose that takes academic writing in new directions.

- Engages effectively with audiences both within and beyond academe.

- Writes confidently and contently, without the agony, angst, and uncertainty that characterize the writing lives of so many academics.

- Actively mentors colleagues and graduate students to become better writers.

I particularly sought out academics from the following cohorts: self-perceived "academic outsiders" (for example, researchers from cultural, ethnic, and/or gender groups underrepresented within their own disciplines); academics who publish in English although it is not their first language; early- to midcareer faculty who gracefully balance their workloads with significant caring responsibilities; and scholars who have followed nontraditional career paths into or through academe.

The remainder of the interviews (45 percent) took place with people whom I approached directly. Most of these were successful academics with whom I was already acquainted, either personally or by reputation: for example, writers whose exemplary prose had featured in my previous books; colleagues at my home university who work in academic disciplines other than my own; and scholars from my home discipline (modernist literature) who have won accolades for their work. There were also some opportunistic, spur-of-the-moment interviews, thanks to the digital "smart pen" recorder that I carried with me at all times during my travels: the conference delegate I met on a long taxi ride in Bangkok who had interesting things to say about academic writing and publication in his home country; the famous figure I approached after a keynote address for an on-the-spot interview in a corner of the conference hotel lobby; the visiting overseas scholar who dropped by my office to introduce herself and ended up staying for an hour-long interview; the three early-career researchers with whom I had just shared a lively lunch at a write-on-site session in a Wellington café.

My ambition was to interview roughly equal numbers of men and women drawn from across the widest possible range of disciplines. The latter, however, turned out to be something of a challenge, thanks to the siloed nature of academic life. Most of my on-the-ground institutional contacts—the people I relied on to help me set up interviews and workshops at their home universities—were social scientists or humanities scholars whom I knew through my own academic networks in educational development and literary studies, respectively. The academic developers were generally able to recommend a few scientists whom they knew through their teaching networks; however, the literary scholars often struggled to name even a single colleague outside the humanities. Also, they did not always follow directions. One generous host, upon being asked to line up interviews with a few exemplary scientists and social scientists at his university, instead sent an email around his own department announcing that he was hosting a visiting researcher who was conducting research on scholarly writing, and would anyone like to be interviewed? Half a dozen or so of his closest colleagues put their hands up; not wanting to seem rude, I interviewed them all—and was glad I did, although my interview cohort was already overstocked with humanists.

At the time of the interviews, ninety-six of my interview subjects were either employed in or recently retired from academic positions in higher education, three were full-time academic editors, two were graduate students, and one was a postdoctoral fellow. (Educational developers with PhDs were classified in the interview cohort as academics, even if they were not employed on faculty contracts.) Most of the interviews lasted between sixty and ninety minutes and covered some or all of the following questions:

1. Briefly describe your academic background, current position, and primary research area(s). Who are the main audiences for whom you write? Have these audiences changed over time?

2. Describe your professional formation as a writer. How, when, and from whom did you learn to write in your

discipline? Have you ever undertaken any formal learning in academic writing (e.g., books, workshops, courses), either pre- or post-PhD?

3. Describe your academic work habits. How, when, and where do you make time for your writing? How have these habits changed or developed over time? How do you maintain "work-life balance"?

4. What are the main emotions that you associate with your academic writing? How have these emotions changed or developed over time?

5. (If applicable) Describe one or more risks, innovations, or unconventional moves that you have undertaken as an academic writer. What were the consequences? Did you take such risks early in your career or only after you became established as an academic?

6. Describe a piece of writing of which you are especially proud. What are its defining characteristics? Is there a piece of writing of which you are not so proud?

7. Describe a situation in which you received a particularly negative response or rejection as a writer. How did you react? How about examples of positive responses?

8. (If applicable) Please talk a little bit about your experiences as a non-native-English speaker writing in English. What barriers have you faced? What particular strategies have you employed to overcome those barriers?

9. What advice would you give to an early-career academic on how to become a more engaging, confident, and/or prolific writer?

All one hundred interviewees agreed to be interviewed "on the record"; in return for their trust, I have made sure that every single one of them is quoted by name somewhere in the book. The disciplinary affiliations listed after their names reflect either their academic appointment at the time of the interview or their current appointment at the time of publication, depending on their own preference.

QUESTIONNAIRES

In contrast to the interviews, which took place by invitation only and generally unfolded at a leisurely pace, most of the 1,223 data questionnaires were completed in under ten minutes by anonymous volunteers taking part in writing-development workshops that I offered at their home universities or at discipline-based conferences. Three of the same questions that I asked in the interviews—on learning to write, daily writing habits, and writing-related emotions—also appeared, in slightly modified form, as questionnaire prompts. About halfway through the data-collection process, I added a fourth prompt: a self-diagnostic BASE exercise similar to the one that appears on page 9. The results of that survey are not discussed in this book, except very briefly in the Introduction.

DEMOGRAPHICS

Nearly half of the interview subjects (47 percent) and around a quarter of the questionnaire respondents (26 percent) identified themselves as residents of North America, whereas nearly half of the questionnaire respondents (49 percent) and around a quarter of the interview subjects (25 percent) lived in Australia or New Zealand (see Table 1). This demographic disparity occurred due to circumstances rather than design: I conducted most of the interviews during research trips to North America, Europe, and Asia in 2011 through 2013; later in the data-gathering process, when my interview roster was nearly full, I was invited to run a number of well-attended writing workshops at universities in Australasia.

Initially, I intended to focus the data collection on faculty writers only. However, the colleagues at my host institutions frequently asked me to open up my writing workshops to graduate students and postdoctoral researchers as well, and before long, I discovered that other writers were also sneaking through the door: departmental administrators, research coordinators, laboratory assistants. The questionnaire respondents thus ended up representing a far more eclectic mix of academic writers than the interview group did: not just tenured or tenure-track faculty (53 percent) but also PhD students (25 percent), postdoctoral researchers (15 percent), and "other writers" employed in a variety of academic contexts (7 percent).

Table 1. Summary of survey group demographics

Demographic category	Interviews (n = 100)	Questionnaires (n = 1,223)
Country of residence		
North America	47%	26%
United Kingdom/Ireland	11%	8%
Europe	13%	13%
Australia/New Zealand	25%	50%
Asia/Africa/South America	4%	3%
Academic role		
Faculty/academic staff	94%	53%
Research fellow/postdoc	1%	15%
MA/PhD student	2%	25%
Other	3%	7%
First language		
English (L1)	75%	68%
Other languages (L2)	25%	32%
Discipline		
Social sciences	33%	37%
Arts/humanities	36%	31%
Sciences	31%	32%
Gender		
Male	51%	31%
Female	49%	69%

Despite notable differences in selection criteria and venue, the two survey cohorts came out looking remarkably similar in two key respects: namely, their ratio of L1 to L2 English speakers and their disciplinary balance. Only 17 percent of the interviewees and 16 percent of the questionnaire respondents reported that they reside in non-English-speaking countries, yet L2 speakers made up between a quarter and a third of all respondents (25 percent interviews, 32 percent questionnaires), a salient reminder of the dominance of English in international academe. (At a large writing workshop that I ran for early-career academics at Oxford University, more than half of the participants came from non-English-speaking backgrounds.) Likewise, the distribution of social scientists, humanists, and scientists in the two groups varied by only a few percentage points (interviews 33/36/31, questionnaires 39/35/26). Apparently, no single disciplinary group holds a monopoly on writing confidence or competence.

The most striking demographic difference between the two survey groups emerged in the category of gender. Whereas the interview cohort consisted, by design, of almost exactly equal proportions of women and men (49/51), the ratio of female to male workshop participants came out at more than two to one (69/31). This "two-to-one rule" held fast across countries, disciplines, and academic ranks; I can now walk into a writing workshop at just about any academic institution in Europe, North America, or Australasia and confidently predict that approximately two-thirds of the participants will be female. (The only exception that I noted during the data collection occurred at a research conference where my presentation was billed as a "keynote address" rather than a writing workshop; there, the men outnumbered the women.) Similarly lopsided gender imbalances have been anecdotally reported elsewhere in the academic-development literature but have never before, to my knowledge, been documented on such a wide scale. Are female academics significantly less confident about their writing than their male counterparts are? Significantly more confident about seeking professional development? Perhaps some combination of the two?

DATA CODING

Responses to the three questionnaire prompts, along with corresponding data from the interviews, went through several iterations of refinement and coding.

1. Learning to write

Respondents in both groups were asked to describe their "professional formation" as writers: "How, when, and from whom did you learn to write in your discipline? Have you ever undertaken any formal learning in academic writing (e.g., books, workshops, courses), either pre- or post-PhD?" We identified three categories of respondents (see Figure 4 on page 64):

- *Formal learning.* Researchers who have undergone systematic, sustained training in graduate- or postgraduate-level research writing and publication, such as accredited writing courses or institutionally sponsored mentoring programs.

- *Semiformal learning.* Researchers who have experienced no "formal learning" but have taken advantage of other opportunities to develop their academic writing knowledge and skills: for example, by reading books on academic writing or by attending occasional academic-development workshops (not counting the workshop at which they filled out the questionnaires).

- *Informal learning.* Researchers whose learning has occurred entirely through ad hoc, opportunistic, noninstitutionalized processes such as informal mentoring, feedback from peer reviewers, self-reflection, and that old favorite of the sink-or-swim academic, trial and error.

Each respondent was assigned to just one category, with each category subsuming the one(s) below it. Hence, an academic who learned about writing from a family member, has read a number of books on scholarly writing, and recently completed an accredited academic writing course would be categorized under "formal learning," despite having also undergone informal and semiformal learning experiences.

2. Writing habits

In contrast to the previous question, which elicited fairly straightforward answers, this prompt—"Briefly describe your academic writing habits. Where, when, and how often do you write?"—yielded responses so slippery and varied that they proved almost impossible to code. "How Academics Write," the original title of my research project, turns out to be a phrase that can mean very different things to different people. Even a prompt as explicit as "where, when, and how often do you write?" provoked responses that often raised new questions or answered questions that had not been asked:

> Frequently. Intermittently. But not daily. [How often is "frequently"? What does "intermittently" mean?]

When I get stuck, I prefer to write with pen and paper, sitting on the grass outside. [Here a comment about process—"getting stuck"—morphs into a description of writing tools and venues.]

I work on sections of writing in papers; start with skeleton/map of a paper then flesh each section out. [This respondent has interpreted a question about behavioral habits as a question about craft.]

Although respondents were explicitly asked to exclude any non-research-related writing tasks such as email correspondence and administrative documentation, some persisted in recording such tasks anyway—a symptom of the messiness, complexity, and unbounded nature of academic research. Who is to say that our email correspondence about a forthcoming conference "doesn't count" as research writing or that the new undergraduate course we are teaching this semester will not feed the academic publication machine somewhere down the line?

3. Writing-related emotions

The third prompt for both groups was deliberately open-ended: "Briefly describe the main emotions that you associate with your academic writing." Despite the differing formats of the two sets of responses—the interviewees spoke at length about their emotions and often mentioned emotional affect in other parts of their interviews as well, whereas the questionnaire respondents had just two or three minutes to jot down a few words or phrases—this item proved relatively straightforward to code, as most emotion words can be readily classified as either negative or positive. There were, to be sure, some challenging exceptions: for example, the word *challenging* can be interpreted as negative, positive, or emotionally ambivalent, depending on context. Respondents also recorded a number of words and phrases that do not actually describe emotions but are often charged with emotion, such as *procrastination* (coded as negative) and *flow* (coded as positive).

The word-frequency diagrams on pages 155 and 156 (Figures 6 and 7) were generated using Wordle (www.wordle.net). Because respondents often described the same emotion using different forms of the same word (for example, *frustrating, frustrated, frustration*), all variant words were consolidated into a single form on the basis of frequency of occurrence, favoring noun forms where possible. Similar words with semantic differences, such as *joy* and *enjoy*, were not consolidated. Emotions that were described using a phrase—*not enough time, not good enough*—were replaced with an equivalent term such as *time* or *inadequate*.

DEMOGRAPHIC CODING

- *Country of residence.* This indicates the country where the respondent worked or studied at the time of the data collection, not necessarily where the data collection took place. For example, a French PhD student studying in Scotland would be classified under "UK/Ireland"; a South African academic interviewed in Thailand would be classified under "Asia/Africa/South America." In cases in which a questionnaire respondent wrote down two countries (e.g., "Finland/New Zealand"), the current workplace trumped the other country listed, when such information was available.

- *Academic role.* "Faculty/academic staff" applies to part-time, full-time, and retired academics, including adjunct faculty and full-time administrators in senior academic roles. "Research fellow/postdoc" designates post-PhD academics in research-only positions. "MA/PhD student" indicates students currently enrolled in graduate study. "Other" includes undergraduates, academic support staff, full-time editors, and anyone else who did not fit into one of the preceding categories. Each category is trumped by the one above: hence, a PhD student who holds a faculty appointment is counted as "Faculty/academic staff."

- *First language.* "English" denotes both English-only speakers and multilingual respondents who identified English as their first language (L1); "Other language(s)" designates speakers of English as an additional or secondary language (L2). In the interview cohort, bilingual speakers of English and another language were designated as L1 or L2 depending on whether they spent their early years in an English-speaking home environment, where such information was available. Twenty questionnaire respondents out of 1,223 (1.6 percent) listed two languages in response to the question, "What is your first language?" These were classified as L2.

- *Discipline.* Nearly one-quarter of the questionnaire respondents identified themselves as cross-disciplinary researchers. However, we ended up categorizing all respondents according to just one disciplinary category each—*social science*, *arts/humanities*, or *science*—even with the knowledge that many interdisciplinary scholars (myself included) would be appalled by such taxonomic shoe-horning. Our classification rubric was based on participants' home departments, which in turn were coded according to the disciplinary affiliations of equivalent departments at the University of Auckland. Thus, for example, nursing scholars and psychologists were all classified under science (as Nursing is situated in the Faculty of Medicine and Psychology in the Faculty of Science), whatever their highest degree or preferred research methodology.

- *Gender.* All respondents classified themselves as either male or female.

Notes

PREFACE

1   Charles Bukowski, "Air and Light and Time and Space," in *The Last Night of the Earth Poems* (New York: Ecco, 2002), 44.

INTRODUCTION

1   Helen Sword, *Stylish Academic Writing* (Cambridge, MA: Harvard University Press, 2012); Helen Sword, *The Writer's Diet: A Guide to Fit Prose* (Chicago: University of Chicago Press, 2016). For writing resources and tools based on these books, see also the Writer's Diet website at www.writersdiet.com.

2   In an interview with Noah Charney for *The Daily Beast*'s "How I Write" column (v 17, 2013), historian Tony Grafton is quoted as saying, "If I'm writing full-time I'll get about 3,500 words per morning, four mornings a week" (http://www.thedailybeast.com/articles/2013/07/17/anthony-grafton-how-i-write.html). Blogger L. D. Burnett subsequently coined the phrase "the Grafton Line" and created the Twitter hashtag #graftonline for writers who wish to post their own daily word counts (*Saved by History Blog*, July 21, 2013); blogger Claire Potter in turn publicized the phrase via her widely read *Tenured Radical Blog* (July 22, 2013).

PART I: BEHAVIORAL HABITS

1   Robert Boice, *Professors as Writers: A Self-Help Guide to Productive Writing* (Stillwater, OK: New Forums, 1990). For a more detailed account of this study, see Robert Boice, "Procrastination, Busyness and Bingeing," *Behaviour Research and Therapy* 27, no. 6 (1989): 605–611. For a critical analysis of its methodology and reception history, see Helen Sword, "Write Every Day: A Mantra Dismantled," *International Journal for Academic Development* 21, no. 4 (2016): 312–322.

2   Julia Cameron, *The Artist's Way: A Spiritual Path to Higher Creativity* (New York: Tarcher/Putnam, 1992), 148.

3   Boice, *Professors as Writers*, 31.

4   Paul J. Silvia, *How to Write a Lot: A Practical Guide to Productive Academic Writing* (Washington, DC: American Psychological Association, 2007), 24–26, 12, 14.

5   Boice, *Professors as Writers*, 128.

1. FINDING TIME TO WRITE

1   Robert Boice, *Professors as Writers: A Self-Help Guide to Productive Writing* (Stillwater, OK: New Forums, 1990), 41–47; Paul J. Silvia, *How to Write a Lot: A Practical Guide to Productive Academic Writing* (Washington, DC: American Psychological Association, 2007), 35–40; Patricia Goodson, *Becoming an Academic Writer: 50 Exercises for Paced, Productive, and Powerful Writing* (London: Sage, 2013), 21; Joan Bolker, *Writing Your Dissertation in Fifteen Minutes a Day: A Guide to Starting, Revising, and Finishing Your Doctoral Thesis* (New York: Holt, 1998), 38; Stephen King, *On Writing: A Memoir of the Craft* (New York: Simon and Schuster, 2000), 148.

2   Francis Crick, "The Impact of Linus Pauling on Molecular Biology," *Proceedings of the Conference on the Life and Work of Linus Pauling (1901–1994): A Discourse on the Art of Biography* (Corvallis: Oregon State University Libraries Special Collections, 1996).

3   Henry Miller, *Henry Miller on Writing* (New York: New Directions, 1964), 141.

4   Boice, *Professors as Writers*, 124, 121.

5   Sylvia Plath, "Appendix 2: Script for the BBC Broadcast: 'New Poems by Sylvia Plath,'" in *Ariel: The Restored Edition* (New York: HarperCollins, 2004), 195.

6   Ferris Jabr, "Why Your Brain Needs More Downtime," *Scientific American*, October 15, 2013, http://www.scientificamerican.com/article/mental-downtime/.

7   Anthony Burgess, "The Art of Fiction No. 48," interview by John Cullinan, *Paris Review* 56 (1973): 121.

8   Boice, *Professors as Writers*; Tara Gray, *Publish and Flourish: Become a Prolific Writer* (Las Cruces: New Mexico State University Teaching Academy, 2015); Silvia, *How to Write a Lot*; Eviatar Zerubavel,

The Clockwork Muse: A Practical Guide to Writing Theses, Dissertations, and Books (Cambridge, MA: Harvard University Press, 1999); Bolker, *Writing Your Dissertation*; Rowena Murray, *Writing for Academic Journals*, 3rd ed. (Berkshire, UK: Open University Press, 2013); Wendy L. Belcher, *Writing Your Journal Article in 12 Weeks: A Guide to Academic Publishing Success* (Los Angeles: Sage, 2009); Keith Hjortshoj, *Understanding Writing Blocks* (New York: Oxford University Press, 2001); Daniel Kahneman, *Thinking, Fast and Slow* (New York: Farrar, Straus and Giroux, 2001); Maggie Berg and Barbara Seeber, *Slow Professor: Challenging the Culture of Speed in the Academy* (Toronto: University of Toronto Press, 2016); John Perry, *The Art of Procrastination: A Guide to Effective Dawdling, Lollygagging and Postponing* (New York: Workman, 2012); John Perry Structured Procrastination website, accessed June 21, 2016, http://www.structuredprocrastination.com/.

2. THE POWER OF PLACE

1 Virginia Woolf, *A Room of One's Own* (1929; London: Penguin, 1993), 79.

2 Paul J. Silvia, *How to Write a Lot: A Practical Guide to Productive Academic Writing* (Washington, DC: American Psychological Association, 2007), 20, 21.

3 Mason Currey, *Daily Rituals: How Artists Work* (New York: Knopf, 2013), 39, 41, 114, 122, 182–183; Ian Fleming Publications Ltd., "Jamaica (1946–1964)," Ian Fleming website, accessed June 21, 2016, http://www.ianfleming.com/ian-fleming/ian-fleming-inside/jamaica-1946-1964/.

4 Stephen King, *On Writing: A Memoir of the Craft* (New York: Simon and Schuster, 2000), 177.

5 Ronald T. Kellogg, *The Psychology of Writing* (Oxford: Oxford University Press, 1994), 186.

6 Fausto Massimini, Mihaly Csikszentmihalyi, and Antonella Delle Fave, "Flow and Biocultural Evolution," in *Optimal Experience: Psychological Studies of Flow in Consciousness*, ed. Mihaly Csikszentmihalyi and Isabella Selega Csikszentmihalyi (Cambridge: Cambridge University Press, 1988), 68.

7 Don Campbell, *The Mozart Effect: Tapping the Power of Music to Heal the Body, Strengthen the Mind, and Unlock the Creative Spirit* (New York: HarperCollins, 2001), 271. (For a meta-analysis questioning

the validity of Campbell's research, see Jakob Pietschnig, Martin Voracek, and Anton Formann, "Mozart Effect–Shmozart Effect: A Meta-
analysis," *Intelligence* 38, no. 3 [2010]: 314–323.)

8 Samuel Taylor Coleridge, "Kubla Khan," in *The Complete Poems*,
ed. William Keach (London: Penguin, 1997), 248.

9 Bruce Holland Rogers, "Cloistered Writing: When You Need a Dose
of Discipline, Take a Writing Retreat—At Home," *Writer* 118, no. 11
(2005): 15.

10 Currey, *Daily Rituals*, 13, 20, 25, 115.

11 Richard Louv, *The Nature Principle: Human Restoration and the End
of Nature-Deficit Disorder* (New York: Algonquin Books, 2012), 58.

12 Anne Morrow Lindbergh, *Gift from the Sea* (New York: Pantheon
Books, 1955); William Zinsser, *Writing Places: The Life Journey of a
Writer and Teacher* (New York: Harper, 2010); W. B. Yeats, "The Lake
Isle of Innisfree," in *The Collected Poems of W. B. Yeats*, ed. Richard J.
Finneran (New York: Scribner, 1996), 39; Henry David Thoreau,
Walden, 150th anniversary ed. (Princeton, NJ: Princeton University
Press, 2004), 1.

3. RHYTHMS AND RITUALS

1 Robert Boice, *Professors as Writers: A Self-Help Guide to Produc-
tive Writing* (Stillwater, OK: New Forums, 1990), 42; Rowena Murray,
Writing for Academic Journals, 3rd ed. (Berkshire, UK: Open University
Press, 2013), 104; Dorothea Brande, *Becoming a Writer* (New York:
Harcourt Brace, 1934), 72–73; Peter Elbow, *Writing with Power: Tech-
niques for Mastering the Writing Process* (Oxford: Oxford University
Press, 1998), 13.

2 Charles Darwin, *Autobiography and Selected Letters*, ed. Francis
Darwin (New York: Dover, 1958), 53.

3 Paul J. Silvia, *How to Write a Lot: A Practical Guide to Productive
Academic Writing* (Washington, DC: American Psychological Association, 2007), 76.

4 Eric Hayot, *The Elements of Academic Style: Writing for the Humanities* (New York: Columbia University Press, 2014), 32.

5 George Greenstein, "Writing Is Thinking: Using Writing to Teach
Science," *Astronomy Education Review* 12, no. 1 (2013); Richard
Menary, "Writing as Thinking," *Language Sciences* 29, no. 5 (2007):

621–632; Pam A. Mueller and Daniel M. Oppenheimer, "The Pen Is Mightier than the Keyboard," *Psychological Science* 25, no. 6 (2014): 1159–1168.

6 Cecile Badenhorst, *Productive Writing: Becoming a Prolific Academic Writer* (Pretoria, South Africa: Van Schaik, 2010).

7 Gilles Deleuze and Félix Guattari, *A Thousand Plateaus: Capitalism and Schizophrenia* (London: Athlone, 1988), 5–7.

8 Eviatar Zerubavel, *The Clockwork Muse: A Practical Guide to Writing Theses, Dissertations, and Books* (Cambridge, MA: Harvard University Press, 1999), 33–35.

9 Boice, *Professors as Writers*, 79.

10 Tara Gray, *Publish and Flourish: Become a Prolific Writer* (Las Cruces: New Mexico State University Teaching Academy, 2015), 12.

11 Murray, *Writing for Academic Journals*, 73.

12 James Hartley and Alan Branthwaite, "The Psychologist as Wordsmith: A Questionnaire Study of the Writing Strategies of Productive British Psychologists," *Higher Education* 18, no. 4 (1989), 427; Ronald T. Kellogg, *The Psychology of Writing* (Oxford: Oxford University Press, 1994), 193.

13 Robert Boice, "Contingency Management in Writing and the Appearance of Creative Ideas: Implications for the Treatment of Writing Blocks," *Behaviour Research and Therapy* 21, no. 5 (1983): 537–543.

14 Brad Isaac, "Jerry Seinfeld's Productivity Secret," *Lifehacker Blog*, July 24, 2007, http://lifehacker.com/281626/jerry-seinfelds-productivity -secret.

15 Anne Lamott, *Stitches: A Handbook on Meaning, Hope, and Repair* (New York: Riverhead, 2013), 82.

16 Joan Bolker attributes this phrase to Kenneth Skier, who taught writing for many years at MIT (Bolker, *Writing Your Dissertation,* 163).

17 Charles Duhigg, *The Power of Habit: Why We Do What We Do and How to Change* (London: Heinemann, 2012), 20.

18 "Big jets": Maria Gardiner and Hugh Kearns, "Turbocharge Your Writing Today," *Nature* 475 (2011): 129; "rocks in a jar": Stephen R.

Covey, A. Roger Merrill, and Rebecca R. Merrill, *First Things First* (New York: Simon and Schuster, 1995), 89.

19 Margaret Atwood's metaphor of "going down the writing burrow" is discussed by Pat Thomson on her blog: "A Metaphor for Thesis Completion?," *Patter Blog*, March 13, 2014, https://patthomson.net/2014/03/13/a-metaphor-for-thesis-completion/.

20 Anne Lamott, *Bird by Bird: Some Instructions on Writing and Life* (New York: Knopf Doubleday, 2007); Annie Dillard, *The Writing Life* (New York: Simon and Schuster, 2000); Stephen King, *On Writing: A Memoir of the Craft* (New York: Simon and Schuster, 2000); Dani Shapiro, *Still Writing: The Perils and Pleasures of a Creative Life* (New York: Grove Atlantic, 2014); bell hooks, *Remembered Rapture: The Writer at Work* (New York: Holt, 2013); Robert S. Boynton, *The New New Journalism: Conversations with America's Best Nonfiction Writers on Their Craft* (New York: Knopf Doubleday, 2007); Gary Olson and Lynn Worsham, eds., *Critical Intellectuals on Writing* (Albany: State University of New York Press, 2010); Mason Currey, *Daily Rituals: How Artists Work* (New York: Knopf, 2013); *Writers on Writing: Collected Essays from the* New York Times (New York: Holt, 2002; Hilton Obenzinger, *How We Write: The Varieties of Writing Experience* (Palo Alto, CA: Stanford University Press, 2015).

PART II: ARTISANAL HABITS

1   Ted Hughes, introduction to *Sylvia Plath: The Collected Poems*, ed. Ted Hughes (New York: Buccaneer Books, 1998), 13.

2   Journalist Janet Malcolm experimented with a similar process in her *New Yorker* article about painter David Salle, "Forty-One False Starts," *New Yorker*, July 11, 1994, http://www.newyorker.com/magazine/1994/07/11/forty-one-false-starts.

3   Rowena Murray, *Writing for Academic Journals*, 3rd ed. (Berkshire, UK: Open University Press, 2013), chap. 3.

4   W. B. Yeats, "Adam's Curse," in *The Collected Poems of W. B. Yeats*, ed. Richard J. Finneran (New York: Scribner, 1996), 80; Ernest Hemingway, "Appendix II: The Alternative Endings," in *A Farewell to Arms: The Hemingway Library Edition*, ed. Seán Hemingway (New York: Scribner, 2012), 303.

5   Throughout this book, I follow the convention of using *L1* to designate speakers of English as a first or primary language and *L2* to designate speakers of English as an additional or secondary language.

4. LEARNING TO WRITE

1   Peter J. Richerson and Robert Boyd, *Not by Genes Alone: How Culture Transformed Human Evolution* (Chicago: University of Chicago Press, 2005), 120.

2   On constructivism, see John Biggs and Catherine Tang, *Teaching for Quality Learning at University* (Berkshire, UK: Open University Press, 2011); on situated learning, see Jean Lave and Étienne Wenger, *Situated Learning: Legitimate Peripheral Participation* (Cambridge: Cambridge University Press, 1991); on reflective practice, see Chris Argyris and Donald A. Schön, *Organizational Learning: A Theory of Action Perspective* (Reading, MA: Addison-Wesley, 1978).

3   Stephen R. Covey, *The Seven Habits of Highly Effective People* (New York: Simon and Schuster, 2004), 277.

4   Stephen Pinker, *The Sense of Style: A Thinking Person's Guide to Writing in the Twenty-First Century* (New York: Penguin, 2015).

5   Roy Peter Clark, *Writing Tools: 50 Essential Strategies for Every Writer* (New York: Little, Brown, 2008); Patricia Goodson, *Becoming an Academic Writer: 50 Exercises for Paced, Productive, and Powerful Writing*, 2nd ed. (London: Sage, 2013); Peter Elbow, *Writing with Power: Techniques for Mastering the Writing Process* (Oxford: Oxford University Press, 1998); Ralph Keyes, *The Courage to Write: How Writers Transcend Fear*, rev. ed. (New York: Holt, 2003); Anne Ellen Geller and Michele Eodice, eds., *Working with Faculty Writers* (Boulder, CO: Utah State University Press, 2013); Barbara Kamler and Pat Thomson, *Helping Doctoral Students Write: Pedagogies for Supervision*, 2nd ed. (London: Routledge, 2014); Susan Carter and Deborah Laurs, eds., *Giving Feedback on Research Writing: A Handbook for Supervisors and Advisors* (London: Routledge, 2017); Barbara E. Fassler Walvoord, *Helping Students Write Well: A Guide for Teachers in All Disciplines*, 2nd ed. (New York: Modern Language Association of America, 1986); William Zinsser, *Writing to Learn* (New York: HarperCollins, 2001); Kim Sterelny, *The Evolved Apprentice* (Cambridge, MA: MIT Press, 2014).

5. THE CRAFT OF WRITING

1   Tim Ingold, *Lines: A Brief History* (Abingdon, UK: Routledge, 2015), 4.

2   Carol S. Dweck, *Mindset: The New Psychology of Success* (New York: Ballantine, 2008), 14.

3   William Strunk Jr. and E. B. White, *The Elements of Style*, 4th ed. (Boston: Allyn and Bacon, 2000); Ernest Gowers, *The Complete Plain Words*, 2nd ed. (London: Her Majesty's Stationery Office, 1973); Joseph M. Williams, *Style: Lessons in Clarity and Grace*, 9th ed. (New York: Pearson Longman, 2007); William Zinsser, *On Writing Well: An Informal Guide to Writing Nonfiction* (New York: Harper and Row, 1980); Bruce Ross-Larson, *Stunning Sentences* (New York: Norton, 1999); Stanley Fish, *How to Write a Sentence: And How to Read One* (New York: HarperCollins, 2011); Claire Cook, *Line by Line: How to Improve Your Own Writing* (Boston: Modern Language Association of America, 1985); Joseph Harris, *Rewriting: How to Do Things with Texts* (Boulder, CO: Utah State University Press, 2006); Richard A. Lanham, *Revising Prose*, 3rd ed. (New York: Macmillan, 1992); Jay Woodruff, *A Piece of Work: Five Writers Discuss Their Revisions* (Iowa City: University of Iowa Press, 1993); Eric Hayot, *The Elements of Academic Style: Writing for the Humanities* (New York: Columbia University Press, 2014); Stephen J. Pyne, *Voice and Vision: A Guide to Writing History and Other Serious Non-fiction* (Cambridge, MA: Harvard University Press, 2009); Bryan A. Garner, *Legal Writing in Plain English: A Text with Exercises* (Chicago: University of Chicago Press, 2013); Howard S. Becker, *Writing for Social Scientists: How to Start and Finish Your Thesis, Book, or Article*, 2nd ed. (Chicago: University of Chicago Press, 2007); Michael Billig, *Learn to Write Badly: How to Succeed in the Social Sciences* (New York: Cambridge University Press, 2013); Robert Goldbort, *Writing for Science* (New Haven, CT: Yale University Press, 2006); Anne E. Greene, *Writing Science in Plain English* (Chicago: University of Chicago Press, 2013); Harold Rabinowitz and Suzanne Vogel, *The Manual of Scientific Style: A Guide for Authors, Editors, and Researchers* (Cambridge, MA: Academic Press, 2009); Joshua Schimel, *Writing Science: How to Write Papers That Get Cited and Proposals That Get Funded* (New York: Oxford University Press, 2012).

6. THE OTHER TONGUE

1   Stacey Cozart, Gry Sandholm Jensen, Tine Wirenfeldt Jensen, and Gitte Wichmann-Hansen, "Grappling with Identity Issues: Danish Doctoral Student Views on Writing in L2 English" (paper presented at the English in Europe Conference, Copenhagen, April 2013). The quotations come from Danish doctoral students who attended an introductory course in academic writing in English at the Faculty of Arts at Aarhus University in 2011 and 2012.

2   Stephen Bailey, *Academic Writing: A Handbook for International Students*, 4th ed. (London: Routledge, 2014); Caroline Brandt, *Read,*

Research and Write: Academic Skills for ESL Students in Higher Education (London: Sage, 2009); Ernest Hall and Carrie S. Y. Jung, *Reflecting on Writing: Composing in English for ESL Students* (Ann Arbor: University of Michigan Press, 2000); Sheryl Holt, *Success with Graduate and Scholarly Writing: A Guide for Non-native Writers of English* (Burnsville, MN: Aspen, 2004); Hilary Glasman-Deal, *Science Research Writing for Non-native Speakers of English* (London: Imperial College Press, 2010); Valerie Matarese, ed., *Supporting Research Writing: Roles and Challenges in Multilingual Settings* (Oxford, UK: Chandos, 2013); Norman W. Evans, Neil J. Anderson, and William G. Eggington, eds., *ESL Readers and Writers in Higher Education: Understanding Challenges, Providing Support* (London: Routledge, 2015); Donna M. Johnson and Duane H. Roen, eds., *Richness in Writing: Empowering ESL Students* (New York: Longman, 1989); John Flowerdew and Matthew Peacock, *Research Perspectives on English for Academic Purposes* (Cambridge: Cambridge University Press, 2001), Claire J. Kramsch, *The Multilingual Subject* (Oxford: Oxford University Press, 2010); Theresa Lillis and Mary Jane Curry, *Academic Writing in a Global Context: The Politics and Practices of Publishing in English* (New York: Routledge, 2010); Ramona Tang, ed., *Academic Writing in a Second or Foreign Language: Issues and Challenges Facing ESL/EFL Academic Writers in Higher Education Contexts* (New York: Continuum, 2012); Vaughan Rapatahana and Pauline Bunce, *English Language as Hydra: Its Impacts on Non-English Language Cultures* (Bristol, UK: Multilingual Matters, 2012).

PART III: SOCIAL HABITS

1   Mason Currey, *Daily Rituals: How Artists Work* (New York: Knopf, 2013); Gary Olson and Lynn Worsham, eds., *Critical Intellectuals on Writing* (New York: State University of New York Press, 2010); Robert S. Boynton, *The New New Journalism: Conversations with American's Best Nonfiction Writers on Their Craft* (New York: Knopf Doubleday, 2007); Mark Kramer and Wendy Call, eds., *Telling True Stories: A Nonfiction Writers' Guide from the Nieman Foundation at Harvard University* (New York: Plume, 2007); Hilton Obenzinger, *How We Write: The Varieties of Writing Experience* (Palo Alto, CA: Stanford University Press, 2015).

7. WRITING FOR OTHERS

1   Christopher Grey, *A Very Short, Fairly Interesting, and Reasonably Cheap Book about Studying Organisations*, 3rd ed. (London: Sage, 2013), 3.

2   See, for example, Ken Hyland, "Stance and Engagement: A Model of Interaction in Academic Discourse," *Discourse Studies* 7, no. 2 (2005):

173–192; Alecia Marie Magnifico, "Writing for Whom? Cognition, Motivation, and a Writer's Audience," *Educational Psychologist* 45, no. 3 (2010): 167–184; and Peter Vandenberg, "Coming to Terms: Audience," *English Journal* 84, no. 4 (1995): 79–80.

3   Dan Melzer, *Assignments across the Curriculum: A National Study of College Writing* (Boulder, CO: Utah State University Press, 2014), 106.

4   Gillie Bolton with Stephen Rowland, *Inspirational Writing for Academic Publication* (London: Sage, 2014), 69.

5   William P. Germano, *Getting It Published: A Guide for Scholars and Anyone Else Serious about Serious Books*, 2nd ed. (Chicago: University of Chicago Press, 2008); Kathleen A. Kendall-Tackett, *How to Write for a General Audience: A Guide for Academics Who Want to Share Their Knowledge with the World and Have Fun Doing It* (Washington, DC: American Psychology Association, 2007); Lynn P. Nygaard, *Writing for Scholars: A Practical Guide to Making Sense and Being Heard* (Oslo: Universitetsforlaget, 2008); Laurel Richardson, *Writing Strategies: Reaching Diverse Audiences* (Newbury Park, CA: Sage, 1990); Ann Curthoys and Ann McGrath, *How to Write History That People Want to Read* (Basingstoke, UK: Palgrave Macmillan, 2011); Dennis Meredith, *Explaining Research: How to Reach Key Audiences to Advance Your Work* (New York: Oxford University Press, 2010); Robert J. Nash, *Liberating Scholarly Writing: The Power of Personal Narrative* (New York: Teachers College Press, 2004); Gerald Graff, *Clueless in Academe: How Schooling Obscures the Life of the Mind* (New Haven, CT: Yale University Press, 2003); Marjorie Garber, *Academic Instincts* (Princeton, NJ: Princeton University Press, 2003); Sarah Perrault, *Communicating Popular Science: From Deficit to Democracy* (New York: Palgrave Macmillan, 2013); Angelika Bammer and Ruth-Ellen Boetcher Joeres, eds., *The Future of Scholarly Writing: Critical Interventions* (New York: Springer, 2015); Jonathan Culler and Kevin Lamb, eds., *Just Being Difficult? Academic Writing in the Public Arena* (Stanford, CA: Stanford University Press, 2003).

8. WRITING WITH OTHERS

1   See, for example, Jeanette Harris, "Towards a Working Definition of Collaborative Writing," in *Author-ity and Textuality: Current Views of Collaborative Writing*, ed. James S. Leonard, Christine E. Wharton, Robert Murray, and Jeanette Harris (West Cornwall, CT: Locust Hill, 1994), 77–84; Lisa Ede and Andrea Lunsford, *Singular Texts/Plural Authors* (Carbondale: Southern Illinois University Press, 1990), 70.

2 James S. Leonard, Christine E. Wharton, Robert Murray, and Jeanette Harris, eds., *Author-ity and Textuality: Current Views of Collaborative Writing* (West Cornwall, CT: Locust Hill, 1994); Jane Speedy and Jonathan Wyatt, eds., *Collaborative Writing as Inquiry* (Newcastle upon Tyne, UK: Cambridge Scholars, 2014); Bruce Speck, Teresa R. Johnson, Catherine P. Dice, and Leon B. Heaton, *Collaborative Writing: An Annotated Bibliography* (Greenwich, CT: Information Age, 2008); Ede and Lunsford, *Singular Texts*; Andrea Lunsford and Lisa Ede, *Writing Together: Collaboration in Theory and Practice* (Boston: Bedford Books, 2011); Ernest Lockridge and Laurel Richardson, *Travels with Ernest: Crossing the Literary/Sociological Divide* (Walnut Creek, CA: AltaMira, 2004); Ken Gale and Jonathan Wyatt, *Between the Two: A Nomadic Inquiry into Collaborative Writing and Subjectivity* (Newcastle upon Tyne, UK: Cambridge Scholars, 2010); Douglas Hofstadter and Daniel Dennett, *The Mind's I* (New York: Basic Books, 1981); Sandra M. Gilbert and Susan Gubar, *The Madwoman in the Attic: The Woman Writer and the Nineteenth-Century Literary Imagination* (New Haven, CT: Yale University Press, 1980); Anthony Grafton and Joanna Weinberg, *"I Have Always Loved the Holy Tongue": Isaac Casaubon, the Jews, and a Forgotten Chapter in Renaissance Scholarship* (Cambridge, MA: Harvard University Press, 2011).

9. WRITING AMONG OTHERS

1 Francesco Cirillo, "The Pomodoro Technique," revision 1.3, June 15, 2007, http://baomee.info/pdf/technique/1.pdf.

2 See, for example, Matthew R. McGrail, Claire M. Rickard, and Rebecca Jones, "Publish or Perish: A Systematic Review of Interventions to Increase Academic Publication Rates," *Higher Education Research Development* 25, no. 1 (2006): 19–35; Rowena Murray and Mary Newton, "Writing Retreat as Structured Intervention: Margin or Mainstream?," *Higher Education Research & Development* 28, no. 5 (2009): 541–553; Virginia Dickson-Swift. Erica L. James, Sandra Kippen, Lyn Talbot, Glenda Verrinder, and Bernadette Ward, "A Non-residential Alternative to Off Campus Writers' Retreats for Academics," *Journal of Further and Higher Education* 33, no. 3 (2009): 229–239; Iain Macleod, Laura Steckley, and Rowena Murray, "Time Is Not Enough: Promoting Strategic Engagement with Writing for Publication," *Studies in Higher Education* 37, no. 6 (2012): 641–654; Wendy Belcher, "Reflections on Ten Years of Teaching Writing for Publication to Graduate Students and Junior Faculty," *Journal of Scholarly Publishing* 40, no. 2 (2009): 184–199.

3 Barbara Grant and Sally Knowles, "Flights of Imagination: Academic Women Be(com)ing Writers," *International Journal for Academic*

Development 5, no. 1 (2000): 6–19; Grant and Knowles, "Walking the Labyrinth: The Holding Embrace of Academic Writing Retreats" in *Writing Groups for Doctoral Education and Beyond: Innovations in Practice and Theory*, ed. Claire Aitchison and Cally Guerin (New York: Routledge, 2014), 110–127.

4   Jean Lave and Étienne Wenger, *Situated Learning: Legitimate Peripheral Participation* (Cambridge: Cambridge University Press, 1991), 94.

5   Judy Reeves, *Writing Alone, Writing Together: A Guide for Writers and Writing Groups* (Novato, CA: New World Library, 2002); Pat Schneider, *Writing Alone and with Others* (New York: Oxford University Press, 2005); Julie Phillips, *The Writers' Group Handbook: Getting the Best for and from Your Writing Group* (Hampshire, UK: John Hunt, 2014); Barbara M. Grant, *Academic Writing Retreats: A Facilitator's Guide* (Milperra, NSW: Higher Education Research and Development Society of Australasia, 2008); Rowena Murray, *Writing in Social Spaces: A Social Processes Approach to Academic Writing* (London: Routledge, 2014); DeNel Rehberg Sedo, *Reading Communities from Salons to Cyberspace* (Basingstoke, UK: Palgrave Macmillan, 2011); Andrew Abbott, *Chaos of Disciplines* (Chicago: University of Chicago Press, 2001); Anna Duszak, ed., *Cultures and Styles of Academic Discourse* (Berlin: Mouton de Gruyter, 1997); Ken Hyland, *Disciplinary Discourses: Social Interactions in Academic Writing* (Ann Arbor: University of Michigan Press, 2004); Michèle Lamont, *How Professors Think: Inside the Curious World of Academic Judgment* (Cambridge, MA: Harvard University Press, 2010); Steven Mailloux, *Disciplinary Identities: Rhetorical Paths of English, Speech, and Composition* (New York: Modern Language Association, 2006); Tony Becher and Paul Trowler, *Academic Tribes and Territories: Intellectual Enquiry and the Culture of Disciplines*, 2nd ed. (Philadelphia: Open University Press, 2003).

PART IV: EMOTIONAL HABITS

1   Sir Arthur Quiller-Couch, *On the Art of Writing: Lectures Delivered in the University of Cambridge 1913–1914* (Cambridge: Cambridge University Press, 1916), 234–35; William Morris, "The Beauty of Life," in *Hopes and Fears for Art* (London: Longmans, Green, 1919), 114.

10. THE PLEASURE PRINCIPLE

1   Katty Kay and Claire Shipman, *The Confidence Code: The Science and Art of Self-Assurance—What Women Should Know* (New York: HarperCollins, 2014).

2 Paul J. Silvia, *How to Write a Lot: A Practical Guide to Productive Academic Writing* (Washington, DC: American Psychological Association, 2007), 7.

3 Mihaly Csikszentmihalyi, *Creativity: Flow and the Psychology of Discovery and Invention* (New York : Harper Perennial, 1997).

4 Alice Brand, *The Psychology of Writing: The Affective Experience* (New York: Greenwood, 1989), 45.

5 Ronald T. Kellogg, *The Psychology of Writing* (Oxford: Oxford University Press, 1994). See also Laura R. Micciche, *Doing Emotion: Rhetoric, Writing, Teaching* (Portsmouth, NH: Boynton/Cook, 2007); Dale Jacobs and Laura R. Micciche, eds., *A Way to Move: Rhetorics of Emotion and Composition Studies* (Portsmouth, NH: Heinemann, 2003); Angela Dwyer, Bridget Lewis, Fiona McDonald, and Marcelle Burns, "It's Always a Pleasure: Exploring Productivity and Pleasure in a Writing Group for Early Career Academics," *Studies in Continuing Education* 34, no. 2 (2012): 129–144; Jenny Cameron, Karen Nairn, and Jane Higgins, "Demystifying Academic Writing: Reflections on Emotions, Know-How and Academic Identity," *Journal of Geography in Higher Education* 33, no. 2 (2009): 269–284; Alice Flaherty, *The Midnight Disease: The Drive to Write, Writer's Block, and the Creative Brain* (Boston: Houghton Mifflin, 2004); Anna Neumann, "Professing Passion: Emotion in the Scholarship of Professors at Research Universities," *American Educational Research Journal* 43, no. 3 (2006): 381–424; Robert S. Root-Bernstein and Michele Root-Bernstein, "Learning to Think with Emotion," *Chronicle of Higher Education* 46, no. 19 (2000): 64; Rebekah Widdowfield, "The Place of Emotions in Academic Research," *Area* 32, no. 2 (2000): 199–208.

6 Robert Boice, "Which Is More Productive, Writing in Binge Patterns of Creative Illness or in Moderation?," *Written Communication* 14, no.4 (1997): 436; Silvia, *How to Write a Lot*, 102.

7 Silvia, *How to Write a Lot*, 4.

8 On positivity and creativity, see Barbara Fredrickson, *Positivity* (New York: Crown Archetype, 2009); on intrinsic motivation, Richard Ryan and Edward Deci, "Self-Determination Theory and the Facilitation of Intrinsic Motivation, Social Development, and Well-Being," *American Psychologist* 55 no. 1 (2000): 68–78; on the relationship between positive affect and luck, Richard Wiseman, *The Luck Factor: The Scientific Study of the Lucky Mind* (New York: Random House, 2011). See also the "Things to Read" section at the end of Chapter 11.

9 Fredrickson, *Positivity*, 12.

10 Barbara L. Fredrickson and Christine Branigan, "Positive Emotions Broaden the Scope of Attention and Thought-Action Repertoires," *Cognition and Emotion* 19, no. 3 (2005): 313–332.

11 James Axtell, *The Pleasures of Academe: A Celebration and Defense of Higher Education* (Lincoln: University of Nebraska Press, 1998); Kim Stafford, *The Muses among Us: Eloquent Listening and Other Pleasures of the Writer's Craft* (Athens: University of Georgia Press, 2003); Roland Barthes, *The Pleasure of the Text*, trans. Richard Miller (1973; New York: Hill and Wang, 1975); Roland Barthes, *The Grain of the Voice: Interviews 1962–1980*, trans. Linda Coverdale (New York: Hill and Wang, 1986), 178; Ray Bradbury, *Zen in the Art of Writing* (Santa Barbara, CA: Joshua Odell, 1994); Bill Bryson, *Mother Tongue* (London: Penguin 1991); Anthony Burgess, *A Mouthful of Air: Language and Languages, Especially English* (London: Cornerstone, 1992); Roy Peter Clark, *The Glamour of Grammar: A Guide to the Magic and Mystery of Practical English* (London: Hachette UK, 2010); Karen E. Gordon, *The Deluxe Transitive Vampire: The Ultimate Handbook of Grammar for the Innocent, the Eager, and the Doomed* (New York: Pantheon Books, 1993); Constance Hale, *Sin and Syntax: How to Craft Wicked Good Prose*, rev. ed. (New York: Three Rivers, 2013); Lynne Truss, *Eats, Shoots & Leaves: The Zero Tolerance Approach to Punctuation* (London: Profile Books, 2003).

11. RISK AND RESILIENCE

1 Howard S. Becker, *Writing for Social Scientists: How to Start and Finish Your Thesis, Book, or Article*, 2nd ed. (Chicago: University of Chicago Press, 2007), 110, 113.

2 Richard Wiseman, *The Luck Factor: The Scientific Study of the Lucky Mind* (New York: Random House, 2011), 21–37.

3 Quoted in Doreen Marcial Poreba, *Idiot's Guides: Unlocking Your Creativity* (London: Penguin, 2015), 292.

4 See, for example, Princeton psychologist Johannes Haushofer's "CV of failures," which he posted on Twitter in April 2016. "CV of Failures: Princeton Professor Publishes Résumé of His Career Lows," *Guardian*, April 30, 2016.

5 Stanley Fish, *Versions of Academic Freedom: From Professionalism to Revolution* (Chicago: University of Chicago Press, 2014); Linda Cooper and Lucia Thesen, *Risk in Academic Writing: Postgraduate Students,*

Their Teachers and the Making of Knowledge (Bristol, UK: Multilingual Matters, 2013); Mark Edmundson, *Why Write? A Master Class on the Art of Writing and Why It Matters* (New York: Bloomsbury, 2016); Jordan Rosenfeld, *A Writer's Guide to Persistence: How to Create a Lasting and Productive Writing Practice* (Blue Ash, OH: F+W Media, 2015); Elizabeth Gilbert, *Big Magic: Creative Living beyond Fear* (New York: Riverhead Books, 2015); Joni B. Cole, *Toxic Feedback: Helping Writers Survive and Thrive* (Hanover, NH: University Press of New England, 2006); Catherine Wald, *The Resilient Writer: Tales of Rejection and Triumph from 23 Top Authors* (New York: Persea Books, 2005); Barbara Fredrickson, *Positivity* (New York: Crown Archetype, 2009); Scott Barry Kaufman and Carolyn Gregoire, *Wired to Create: Unraveling the Mysteries of the Creative Mind* (New York: TarcherPerigree, 2015); Brené Brown, *Rising Strong* (New York: Spiegel and Grau, 2015); Emma Seppala, *The Happiness Track: How to Apply the Science of Happiness to Accelerate Your Success* (London: Piatkus Books, 2016; Amy Cuddy, *Presence: Bringing Your Boldest Self to Your Biggest Challenges* (Boston: Little, Brown, 2015); Anders Ericsson and Robert Pool, *Peak: Secrets from the New Science of Expertise* (New York: Random House, 2016); Angela Duckworth, *Grit: The Power of Passion and Perseverance* (New York: Scribner, 2016); Wiseman, *Luck Factor*; Mihaly Csikszentmihalyi, *Flow: The Psychology of Happiness* (New York: Random House, 2013); Martin E. P. Seligman, *Flourish: A Visionary New Understanding of Happiness and Well-Being* (New York: Simon and Schuster, 2012).

12. METAPHORS TO WRITE BY

1 William Shakespeare, *A Midsummer Night's Dream*, act 5, scene 1, lines 16–17.

2 George Lakoff and Mark Johnson, *Metaphors We Live By* (Chicago: University of Chicago Press, 1980), 144, 158.

3 Ibid., 10.

4 "Turbocharge your writing": Maria Gardiner and Hugh Kearns, "Turbocharge Your Writing Today," *Nature* 475 (2011): 129–130; "Fly in your writercopter": Hillary Rettig, *The Seven Secrets of the Prolific: The Definitive Guide to Overcoming Procrastination, Perfectionism, and Writer's Block* (Infinite Art, 2011), 102–104.

5 Barbara Kamler and Pat Thomson, *Helping Doctoral Students Write: Pedagogies for Supervision*, 2nd ed. (London: Routledge, 2014), 30, 36.

6 Parker J. Palmer, *The Courage to Teach: Exploring the Inner Land-scape of a Teacher's Life*, 10th anniversary ed. (San Francisco: Jossey-Bass, 2007), 153–154.

7 Ibid., 154.

8 Johann Wolfgang von Goethe, *Elective Affinities* (Oxford: Oxford University Press, 2008), 122; Sir Arthur Conan Doyle, *A Study in Scarlet* (London: Bibliolis Books, 2010), 52.

9 Daniel P. McAdams, *The Redemptive Self: Stories Americans Live By* (Oxford: Oxford University Press, 2006) 26–27, 44.

10 Robert Neimeyer, "Re-storying Loss: Fostering Growth in the Post-traumatic Narrative" in *The Handbook of Posttraumatic Growth: Research and Practice*, ed. Lawrence G. Calhoun and Richard G. Tedeschi (Mahwah, NJ: Lawrence Erlbaum, 2006), 68–80; Lila Jacobs, José Cintrón, and Cecil E. Canton, eds., *The Politics of Survival in Academia: Narratives of Inequity, Resilience, and Success* (Lanham, MD: Rowan and Littlefield, 2002).

11 Anne Lamott, *Bird by Bird: Some Instructions on Writing and Life* (New York: Knopf Doubleday, 2007), 21.

12 For more on how concrete language can aid readers' understanding of abstract concepts, see Stephen Pinker, *The Sense of Style: The Thinking Person's Guide to Writing in the 21st Century* (New York: Penguin, 2015); Mark Sadoski, Ernest T. Goetz, and Joyce B. Fritz, "Impact of Concreteness on Comprehensibility, Interest, and Memory for Text: Implications for Dual Coding Theory and Text Design," *Journal of Educational Psychology* 85, no. 2 (1993): 291–304.

13 Denis Donoghue, *Metaphor* (Cambridge, MA: Harvard University Press, 2014); Andrew Goatly, *The Language of Metaphors*, 2nd ed. (London: Routledge, 2011); Alan Wall, *Myth, Metaphor, and Science* (Chester, UK: Chester Academic Press, 2009); Rick Wormeli, *Metaphors & Analogies: Power Tools for Teaching Any Subject* (Portland, ME: Stenhouse, 2009); L. David Ritchie, *Metaphor* (Cambridge: Cambridge University Press, 2013); Raymond W. Gibbs Jr., ed., *The Cambridge Handbook of Metaphor and Thought* (Cambridge: Cambridge University Press, 2008); Murray Knowles and Rosamund Moon, *Introducing Metaphor* (London: Routledge, 2006); J. Berenike Herrmann and Tony Berber Sardinha, eds., *Metaphor in Specialist Discourse* (Amsterdam: John Benjamins, 2015); Timothy D. Giles, *Motives for Metaphor in Scientific and Technical Communication* (Amityville, NY: Baywood,

2007); Lakoff and Johnson, *Metaphors We Live By*; George Lakoff, *Women, Fire and Dangerous Things: What Categories Reveal about the Mind* (Chicago: University of Chicago Press, 1987).

CONCLUSION

1   Pierre Bourdieu, *Outline of a Theory of Practice* (Cambridge: Cambridge University Press, 2002), 72–78.

2   Helena K. Rene, *China's Sent-Down Generation: Public Administration and the Legacies of Mao's Rustication Program* (Washington, DC: Georgetown University Press, 2013).

3   Jung H. Yun and Mary Deane Sorcinelli, "When Mentoring Is the Medium: Lessons Learned from a Faculty Development Initiative," *To Improve the Academy* 27 (2009): 365–384.

4   Jean-Michel Fortin and David J. Currie, "Big Science vs. Little Science: How Scientific Impact Scales with Funding," *PLOS ONE* 8, no. 6 (2013): e65263, doi:10.1371/journal.pone.0065263.

5   Martin Heidegger, "Building Dwelling Thinking," in *Poetry, Language, Thought*, trans. Albert Hofstadter (New York: Harper Colophon Books, 1971), 143.

6   Ibid., 152.

7   Martin Heidegger, ". . . Poetically Man Dwells . . ." ibid., 212, 224–225. The title of Heidegger's essay comes from Friedrich von Hölderlin's poem "In lieblicher Blaue" ("In Lovely Blueness") in *Sämtliche Werke*, vol. 2, *Gedichte nach 1800*, ed. Friedrich Beißner (Stuttgart: Kohlhammer, 1953), 372.

8   Emily Dickinson, "I Dwell in Possibility," in *Dickinson: Selected Poems and Commentaries*, ed. Helen Vendler (Cambridge, MA: Harvard University Press, 2010), 222.

9   Pierre Bourdieu, *Homo Academicus*, trans. Peter Collier (Stanford, CA: Stanford University Press, 1988).

AFTERWORD

1   Malvina Reynolds, "Little Boxes" (Schroder Music Company, 1962, 1990).

Bibliography

Abbott, Andrew. *Chaos of Disciplines.* Chicago: University of Chicago Press, 2001.

Argyris, Chris, and Donald A. Schön. *Organizational Learning: A Theory of Action Perspective.* Reading, MA: Addison-Wesley, 1978.

Axtell, James. *The Pleasures of Academe: A Celebration and Defense of Higher Education.* Lincoln: University of Nebraska Press, 1998.

Badenhorst, Cecile. *Productive Writing: Becoming a Prolific Academic Writer.* Pretoria, South Africa: Van Schaik, 2010.

Bailey, Stephen. *Academic Writing: A Handbook for International Students.* 4th ed. London: Routledge, 2014.

Bammer, Angelika, and Ruth-Ellen Boetcher Joeres, eds. *The Future of Scholarly Writing: Critical Interventions.* New York: Springer, 2015.

Barthes, Roland. *The Grain of the Voice: Interviews 1962–1980.* Translated by Linda Coverdale. New York: Hill and Wang, 1986.

———. *The Pleasure of the Text.* Translated by Richard Miller. 1973. New York: Hill and Wang, 1975.

Becher, Tony, and Paul Trowler. *Academic Tribes and Territories: Intellectual Enquiry and the Culture of Disciplines.* 2nd ed. Philadelphia: Open University Press, 2003.

Becker, Howard S. *Writing for Social Scientists: How to Start and Finish Your Thesis, Book, or Article.* 2nd ed. Chicago: University of Chicago Press, 2007.

Belcher, Wendy. "Reflections on Ten Years of Teaching Writing for Publication to Graduate Students and Junior Faculty." *Journal of Scholarly Publishing* 40, no. 2 (2009): 184–199.

————. *Writing Your Journal Article in 12 Weeks: A Guide to Academic Publishing Success*. Los Angeles: Sage, 2009.

Berg, Maggie, and Barbara Seeber. *Slow Professor: Challenging the Culture of Speed in the Academy*. Toronto: University of Toronto Press, 2016.

Biggs, John, and Catherine Tang. *Teaching for Quality Learning at University*. Berkshire, UK: Open University Press, 2011.

Billig, Michael. *Learn to Write Badly: How to Succeed in the Social Sciences*. New York: Cambridge University Press, 2013.

Boice, Robert. "Contingency Management in Writing and the Appearance of Creative Ideas: Implications for the Treatment of Writing Blocks." *Behaviour Research and Therapy* 21, no. 5 (1983): 537–543.

————. "Procrastination, Busyness and Bingeing." *Behaviour Research and Therapy* 27, no. 6 (1989): 605–611.

————. *Professors as Writers: A Self-Help Guide to Productive Writing*. Stillwater, OK: New Forums, 1990.

————. "Which Is More Productive, Writing in Binge Patterns of Creative Illness or in Moderation?" *Written Communication* 14, no. 4 (1997): 435–459.

Bolker, Joan. *Writing Your Dissertation in Fifteen Minutes a Day: A Guide to Starting, Revising, and Finishing Your Doctoral Thesis*. New York: Holt, 1998.

Bolton, Gillie, with Stephen Rowland. *Inspirational Writing for Academic Publication*. London: Sage, 2014.

Bourdieu, Pierre. *Homo Academicus*. Translated by Peter Collier. Stanford, CA: Stanford University Press, 1988.

————. *Outline of a Theory of Practice*. Cambridge: Cambridge University Press, 2002.

Boynton, Robert S. *The New New Journalism: Conversations with America's Best Nonfiction Writers on Their Craft*. New York: Knopf Doubleday, 2007.

Bradbury, Ray. *Zen in the Art of Writing*. Santa Barbara, CA: Joshua Odell, 1994.

Brand, Alice. *The Psychology of Writing: The Affective Experience*. New York: Greenwood, 1989.

Brande, Dorothea. *Becoming a Writer.* New York: Harcourt Brace, 1934.

Brandt, Caroline. *Read, Research and Write: Academic Skills for ESL Students in Higher Education.* London: Sage, 2009.

Brown, Brené. *Rising Strong.* New York: Spiegel and Grau, 2015.

Bryson, Bill. *Mother Tongue.* London: Penguin, 1991.

Bukowski, Charles. *The Last Night of the Earth Poems.* New York: Ecco, 2002.

Burgess, Anthony. "The Art of Fiction No. 48." Interview by John Cullinan. *Paris Review* 56 (1973): 121.

————. *A Mouthful of Air: Language and Languages, Especially English.* London: Cornerstone, 1992.

Cameron, Jenny, Karen Nairn, and Jane Higgins. "Demystifying Academic Writing: Reflections on Emotions, Know-How and Academic Identity." *Journal of Geography in Higher Education* 33, no. 2 (2009): 269–284.

Cameron, Julia. *The Artist's Way: A Spiritual Path to Higher Creativity.* New York: Tarcher/Putnam, 1992.

Campbell, Don. *The Mozart Effect: Tapping the Power of Music to Heal the Body, Strengthen the Mind, and Unlock the Creative Spirit.* New York: HarperCollins, 2001.

Carter, Susan, and Deborah Laurs, eds. *Giving Feedback on Research Writing: A Handbook for Supervisors and Advisors.* London: Routledge, 2017.

Charney, Noah. "Anthony Grafton: How I Write." *The Daily Beast,* July 17, 2013. http://www.thedailybeast.com/articles/2013/07/17/anthony -grafton-how-i-write.html.

Cirillo, Francesco. "The Pomodoro Technique." Revision 1.3. June 15, 2007. http://baomee.info/pdf/technique/1.pdf.

Clark, Roy Peter. *The Glamour of Grammar: A Guide to the Magic and Mystery of Practical English.* London: Hachette UK, 2010.

————. *Writing Tools: 50 Essential Strategies for Every Writer.* New York: Little, Brown, 2008.

Cole, Joni B. *Toxic Feedback: Helping Writers Survive and Thrive.* Hanover, NH: University Press of New England, 2006.

Coleridge, Samuel Taylor. "Kubla Khan." In *The Complete Poems*, edited by William Keach, 249–251. London: Penguin, 1997.

Cook, Claire K. *Line by Line: How to Improve Your Own Writing.* Boston: Modern Language Association of America, 1985.

Cooper, Linda, and Lucia Thesen. *Risk in Academic Writing: Postgraduate Students, Their Teachers and the Making of Knowledge.* Bristol, UK: Multilingual Matters, 2013.

Covey, Stephen R. *The Seven Habits of Highly Effective People.* New York: Simon and Schuster, 2004.

Covey, Stephen R., A. Roger Merrill, and Rebecca R. Merrill. *First Things First.* New York: Simon and Schuster, 1995.

Cozart, Stacey, Gry Sandholm Jensen, Tine Wirenfeldt Jensen, and Gitte Wichmann-Hansen. "Grappling with Identity Issues: Danish Doctoral Student Views on Writing in L2 English." Paper presented at the English in Europe Conference, Copenhagen, April 2013.

Crick, Francis. "The Impact of Linus Pauling on Molecular Biology." In *Proceedings of the Conference on the Life and Work of Linus Pauling (1901–1994): A Discourse on the Art of Biography* (Corvallis: Oregon State University Libraries Special Collections, 1996).

Csikszentmihalyi, Mihaly. *Creativity: Flow and the Psychology of Discovery and Invention.* New York: Harper Perennial, 1997.

———. *Flow: The Psychology of Happiness.* New York: Random House, 2013.

Cuddy, Amy. *Presence: Bringing Your Boldest Self to Your Biggest Challenges.* Boston: Little, Brown, 2015.

Culler, Jonathan, and Kevin Lamb, eds. *Just Being Difficult? Academic Writing in the Public Arena.* Stanford, CA: Stanford University Press, 2003.

Currey, Mason. *Daily Rituals: How Artists Work.* New York: Knopf, 2013.

Curthoys, Ann, and Ann McGrath. *How to Write History That People Want to Read.* Basingstoke, UK: Palgrave Macmillan, 2011.

"CV of Failures: Princeton Professor Publishes Résumé of His Career Lows." *Guardian*, April 30, 2016.

Darwin, Charles. *Autobiography and Selected Letters.* Edited by Francis Darwin. New York: Dover, 1958.

Deleuze, Gilles, and Félix Guattari. *A Thousand Plateaus: Capitalism and Schizophrenia*. London: Athlone, 1988.

Dickinson, Emily. *Dickinson: Selected Poems and Commentaries*. Edited by Helen Vendler. Cambridge, MA: Harvard University Press, 2010.

Dickson-Swift, Virginia, Erica L. James, Sandra Kippen, Lyn Talbot, Glenda Verrinder, and Bernadette Ward. "A Non-residential Alternative to Off Campus Writers' Retreats for Academics." *Journal of Further and Higher Education* 33, no. 3 (2009): 229–239.

Dillard, Annie. *The Writing Life*. New York: Simon and Schuster, 2000.

Donoghue, Denis. *Metaphor*. Cambridge, MA: Harvard University Press, 2014.

Doyle, Sir Arthur Conan. *A Study in Scarlet*. London: Bibliolis Books, 2010.

Duckworth, Angela. *Grit: The Power of Passion and Perseverance*. New York: Scribner, 2016.

Duhigg, Charles. *The Power of Habit: Why We Do What We Do and How to Change*. London: Heinemann, 2012.

Duszak, Anna, ed. *Cultures and Styles of Academic Discourse*. Berlin: Mouton de Gruyter, 1997.

Dweck, Carol S. *Mindset: The New Psychology of Success*. New York: Ballantine, 2008.

Dwyer, Angela, Bridget Lewis, Fiona McDonald, and Marcelle Burns. "It's Always a Pleasure: Exploring Productivity and Pleasure in a Writing Group for Early Career Academics." *Studies in Continuing Education* 34, no. 2 (2012): 129–144.

Ede, Lisa, and Andrea Lunsford. *Singular Texts/Plural Authors*. Carbondale: Southern Illinois University Press, 1990.

Edmundson, Mark. *Why Write? A Master Class on the Art of Writing and Why It Matters*. New York: Bloomsbury, 2016.

Elbow, Peter. *Writing with Power: Techniques for Mastering the Writing Process*. Oxford: Oxford University Press, 1998.

Ericsson, Anders, and Robert Pool. *Peak: Secrets from the New Science of Expertise*. New York: Random House, 2016.

Evans, Norman W., Neil J. Anderson, and William G. Eggington, eds. *ESL Readers and Writers in Higher Education: Understanding Challenges, Providing Support*. London: Routledge, 2015.

Fish, Stanley. *How to Write a Sentence: And How to Read One*. New York: HarperCollins, 2011.

——. *Versions of Academic Freedom: From Professionalism to Revolution*. Chicago: University of Chicago Press, 2014.

Flaherty, Alice. *The Midnight Disease: The Drive to Write, Writer's Block, and the Creative Brain*. Boston: Houghton Mifflin, 2004.

Flowerdew, John, and Matthew Peacock. *Research Perspectives on English for Academic Purposes*. Cambridge: Cambridge University Press, 2001.

Fortin, Jean-Michel, and David J. Currie. "Big Science vs. Little Science: How Scientific Impact Scales with Funding." *PLOS ONE* 8, no. 6 (2013): e65263. doi:10.1371/journal.pone.0065263.

Fredrickson, Barbara. *Positivity*. New York: Crown Archetype, 2009.

Fredrickson, Barbara, and Christine Branigan. "Positive Emotions Broaden the Scope of Attention and Thought-Action Repertoires." *Cognition and Emotion* 19, no. 3 (2005): 313–332.

Gale, Ken, and Jonathan Wyatt. *Between the Two: A Nomadic Inquiry into Collaborative Writing and Subjectivity*. Newcastle upon Tyne, UK: Cambridge Scholars, 2010.

Garber, Marjorie. *Academic Instincts*. Princeton, NJ: Princeton University Press, 2003.

Gardiner, Maria, and Hugh Kearns. "Turbocharge Your Writing Today." *Nature* 475 (2011): 129–130.

Garner, Bryan A. *Legal Writing in Plain English: A Text with Exercises*. Chicago: University of Chicago Press, 2013.

Geller, Anne Ellen, and Michele Eodice. *Working with Faculty Writers*. Boulder, CO: Utah State University Press, 2013.

Germano, William. *Getting It Published: A Guide for Scholars and Anyone Else Serious about Serious Books*. 2nd ed. Chicago: University of Chicago Press, 2008.

Gibbs, Raymond W., Jr., ed. *The Cambridge Handbook of Metaphor and Thought*. Cambridge: Cambridge University Press, 2008.

Gilbert, Elizabeth. *Big Magic: Creative Living beyond Fear.* New York: Riverhead Books, 2015.

Gilbert, Sandra M., and Susan Gubar. *The Madwoman in the Attic: The Woman Writer and the Nineteenth-Century Literary Imagination.* New Haven, CT: Yale University Press, 1980.

Giles, Timothy D. *Motives for Metaphor in Scientific and Technical Communication.* Amityville, NY: Baywood, 2007.

Glasman-Deal, Hilary. *Science Research Writing for Non-native Speakers of English.* London: Imperial College Press, 2010.

Goatly, Andrew. *The Language of Metaphors.* 2nd ed. London: Routledge, 2011.

Goethe, Johann Wolfgang von. *Elective Affinities.* Oxford: Oxford University Press, 2008.

Goldbort, Robert. *Writing for Science.* New Haven, CT: Yale University Press, 2006.

Goodson, Patricia. *Becoming an Academic Writer: 50 Exercises for Paced, Productive, and Powerful Writing.* London: Sage, 2013.

Gordon, Karen E. *The Deluxe Transitive Vampire: The Ultimate Handbook of Grammar for the Innocent, the Eager, and the Doomed.* New York: Pantheon Books, 1993.

Gowers, Ernest. *The Complete Plain Words.* 2nd ed. London: Her Majesty's Stationery Office, 1973.

Graff, Gerald. *Clueless in Academe: How Schooling Obscures the Life of the Mind.* New Haven, CT: Yale University Press, 2003.

Grafton, Anthony, and Joanna Weinberg. *"I Have Always Loved the Holy Tongue": Isaac Casaubon, the Jews, and a Forgotten Chapter in Renaissance Scholarship.* Cambridge, MA: Harvard University Press, 2011.

Grant, Barbara M. *Academic Writing Retreats: A Facilitator's Guide.* Milperra, NSW: Higher Education Research and Development Society of Australasia, 2008.

Grant, Barbara, and Sally Knowles. "Flights of Imagination: Academic Women Be(com)ing Writers." *International Journal for Academic Development* 5, no. 1 (2000): 6–19.

———. "Walking the Labyrinth: The Holding Embrace of Academic Writing Retreats." In *Writing Groups for Doctoral Education and*

Beyond: Innovations in Practice and Theory, edited by Claire Aitchison and Cally Guerin, 110–127. New York: Routledge, 2014.

Gray, Tara. *Publish and Flourish: Become a Prolific Writer.* Las Cruces: New Mexico State University Teaching Academy, 2015.

Greene, Anne E. *Writing Science in Plain English.* Chicago: University of Chicago Press, 2013.

Greenstein, George. "Writing Is Thinking: Using Writing to Teach Science." *Astronomy Education Review* 12, no. 1 (2013).

Grey, Christopher. *A Very Short, Fairly Interesting, and Reasonably Cheap Book about Studying Organisations.* 3rd ed. London: Sage, 2013.

Hale, Constance. *Sin and Syntax: How to Craft Wickedly Good Prose.* Rev. ed. New York: Three Rivers, 2013.

Hall, Ernest, and Carrie S. Y. Jung. *Reflecting on Writing: Composing in English for ESL Students.* Ann Arbor: University of Michigan Press, 2000.

Harris, Jeanette. "Towards a Working Definition of Collaborative Writing." In *Author-ity and Textuality: Current Views of Collaborative Writing*, edited by James S. Leonard, Christine E. Wharton, Robert Murray, and Jeanette Harris., 77–84. West Cornwall, CT: Locust Hill, 1994.

Harris, Joseph. *Rewriting: How to Do Things with Texts.* Boulder, CO: Utah State University Press, 2006.

Hartley, James, and Alan Branthwaite. "The Psychologist as Wordsmith: A Questionnaire Study of the Writing Strategies of Productive British Psychologists." *Higher Education* 18, no. 4 (1989): 423–452.

Hayot, Eric. *The Elements of Academic Style: Writing for the Humanities.* New York: Columbia University Press, 2014.

Heidegger, Martin. *Poetry, Language, Thought.* Translated by Albert Hofstadter. New York: Harper Colophon Books, 1971.

Hemingway, Ernest. *A Farewell to Arms: The Hemingway Library Edition.* Edited by Seán Hemingway. New York: Scribner, 2012.

Herrmann, J. Berenike, and Tony Berber Sardinha, eds. *Metaphor in Specialist Discourse.* Amsterdam: John Benjamins, 2015.

Hjortshoj, Keith. *Understanding Writing Blocks.* New York: Oxford University Press, 2001.

Hofstadter, Douglas, and Daniel Dennett. *The Mind's I*. New York: Basic Books, 1981.

Hölderlin, Friedrich von. *Sämtliche Werke*. Vol. 2, *Gedichte nach 1800*. Edited by Friedrich Beißner. Stuttgart: Kohlhammer, 1953.

Holt, Sheryl. *Success with Graduate and Scholarly Writing: A Guide for Non-native Writers of English*. Burnsville, MN: Aspen, 2004.

hooks, bell. *Remembered Rapture: The Writer at Work*. New York: Holt, 2013.

Hughes, Ted. Introduction to *The Collected Poems*, by Sylvia Plath, 13–17. New York: Buccaneer Books, 1998.

Hyland, Ken. *Disciplinary Discourses: Social Interactions in Academic Writing*. Ann Arbor: University of Michigan Press, 2004.

———. "Stance and Engagement: A Model of Interaction in Academic Discourse." *Discourse Studies* 7, no. 2 (2005): 173–192.

Ian Fleming Publications Ltd. "Jamaica (1946–1964)." Ian Fleming website. Accessed June 21, 2016, http://www.ianfleming.com/ian-fleming /ian-fleming-inside/jamaica-1946-1964/.

Ingold, Tim. *Lines: A Brief History*. Abingdon, UK: Routledge, 2015.

Isaac, Brad. "Jerry Seinfeld's Productivity Secret." *Lifehacker Blog*. July 24, 2007. http://lifehacker.com/281626/jerry-seinfelds-productivity-secret.

Jabr, Ferris. "Why Your Brain Needs More Downtime." *Scientific American*, October 15, 2013. http://www.scientificamerican.com/article/mental -downtime/.

Jacobs, Dale, and Laura R. Micciche, eds. *A Way to Move: Rhetorics of Emotion and Composition Studies*. Portsmouth, NH: Heinemann, 2003.

Jacobs, Lila, José Cintrón, and Cecil E. Canton, eds. *The Politics of Survival in Academia: Narratives of Inequity, Resilience, and Success*. Lanham, MD: Rowan and Littlefield, 2002.

Johnson, Donna M., and Duane H. Roen, eds. *Richness in Writing: Empowering ESL Students*. New York: Longman, 1989.

Kahneman, Daniel. *Thinking, Fast and Slow*. New York: Farrar, Straus and Giroux, 2001.

Kamler, Barbara, and Pat Thomson. *Helping Doctoral Students Write: Pedagogies for Supervision*. 2nd ed. London: Routledge, 2014.

Kaufman, Scott Barry, and Carolyn Gregoire. *Wired to Create: Unraveling the Mysteries of the Creative Mind.* New York: TarcherPerigree, 2015.

Kay, Katty, and Claire Shipman. *The Confidence Code: The Science and Art of Self-Assurance—What Women Should Know.* New York: Harper-Collins, 2014.

Kellogg, Ronald T. *The Psychology of Writing.* Oxford: Oxford University Press, 1994.

Kendall-Tackett, Kathleen. *How to Write for a General Audience: A Guide for Academics Who Want to Share Their Knowledge with the World and Have Fun Doing It.* Washington, DC: American Psychology Association, 2007.

Keyes, Ralph. *The Courage to Write: How Writers Transcend Fear.* Rev. ed. New York: Holt, 2003.

King, Stephen. *On Writing: A Memoir of the Craft.* New York: Simon and Schuster, 2000.

Knowles, Murray, and Rosamund Moon. *Introducing Metaphor.* London: Routledge, 2006.

Kramer, Mark, and Wendy Call, eds. *Telling True Stories: A Nonfiction Writers' Guide from the Nieman Foundation at Harvard University.* New York: Plume, 2007.

Kramsch, Claire J. *The Multilingual Subject.* Oxford: Oxford University Press, 2010.

Lakoff, George. *Women, Fire and Dangerous Things: What Categories Reveal about the Mind.* Chicago: University of Chicago Press, 1987.

Lakoff, George, and Mark Johnson. *Metaphors We Live By.* Chicago: University of Chicago Press, 1980.

Lamont, Michèle. *How Professors Think: Inside the Curious World of Academic Judgment.* Cambridge, MA: Harvard University Press, 2010.

Lamott, Anne. *Bird by Bird: Some Instructions on Writing and Life.* New York: Knopf Doubleday, 2007.

———. *Stitches: A Handbook on Meaning, Hope, and Repair.* New York: Riverhead, 2013.

Lanham, Richard A. *Revising Prose.* 3rd ed. New York: Macmillan, 1992.

Lave, Jean, and Étienne Wenger. *Situated Learning: Legitimate Peripheral Participation*. Cambridge: Cambridge University Press, 1991.

Leonard, James S., Christine E. Wharton, Robert Murray, and Jeanette Harris, eds. *Author-ity and Textuality: Current Views of Collaborative Writing*. West Cornwall, CT: Locust Hill Press, 1994.

Lillis, Theresa, and Mary Jane Curry. *Academic Writing in a Global Context: The Politics and Practices of Publishing in English*. New York: Routledge, 2010.

Lindbergh, Anne Morrow. *Gift from the Sea*. New York: Pantheon Books, 1955.

Lockridge, Ernest, and Laurel Richardson. *Travels with Ernest: Crossing the Literary/Sociological Divide*. Walnut Creek, CA: AltaMira, 2004.

Louv, Richard. *The Nature Principle: Human Restoration and the End of Nature-Deficit Disorder*. New York: Algonquin Books, 2012.

Lu Chi. *Wen Chu: The Art of Writing*. Trans. Sam Hamill. Minneapolis, MN: Milkweed, 2000.

Lunsford, Andrea, and Lisa Ede. *Writing Together: Collaboration in Theory and Practice*. Boston: Bedford Books, 2011.

Macleod, Iain, Laura Steckley, and Rowena Murray. "Time Is Not Enough: Promoting Strategic Engagement with Writing for Publication." *Studies in Higher Education* 37, no. 6 (2012): 641–654.

Magnifico, Alecia Marie. "Writing for Whom? Cognition, Motivation, and a Writer's Audience." *Educational Psychologist* 45, no. 3 (2010): 167–184.

Mailloux, Steven. *Disciplinary Identities: Rhetorical Paths of English, Speech, and Composition*. New York: Modern Language Association, 2006.

Malcolm, Janet. "Forty-One False Starts." *New Yorker*, July 11, 1994. http://www.newyorker.com/magazine/1994/07/11/forty-one-false -starts.

Massimini, Fausto, Mihaly Csikszentmihalyi, and Antonella Delle Fave. "Flow and Biocultural Evolution." In *Optimal Experience: Psychological Studies of Flow in Consciousness*, edited by Mihaly Csikszentmihalyi and Isabella Selega Csikszentmihalyi, 60–81. Cambridge: Cambridge University Press, 1988.

Matarese, Valerie, ed. *Supporting Research Writing: Roles and Challenges in Multilingual Settings.* Oxford, UK: Chandos, 2013.

McAdams, Daniel P. *The Redemptive Self: Stories Americans Live By.* Oxford: Oxford University Press, 2006.

McGrail, Matthew R., Claire M. Rickard, and Rebecca Jones. "Publish or Perish: A Systematic Review of Interventions to Increase Academic Publication Rates." *Higher Education Research Development* 25, no. 1 (2006): 19–35.

Melzer, Dan. *Assignments across the Curriculum: A National Study of College Writing.* Boulder, CO: Utah State University Press, 2014.

Menary, Richard. "Writing as Thinking." *Language Sciences* 29, no. 5 (2007): 621–632.

Meredith, Dennis. *Explaining Research: How to Reach Key Audiences to Advance Your Work.* New York: Oxford University Press, 2010.

Micciche, Laura R. *Doing Emotion: Rhetoric, Writing, Teaching.* Portsmouth, NH: Boynton/Cook, 2007.

Miller, Henry. *Henry Miller on Writing.* New York: New Directions, 1964.

Morris, William. *Hopes and Fears for Art.* London: Longmans, Green, 1919. Project Gutenberg, 2004.

Mueller, Pam A., and Daniel M. Oppenheimer. "The Pen Is Mightier than the Keyboard." *Psychological Science* 25, no. 6 (2014): 1159–1168.

Murray, Rowena. *Writing for Academic Journals.* 3rd ed. Berkshire, UK: Open University Press, 2013.

———. *Writing in Social Spaces: A Social Processes Approach to Academic Writing.* London: Routledge, 2014.

Murray, Rowena, and Mary Newton. "Writing Retreat as Structured Intervention: Margin or Mainstream?" *Higher Education Research & Development* 28, no. 5 (2009): 541–553.

Nash, Robert J. *Liberating Scholarly Writing: The Power of Personal Narrative.* New York: Teachers College Press, 2004.

Neimeyer, Robert. "Re-storying Loss: Fostering Growth in the Posttraumatic Narrative." In *The Handbook of Posttraumatic Growth: Research and Practice,* edited by Lawrence G. Calhoun and Richard G. Tedeschi, 68–80. Mahwah, NJ: Lawrence Erlbaum, 2006.

Neumann, Anna. "Professing Passion: Emotion in the Scholarship of Professors at Research Universities." *American Educational Research Journal* 43, no. 3 (2006): 381–424.

Nygaard, Lynn P. *Writing for Scholars: A Practical Guide to Making Sense and Being Heard.* Oslo: Universitetsforlaget, 2008.

Obenzinger, Hilton. *How We Write: The Varieties of Writing Experience.* Palo Alto, CA: Stanford University Press, 2015.

Olson, Gary, and Lynn Worsham, eds. *Critical Intellectuals on Writing.* Albany: State University of New York Press, 2010.

Palmer, Parker J. *The Courage to Teach: Exploring the Inner Landscape of a Teacher's Life.* 10th anniversary ed. San Francisco: Jossey-Bass, 2007.

Perrault, Sarah. *Communicating Popular Science: From Deficit to Democracy.* New York: Palgrave Macmillan, 2013.

Perry, John. *The Art of Procrastination: A Guide to Effective Dawdling, Lollygagging and Postponing.* New York: Workman, 2012.

———. Structured Procrastination website. Accessed June 21, 2016, http://www.structuredprocrastination.com/.

Phillips, Julie. *The Writers' Group Handbook: Getting the Best for and from Your Writing Group.* Hampshire, UK: John Hunt, 2014.

Pietschnig, Jakob, Martin Voracek, and Anton Formann. "Mozart Effect–Shmozart Effect: A Meta-analysis." *Intelligence* 38, no. 3 (2010): 314–323.

Pinker, Steven. *The Sense of Style: The Thinking Person's Guide to Writing in the 21st Century.* New York: Penguin, 2015.

Plath, Sylvia. *Ariel: The Restored Edition.* New York: HarperCollins, 2004.

Poreba, Doreen Marcial. *Idiot's Guides: Unlocking Your Creativity.* London: Penguin, 2015.

Pyne, Stephen J. *Voice and Vision: A Guide to Writing History and Other Serious Non-fiction.* Cambridge, MA: Harvard University Press, 2009.

Quiller-Couch, Sir Arthur. *On the Art of Writing: Lectures Delivered in the University of Cambridge 1913–1914.* Cambridge: Cambridge University Press, 1916. New York: Dover, 2006.

Rabinowitz, Howard, and Suzanne Vogel. *The Manual of Scientific Style: A Guide for Authors, Editors, and Researchers.* Cambridge, MA: Academic Press, 2009.

Rapatahana, Vaughan, and Pauline Bunce, eds. *English Language as Hydra: Its Impacts on Non-English Language Cultures.* Bristol, UK: Multilingual Matters 2012.

Reeves, Judy. *Writing Alone, Writing Together: A Guide for Writers and Writing Groups.* Novato, CA: New World Library, 2002.

Rene, Helena K. *China's Sent-Down Generation: Public Administration and the Legacies of Mao's Rustication Program.* Washington, DC: Georgetown University Press, 2013.

Rettig, Hillary. *The Seven Secrets of the Prolific: The Definitive Guide to Overcoming Procrastination, Perfectionism, and Writer's Block.* Infinite Art, 2011.

Reynolds, Malvina. "Little Boxes." Schroder Music Company, 1962, 1990.

Richardson, Laurel. *Writing Strategies: Reaching Diverse Audiences.* Newbury Park, CA: Sage, 1990.

Richerson, Peter J., and Robert Boyd. *Not by Genes Alone: How Culture Transformed Human Evolution.* Chicago: University of Chicago Press, 2005.

Ritchie, L. David. *Metaphor.* Cambridge: Cambridge University Press, 2013.

Rogers, Bruce Holland. "Cloistered Writing: When You Need a Dose of Discipline, Take a Writing Retreat—At Home." *Writer* 118, no. 11 (2005): 15–18.

Root-Bernstein, Robert S., and Michele Root-Bernstein. "Learning to Think with Emotion." *Chronicle of Higher Education* 46, no. 19 (2000): 64.

Rosenfeld, Jordan. *A Writer's Guide to Persistence: How to Create a Lasting and Productive Writing Practice.* Blue Ash, OH: F+W Media, 2015.

Ross-Larson, Bruce. *Stunning Sentences.* New York: Norton, 1999.

Ryan, Richard, and Edward Deci. "Self-Determination Theory and the Facilitation of Intrinsic Motivation, Social Development, and Well-Being." *American Psychologist* 55, no. 1 (2000): 68–78.

Sadoski, Mark, Ernest T. Goetz, and Joyce B. Fritz. "Impact of Concreteness on Comprehensibility, Interest, and Memory for Text: Implications for Dual Coding Theory and Text Design." *Journal of Educational Psychology* 85, no. 2 (1993): 291–304.

Sedo, DeNel Rehberg. *Reading Communities from Salons to Cyberspace.* Basingstoke, UK: Palgrave Macmillan, 2011.

Seligman, Martin E. P. *Flourish: A Visionary New Understanding of Happiness and Well-Being.* New York: Simon and Schuster, 2012.

Seppala, Emma. *The Happiness Track: How to Apply the Science of Happiness to Accelerate Your Success.* London: Piatkus Books, 2016.

Schimel, Joshua. *Writing Science: How to Write Papers That Get Cited and Proposals That Get Funded.* New York: Oxford University Press, 2012.

Schneider, Pat. *Writing Alone and with Others.* New York: Oxford University Press, 2005.

Shapiro, Dani. *Still Writing: The Perils and Pleasures of a Creative Life.* New York: Grove Atlantic, 2014.

Silvia, Paul J. *How to Write a Lot: A Practical Guide to Productive Academic Writing.* Washington, DC: American Psychological Association, 2007.

Speck, Bruce, Teresa R. Johnson, Catherine P. Dice, and Leon B. Heaton. *Collaborative Writing: An Annotated Bibliography.* Greenwich, CT: Information Age, 2008.

Speedy, Jane, and Jonathan Wyatt, eds. *Collaborative Writing as Inquiry.* Newcastle upon Tyne, UK: Cambridge Scholars, 2014.

Stafford, Kim. *The Muses among Us: Eloquent Listening and Other Pleasures of the Writer's Craft.* Athens: University of Georgia Press, 2003.

Sterelny, Kim. *The Evolved Apprentice.* Cambridge, MA: MIT Press, 2014.

Strunk, William Jr., and E. B. White. *The Elements of Style.* 4th ed. Boston: Allyn and Bacon, 2000.

Sword, Helen. *Stylish Academic Writing.* Cambridge, MA: Harvard University Press, 2012.

———. "Write Every Day: A Mantra Dismantled." *International Journal for Academic Development* 21, no. 4 (2016): 312–322.

———. *The Writer's Diet: A Guide to Fit Prose*. Chicago: University of Chicago Press, 2016.

Tang, Ramona, ed. *Academic Writing in a Second or Foreign Language: Issues and Challenges Facing ESL / EFL Academic Writers in Higher Education Contexts*. New York: Continuum, 2012.

Thomson, Pat. "A Metaphor for Thesis Completion?" *Patter Blog*. March 13, 2014. https://patthomson.net/2014/03/13/a-metaphor-for -thesis-completion/.

Thoreau, Henry David. *Walden*. 150th anniversary ed. Princeton, NJ: Princeton University Press, 2004.

Truss, Lynne. *Eats, Shoots & Leaves: The Zero Tolerance Approach to Punctuation*. London: Profile Books, 2003.

Vandenberg, Peter. "Coming to Terms: Audience." *English Journal* 84, no. 4 (1995): 79–80.

Wald, Catherine. *The Resilient Writer: Tales of Rejection and Triumph from 23 Top Authors*. New York: Persea Books, 2005.

Wall, Alan. *Myth, Metaphor, and Science*. Chester, UK: Chester Academic Press, 2009.

Walvoord, Barbara E. Fassler. *Helping Students Write Well: A Guide for Teachers in All Disciplines*. 2nd ed. New York: Modern Language Association of America, 1986.

Widdowfield, Rebekah. "The Place of Emotions in Academic Research." *Area* 32, no. 2 (2000): 199–208.

Williams, Joseph M. *Style: Lessons in Clarity and Grace*. 9th ed. New York: Pearson Longman, 2007.

Wiseman, Richard. *The Luck Factor: The Scientific Study of the Lucky Mind*. New York: Random House, 2011.

Woodruff, Jay. *A Piece of Work: Five Writers Discuss Their Revisions*. Iowa City: University of Iowa Press, 1993.

Woolf, Virginia. *A Room of One's Own*. 1929. London: Penguin, 1993.

Wormeli, Rick. *Metaphors & Analogies: Power Tools for Teaching Any Subject*. Portland, ME: Stenhouse, 2009.

Writers on Writing: Collected Essays from the New York Times. New York: Holt, 2002.

Yeats, W. B. *The Collected Poems of W. B Yeats*. Edited by Richard J. Finneran. New York: Scribner, 1996.

Yun, Jung H., and Mary Deane Sorcinelli. "When Mentoring Is the Medium: Lessons Learned from a Faculty Development Initiative." *To Improve the Academy* 27 (2009): 365–384.

Zerubavel, Eviatar. *The Clockwork Muse: A Practical Guide to Writing Theses, Dissertations, and Books*. Cambridge, MA: Harvard University Press, 1999.

Zinsser, William. *On Writing Well: An Informal Guide to Writing Nonfiction*. New York: Harper and Row, 1980.

———. *Writing Places: The Life Journey of a Writer and Teacher*. New York: Harper, 2010.

———. *Writing to Learn*. New York: HarperCollins, 2001.

Acknowledgments

One hundred academic authors and editors generously agreed to be interviewed for this book. Their thoughts, words, and emotions are the foundation stones on which I have built my own house of writing, and I thank them all: Dan Albert, Kurt Albertine, Marialuisa Aliotta, Shanthi Ameratunga, Staffan Andersson, Tim Appenzeller, Kwame Anthony Appiah, Marysol Asencio, Donald Barr, Bill Barton, Ruth Behar, Claudia Bernardi, Ann Blair, Gillie Bolton, Brian Boyd, Margaret Breen, Matthew Clarke, Michael Corballis, Patricia Culligan, Janet Currie, Keith Devlin, Shelda Debowski, Enda Duffy, John Dumay, Maja Elmgren, Sam Elworthy, Margery Fee, Martin Fellenz, Mindy Fullilove, James Garraway, Fabrizio Gilardi, Alison Gopnik, Tony Grafton, Russell Gray, Christopher Grey, Susan Gubar, Kalervo Gulson, Tony Harland, Pauline Harris, Eric Hayot, John Heilbron, Ann-Sofie Henriksson, Cecilia Heyes, Douglas Hofstadter, Marjorie Howes, Maraea Hunia, Janelle Jenstad, Alison Jones, Ludmilla Jordanova, Deborah Kaple, Kevin Kenny, Tabish Khair, Elizabeth Knoll, Sun Kwok, Agnes Lam, Michèle Lamont, Ellen Langer, Carl Leggo, Mary Elizabeth Leighton, Kristina Lejon, Andrea Lunsford, Sarah Maddison, Pania Matthews, Eric Mazur, Inger Mewburn, Robert Miles, Johanna Moisander, Mark Moldwin, Massimo Morelli, Dory Nason, Kathy Nelson, Christer Nilsson, David Pace, Miles Padgett, Rebecca Piekkari, Steven Pinker, Ewan Pohe, Robert Poulin, Leah Price, Michael Reilly, Poia Rewi, Jennifer Meta Robinson, Thomas Aastrup Rømer, Lena Roos, Elizabeth Rose, Victoria Rosner, Stephen Ross, Carlo Rotella, Stephen Rowland, Trudy Rudge, Daromir Rudnyckyj, James Shapiro, Lee Shulman, Julie Stout, Lisa Surridge, Stefan Svallfors, Wim Vanderbauwhede, Lesley Wheeler, Michael Wride, and Mei Fung Yong.

I am grateful also to the 1,223 faculty members, postdocs, graduate students, and other academic writers who responded in thoughtful detail to my anonymous data questionnaire, as well as to the many colleagues who helped me with my data collection at forty-nine colleges

and universities and eight international conferences in fifteen countries. In acknowledging my primary contacts at each of the institu-
tions named, I hope that they will pass on my thanks to the many others
who assisted me in arranging interviews and facilitating writing work-
shops: in Australia, Melanie Haines and Inger Mewburn (Australian
National University), Sally Knowles and Rob Holt (Edith Cowan
University), Kathleen Daly and Victoria Meyer (Griffith University),
Tai Peseta (La Trobe University), Jacqui True (Monash University),
Carolina Matheson and Jan McLean (University of New South
Wales), Kati Kuusisto (Royal Melbourne Institute of Technology),
Simon Barrie (University of Sydney); in Canada, Simon Bates, Isabeau
Iqbal, and Amy Perreault (University of British Columbia), Stephen
Ross (University of Victoria); in Denmark, Stacey Cozart, Gry Sand-
holm Jensen, and Mads Rosendahl Thomsen (Aarhus University); in
England, Kathryn Black and Kathleen Quinlan (University of Oxford);
in Finland, Elizabeth Rose (Aalto University); in Germany, Stefanie
Haacke, Svenja Kaduk, and Swantje Lahm (Bielefeld University); in
China, Iain Doherty (University of Hong Kong); in Ireland, Jade Con-
cannon and Ciara O'Farrell (Trinity College Dublin); in the Nether-
lands, Tania Doller and Andre Lardinois (Radboud University); in
New Zealand, Denise Greenwood, Anita Lacey, Nic Mason, and Janet
McLean (University of Auckland), Gayle Morris and Lynette Reid
(Auckland University of Technology), Bill Hagan (Manukau Institute
of Technology), Lily George and Te Kani Kingi (Massey University),
Tony Harland and Matiu Ratima (University of Otago), Meegan Hall
and Kathryn Sutherland (Victoria University of Wellington), Ann
Cameron and Kao-Yun Liu (Whitireia Polytechnic); in Scotland, Daphne
Loads (University of Edinburgh), John Hamer and Helen Purchase
(University of Glasgow); in Sweden, Katarina Winka (Umeå Univer-
sity), Margareta Erhardsson and Lena Roos (Uppsala University); in
Switzerland, Michel Comte (University of Lucerne), Benno Volk (Swiss
Federal Institute of Technology), Flavia Fossati and Eva Hanifa (Univer-
sity of Zurich); in the United States, Marjorie Howes (Boston College),
Joe Bizup and Lauren Proll (Boston University), Janet Currie (Columbia
University), Margaret Breen (University of Connecticut), Sophie Acord,
Marsha Bryant, and Bonnie Efros (University of Florida), Amy Brand,
Elizabeth Knoll, and Judith Singer (Harvard University), Jonathan
Elmer and Tom Gieryn (Indiana University), Brian Baldi (University of
Massachusetts), Susan Burke and Matthew Kaplan (University of Mich-
igan), Becky Wai-Ling Packard and Mary Deane Sorcinelli (Mount
Holyoke College), Nora Bacon (University of Nebraska), Karen Springen
(Northwestern University), Amanda Irwin Wilkins (Princeton Univer-

sity), David Green (Seattle University), Floyd Cheung (Smith College), Julia Bleakney and Andrea Lunsford (Stanford University), Deandra Little (University of Virginia), Lesley Wheeler (Washington and Lee University). Thanks also to the organizers of the eight academic conferences (in Australia, Canada, New Zealand, Sweden, Thailand, and the United States) where I presented my work in progress and gathered interview and questionnaire data.

Many friends, colleagues, and strangers have engaged with me over the years in lively conversations about writing. In particular, my current and former colleagues at the Centre for Learning and Research in Higher Education at the University of Auckland contributed to my work in innumerable ways, from commenting on my earliest draft chapters to helping me wrangle the statistical data. Tēnā rawa atu te CLeaR whanau: Adam Blake, Susan Carter, Tony Chung, Ashwini Datt, Claire Donald, Cathy Gunn, Wen-Chen Hol, Craig Housley, Barbara Kensington-Miller, Steve Leichtweis, Jen Martin, Matiu Ratima, Sean Sturm, and ʻEma Wolfgramm-Foliaki. Special thanks to Marion Blumenstein, Alistair Kwan, and Evija Trofimova, who helped me see the questionnaires with new eyes; to Lynette Herrero-Torres, Kaye Hodge, Arishma Lal, and Zoë Pollard, who brighten my workdays and lighten my workload in so many ways; and to Graeme Aitken, Dean of the Faculty of Education and Social Work, who has supported my international research ambitions even while modeling how to be a conscientious and caring academic leader closer to home.

Part 1 is informed in part by my article "Write Every Day: A Mantra Dismantled" (*International Journal for Academic Development*, 2016), copyright Taylor and Francis (http://www.tandfonline.com/doi/full/10.1080/1360144X.2016.1210153), and several author quotes are revisited from my article "Narrative Trust" in *Times Higher Education* (5 Sept. 2012). Generous funding from the University of Auckland—a grant-in-aid of Research and Study Leave, a Faculty Research and Development Fund grant, a Hood Travelling Fellowship, and a Summer Research Scholarship—underwrote my travel expenses and supported the work of a summer scholar, Marc Reinhardt, and three superb research assistants. While I framed up the structure of the book, they gibbed the walls, hammered in the nails, and fixed up the creaks and cracks. Warm thanks to Louisa Shen, who was already on the construction site when the very first blueprints were being drawn up, and to Madeleine Ballard and Sophie Van Waardenberg, who helped with the finishing work.

A number of other people also deserve a special shout-out: my agent, John Wright, who trusted me from the beginning to get there in the end; editors Elizabeth Knoll, who commissioned the book on the basis of a ten-page abstract, and Andrew Kinney, who patiently guided the project to completion; graphic designer Gideon Keith, who helped me visualize the BASE; Katrina Vassallo, Angela Piliouras, Andrew Katz, and all the others at Harvard University Press and Westchester Publishing Services who magicked the manuscript into a beautiful book; Michele Leggott and Olive, who keep my love of poetry alive; Janet Lindgren, "my reader in New York," who commented on draft after draft with unflagging wisdom and patience; Selina Tusitala Marsh, with whom I shared many laughter-filled write-on-site sessions over cups of coffee and glasses of wine; and Beate Schuler, whose loan of her father's desk for five days of productive writing in Bad Homburg turned out to be only the starting point of her generosity.

As always, my most heartfelt thanks go to my family: Claire, who sent me the Bukowski poem that gave the book its title; Peter, who lent a sympathetic ear and fixed up a last-minute statistical glitch; David, who kept me laughing through it all; and Richard, who created the nurturing environment of "air and light and time and space" that made it possible for me to bring this book into being. I could not have done it without him.

Index